Maya Deren
and the American Avant-Garde

Edited by **Bill Nichols**

UNIVERSITY OF CALIFORNIA PRESS   BERKELEY   LOS ANGELES   LONDON

University of California Press
Berkeley and Los Angeles, California

University of California Press, Ltd.
London, England

Frontispiece: Maya Deren (1942). Photographed by
Alexander Hammid. Courtesy of Czech Center of
Photography, Prague.

Library of Congress Cataloging-in-Publication Data
Maya Deren and the American avant-garde / edited by
   Bill Nichols.
       p.   cm.
   Some contributions are rev. papers of a 1996
conference held at the San Francisco State University
in conjunction with a film series at the San Francisco
Museum of Modern Art; other contributions were
prepared for this volume.
   The text of Maya Deren's "An anagram of ideas on art,
form and film" is included in the appendix.
   Includes bibliographical references and index.
   ISBN 0-520-22444-2 (cloth : alk. paper)—
   ISBN 0-520-22732-8 (pbk. : alk. paper)
       1. Deren, Maya—Criticism and interpretation.
   I. Nichols, Bill.   II. Deren, Maya.
       Anagram of ideas on art, form and film.

PN1998.3.D47 M39   2001
791.43'0233'092—dc21   2001027112
                                                        CIP

Manufactured in the United States of America

10   09   08   07   06   05   04   03   02   01
10   9   8   7   6   5   4   3   2   1

The paper used in this publication meets the minimum
requirements of ANSI/NISO Z39.48-1992 (R 1997)
(Permanence of Paper).♾

To Eugenia Clarke—
writer, poet, dancer, artist, filmmaker, and,
as my stepdaughter, a constant joy

Contents

A DEREN'S WORK
AND THE ARTS

B DEREN'S WRITINGS
AND FILM THEORY

C DEREN'S FILMS
AND THEIR FORM

Illustrations

Preface

A Word about the Organization of this Book: On Anagrams

The contents of this volume are arranged in the form of an anagram. In homage to Maya Deren's own anagram (*An Anagram of Ideas on Art, Form and Film*), this anagram offers the reader multiple pathways through the essays collected here. As Deren herself noted, "An anagram is a combination of letters in such a relationship that each and every one is simultaneously an element in more than one linear series. . . . The whole is so related to every part that whether one reads horizontally, vertically, diagonally or even in reverse, the logic of the whole is not disrupted, but remains intact" (preface to *An Anagram*). The anagram constructed from the assembled essays is followed by Maya Deren's own *Anagram* as an appendix. Since several of the essays refer to it and since it is a document of continuing importance we have reproduced the original *Anagram* here.[1]

With its arrangement of the essays in vertical columns and horizontal rows, the structure of the anagram allows the book to be subdivided into at least six parts that can be read in any order, as the reader chooses. Each choice will highlight a different set of relationships among the essays. The vertical columns provide a set of conceptual categories: Deren's work and its relation to the other arts, Deren's writing and its relation to film theory, and Deren's films and their specific form. The horizontal rows provide a set of temporal categories: Deren's work in relation to earlier work, Deren's work in relation to work contemporary to her own, and the legacy of her life and work since the 1950s.

If columns A, B, and C are read in succession, then the essays by Michelson, Jackson, Turim, and Soussloff offer a solid historical and theoretical overview to Deren's accomplishments under the heading "A. Deren's Writings and Film Theory"; Franko, Holl, and Wodening specify some of the crosscurrents between Deren and artists working in other media in "B. Deren's Work and the Arts"; while Fischer, Sullivan, Pramaggiore, and Hammer give greater attention to the actual style and structure of Deren's films in "C. Deren's Films and Their Form."

If rows 1, 2, and 3 are read in succession, then the essays by Michelson, Jackson, Franko, and Fischer place Deren within larger historical traditions that preceded her work in "1. The Historical Lens"; the essays by Turim, Holl, and Sullivan explore Deren's relationship with her contemporaries in the 1940s and 1950s in "2. In the Eyes of Her Contemporaries"; and the essays by Soussloff, Wodening, Pramaggiore, and Hammer convey some sense of the subsequent reception and understanding of Deren and her work in "3. The Terms of Her Legend and Legacy."

Maya Deren's own *Anagram* begins on page 267 of this book. The layout and internal pagination are those of the original publication. References to the *Anagram* in the essays here are to these original page numbers.

Note

1. The 1946 publication by Alicat Book Shop Press only offered 750 copies for sale. The *Anagram* is reprinted in *The Legend of Maya Deren*, vol. 1, pt. 2, *Chambers* (1988); in Teresa Hak Kyung Cha, ed., *Apparatus* (New York: Tanam Press, 1980); in George Amberg, *The Art of Cinema* (New York: Arno Press, 1972), and in *Film Culture*, no. 39 (1965). All these sources are currently out of print.

Acknowledgments

Not only is this volume the work of all the contributors, but it is also the product of considerable support, advice, and concrete assistance from many others, both in terms of institutional support and individual assistance. The San Francisco Museum of Modern Art, thanks to the keen interest of former Media Arts Curator Robert Riley, gave generous support to the 1996 film series that revolved around Maya Deren. The Department of Cinema and the School of Creative Arts at San Francisco State facilitated the accompanying conference on Maya Deren that became the basis of this book. An annual conference on a topic chosen by the graduate students themselves has since become a tradition in the department. Both for the conference and the tradition it inspired, I have former graduate student Lisa Carlson to thank. My colleague Pat Ferrero provided financial support in the form of a grant from the Christian Saxton Memorial Fund that allowed us to support a keynote address by Professor Annette Michelson. The Getty Research Institute graciously made its research collections available and provided work space for me during the 1999–2000 academic year.

I received considerable assistance in making editorial decisions from my colleague Akira Lippit. Professor Lippit's love of cinema is only exceeded by his knowledge of it. His suggestions and advice proved invaluable. Professor Annette Michelson attended the initial conference and has remained a steadfast advisor ever since. She introduced me to recent work on Maya Deren from France, most notably Alain-Alcide Sudre's book *Dialogues théorique avec Maya Deren: Du cinéma expérimental au film ethnographique* (Paris: L'Harmattan, 1996) and has given generous advice and encouragement during the long evolution of this project from a onetime conference to the more indelible form of a book.

Once the manuscript was accepted at the University of California Press, an act for which I have two anonymous readers to thank, Eric Smoodin became the steward and champion of the book. As the sponsoring editor, he moved the book forward with genuine dedication to the project. He has been an indispensable ally in the process of bringing the book to completion. Rachel Berchten, Mimi Kusch, and Nola Burger transformed the manuscript into a finished book with unwavering professionalism.

Robert Haller at Anthology Film Archives has provided invaluable assistance both in securing photographs and film stills and in making available to me back issues of *Field of Vision*, especially issue number 4 (fall 1978), which contains his own informative interview with Alexander Hammid. Similarly, Jonas Mekas, the founder of Anthology Film Archives, and Amos Vogel, cofounder of Cinema 16, also helped to locate some of the more elusive images selected. Shelley Rice, who curated *Inverted Odysseys: Claude Cahun, Maya Deren, Cindy Sherman* for the Grey Gallery at New York University, proved extraordinarily generous in helping me locate images of Deren that went beyond the available film stills. Jirí Jaskmanický of the Czech Center of Photography in Prague provided photographs taken by "Sasha" Hammid that were not otherwise available. Jaskmanický's gallery is the exclusive agent for Hammid photographic work. Sasha Hammid himself was also of great help in locating material and in generously granting his permission for the inclusion of his work.

Also of enormous help in obtaining film stills was Catrina Neiman, one of the coeditors of *The Legend of Maya Deren*. She not only generously produced photographs for inclusion in this volume but also provided much-needed assistance in locating other images. Tavia Ito, executor of the Maya Deren estate, helped me secure several photographs that would have been otherwise unattainable. The assistance of these in-dividuals has led to a much more handsome book than I had thought pos-sible. Jane Brakhage Wodening generously allowed me to reprint her ac-count of Maya Deren from the limited edition volume *from The Book of Legends* (New York: Granary Books, 1989).

Finally, to her whose help is least easily captured in words, Catherine Soussloff, I offer my deepest thanks. Her advice and encouragement were greatly needed, immensely appreciated, and are but imperfectly ac-knowledged here.

All the people identified here have the fullest measure of my grati-tude. A love of cinema, and a love of Maya Deren, as artist and as leg-end, intertwine among us all. From that twining, this book appears, its flaws and faults my own, its strengths, the product of the braid others have helped create.

Maya Deren and the American Avant-Garde

Bill Nichols

Introduction

Perspectives

Some facts: Elenora Derenkowsky is born in Kiev in 1917.[1] In 1922 her parents flee to the United States during a series of anti-Semitic pogroms in the Ukraine. Precocious, she writes poetry, marries Gregory Bardacke, a student activist at Syracuse University, moves to New York City, serves as national secretary of the Young Peoples Socialist League (YPSL), divorces Bardacke, completes her B.A. at New York University (1936), earns an M.A. in English literature at Smith College (1939), and takes on freelance jobs that lead to a secretarial position with African American dancer and choreographer Katherine Dunham. She tours with Dunham's road show of *Cabin in the Sky* (1941) and meets Alexander Hammid in Los Angeles. Hammid is an established Czech filmmaker and émigré to the United States. He makes *Aimless Walk* (1930) and *Prague Castle* (1932), among numerous other films, while still in Europe and *The Forgotten Village* (1941) and *Toscanini: Hymn of the Nations* (1944), among others, in the United States. Derenkowsky and he marry, she publishes photographs not unlike those of Tina Modotti, and along with Hammid, makes *Meshes of the Afternoon* (1943). At this point Deren, whose family name was shortened from Derenkowsky in 1928, when her parents became naturalized citizens, changes her name from Elenora to Maya, the Hindu word for illusion.

Deren and Hammid join the European émigré art scene in Greenwich Village, meeting, through Anaïs Nin, a number of the people who

Figure 1. Maya Deren and Alexander Hammid (1942). Photographed by Alexander Hammid. Courtesy of Czech Center of Photography.

appear in *Ritual in Transfigured Time*. Deren writes articles, publishes photographs, and gains a reputation for her handmade clothes, her flamboyant, curly hair, and her fierce convictions. In 1946, after distributing her films to colleges entirely on her own, she books the Village's Provincetown Playhouse for a major public exhibition titled *Three Abandoned Films*—a showing of *Meshes of the Afternoon, At Land*, and *A Study for the Choreography of a Camera*. Her successful public screening inspires Amos Vogel's formation of Cinema 16, the most successful film society of the 1950s. Also in 1946 she wins the first Guggenheim Fellowship for filmmaking, writes her most sustained theoretical essay, *An Anagram of Ideas on Art, Form and Film*, and begins preparations for a film on Haitian Voudoun dance, which she will never complete.

Throughout the 1950s, Deren devotes increasing energy to the cause of avant-garde cinema and forms the Creative Film Foundation to spur further work. Sara Kathryn Arledge is one of the first award winners, followed by Stan Brakhage, Robert Breer, and Shirley Clarke. Deren dies in 1961 of a massive cerebral hemorrhage, a consequence, possibly, of a long-term dependence on amphetamines and sleeping pills prescribed by Dr. Max Jacobson, an arts-scene doctor notorious for his liberal prescription of drugs.

Such facts give rise to a legendary figure: Maya Deren, pioneer of the American avant-garde and feminist inspiration.

As legend, Maya Deren did not contribute to an existing film movement but galvanically launched a new one. Others preceded her (like the Whitney brothers, Mary Ellen Bute, and Sara Kathryn Arledge) but only Maya Deren publicly and insistently proclaimed the need for a new art cinema, envisioned the conceptual and material means to build one, and actively saw to its implementation. (Some described Deren as intimidating, threatening, and "too aggressive," qualities that, in a male leader, might easily be described as compelling, relentless, and impassioned.) For the first public screening she not only rented the Playhouse but also screened her work on her living room wall to critics like James Agee and Manny Farber. Contemporary avant-garde filmmakers or video artists who describe and define their own work in written commentary, who tour, lecture, and self-distribute their work, and who support themselves with fees and grants follow in Deren's footsteps. The New American Cinema of the 1950s took on the shape of an institutional reality that gave sustenance to the creative efforts of Hollis Frampton, Stan Brakhage, Paul Sharits, Robert Frank, Morris Engel, and Jack Smith. Deren demonstrated how such artists could gain common recognition and participate in a shared framework of distribution, exhibition, and critical discourse. Along with the inexhaustible efforts of Jonas Mekas, Amos Vogel, and others, Deren formulated the terms and conditions of an independent cinema that remain with us today.

The historical facts do not contradict the mythic legend of Maya Deren—far from it. Rather, they ground the legend and invest it with an aura of legitimacy. But the relation between the filmmaker of fact and the woman of legend has its complexities. Historical fact gives rise to a legend, as Jane Brakhage Wodening's essay demonstrates so vividly. The legend of her mesmerizing appearances, audacious acts, and transformative rituals amplifies biographical facts into condensed, evocative, more spectacular (and less fully historical) versions of themselves. The legend bears a relation to fact similar to that of dream to its originating instance. The reality of that instance remains embedded in the dream but in a form radically altered by condensation, displacement, and other types of dream work.

The legendary status of Maya Deren as artist also clashes in particularly complicated ways with how Deren herself perpetuated this myth of the visionary hero while also playing down the central role of the cult of personality, and authorship, in her actual work. Her choice of film as a medium contributed to this complication. It allowed her to escape the fetishization of the signed, authenticated, original work of art in favor of mechanically reproducible works (films) whose function approximates that of unsigned, collectively performed acts of magic, myth, and ritual in other cultures. Similarly, she downplayed her own role as actor, or "star," within her own films; to the average viewer, the characters in her films were anonymous figures rather than iconic deities. Deren's philosophy of art, with its de-emphasis of individual psychology and stress on ritual, stands in tension with her promotion of art. Her philosophy, or aesthetic, with its formidable insistence on an ethical dimension to the function of art, continues to be underappreciated, while her legendary status as a feminist pioneer and entrepreneurial promoter seems to fit more comfortably with the realities of a commodity art market and the making of individual reputations.

Deren acted the role of a cinematic Prometheus, stealing the fire of the Hollywood gods for those whom the gods refused to recognize. Her passionate sense of social commitment and moral purpose separates her from the entertainment values of the film industry; from the detached, ironic attitude of her surrealist and dadaist predecessors; from the cool, camp, hip attitudes of her Beat successors; from the "fly-on-the-wall" aesthetic of cinema verité practitioners; and from the abstruseness of contemporary film theory, feminist or otherwise. For her the pursuit of art stemmed from a moral imperative: "No one who presumes to treat of profound human values is exonerated from a moral responsibility for the negative action of failure, as well as the positive action of error" (*An Anagram*, 37). Both her organizational efforts and her creative endeavors attest to an ethical, social commitment that almost certainly found its earliest expression in her political activism as a Socialist.

Even more than her films, Maya Deren's writings became lost to succeeding generations. (Though legendary, they, too, did not conform to the prevailing norms.) And yet her writings, especially *Divine Horsemen: The Living Gods of Haiti, An Anagram of Ideas of Art, Form and Film*, and essays like "Cinematography: The Creative Use of Reality," represent a brilliant body of work comparable to that of Sergei Eisenstein, Dziga Vertov, Jean-Luc Godard, David MacDougall, and Trinh T. Minh-ha. Other pieces, such as her brief (unpublished) essay on fashion, "Psychology of Fashion" (circa 1945), address, with a distinctly feminist cast, the kind of analysis that writers like Roland Barthes were to bring to everyday life and social practices in works like *Mythologies* (1957).

In the 1930s, as a dedicated YPSL member and Trotskyite, Maya Deren was not content with a sideline role. Her willingness to take initiative in areas dominated by men (rather than to distinguish herself in those areas reserved for women) was already in evidence. In 1937 she coauthored and presented to a sizable gathering of (predominantly male) Socialist Party convention members an analysis of the U.S.S.R. that termed it a model of "feudal industrialism" rather than a workers' state. The response was derisive. Here was a flamboyantly dressed young woman of twenty contradicting the views of seasoned male activists two and three times her age. Her speech became the butt of ironic asides and dismissive jokes.

This experience replicated itself in 1953 at a Cinema 16 symposium, "Poetry and the Film." (Both Annette Michelson and Renata Jackson refer to this event in their essays.) Deren claimed that film works on two axes, a horizontal, narrative axis of character and action and a vertical, poetic axis of mood, tone, and rhythm. Later, film scholars recognized this theory as comparable to Roman Jakobson's treatment of the metonymic and metaphoric poles of linguistic organization. Deren's simple claim, however, befuddled her older male "superiors." Dylan Thomas dismissively announced that he was "all for horizontal and vertical," or "up and down," and confessed that the only avant-garde work he'd seen was "in a cellar, or a sewer, or somewhere. I happened to be with Mr. Miller over there." Arthur Miller later added, "To hell with that horizontal and vertical. It doesn't mean anything." Deren entered an overwhelmingly male arena rather than move toward a separate feminist alternative. She fought for her own space within it, but others defined the terms of debate and, when it suited them, chose to disregard her intervention.

Deren defies categories. She was neither feminine in the demure sense nor feminist in the modern sense. She actively contributed to her own legendary status less to advance a myth of herself as artist than to promote a common cause. She withheld acting credits from her films. She took offense when James Agee wrote about her appearance in her own films as though it were self-serving. She wanted viewers to regard her performance as a character as distinct from her persona as an artist.

In fact, Deren's attraction to Voudoun possession ceremonies, to

Figure 2. *Witch's Cradle* (unfinished film, begun 1943). The sequence of images involves a choreographed set of movements between the camera and the man portrayed (Marcel Duchamp). The film was to have explored the magical qualities of various objects in Peggy Guggenheim's Art of This Century gallery, where Duchamp, among others, exhibited. Photograph from *View* magazine (March 1945), courtesy of Catherine M. Soussloff. See figure 9, page 89.

2

dance, play, games, and especially ritual, stemmed from her belief in the vital necessity to decenter our notions of self, ego, and personality. She used both herself and Rita Christiani as the protagonist in *Ritual in Transfigured Time* interchangeably because she wanted to address ritual aspects of journey, quest, and discovery that were less personal than social or collective. She puts this goal, one that undercuts the very legend of "Maya Deren," compellingly in *An Anagram of Ideas:*

> The ritualistic form treats the human being not as the source
> of the dramatic action, but as a somewhat depersonalized element
> in a dramatic whole. The intent of such depersonalization is not
> the destruction of the individual; on the contrary, it enlarges him
> beyond the personal dimension and frees him from the specializa-
> tions and confines of personality. He becomes part of a dynamic
> whole which, like all such creative relationships, in turn, endow
> its parts with a measure of its larger meaning. (20)

It is to endowing Maya Deren, as fact and legend, with this larger meaning that we dedicate this volume.

Re-viewing Maya Deren

The Legend of Maya Deren project and the Maya Deren archives at Boston University have provided the indispensable starting point for almost all contemporary scholarship on Maya Deren. The two-part first volume of *The Legend of Maya Deren*—with its reproduction of her diary entries, poetry, political theorizing, letters, scripts, and other invaluable material—has proved the definitive reference for study of Maya Deren, but after the first volume appeared, tracing her development from her childhood to the completion of her first three films in 1947, the project came to a halt. Subsequent volumes have not yet appeared, although the second volume is scheduled to appear soon.[2]

The anticipated publication of the volumes covering the remainder of her work—including much of her organizational activity on behalf of a new American independent cinema; her debates with Jonas Mekas and others about the nature and direction of independent cinema; her research on dance, magic, and ritual that culminated in her book *Divine Horsemen: The Living Gods of Haiti* in 1953; and the posthumous assembly of portions of her Haitian footage and resource material on her other later films—caused many to postpone their own research on Deren. Further scholarship would clearly benefit from the enormous range of information the *Legend* editors would be sure to provide. But more than ten years have passed since the publication of volume 1, part 2, and a palpable desire exists to return to the life and legend of Maya Deren without further delay. A new generation of scholars has chosen to reassess Deren's achievement from a fresh perspective, one informed by considerable change in the orientation and emphasis of film study generally.

One sign of this desire to reexamine the work of Maya Deren was in 1996 when I cocurated, with Robert Riley, former curator of media arts, a film series organized around the work of Maya Deren at the San Francisco Museum of Modern Art. The series (a set of six programs combining Deren's work with that of others significant to it) proved tremendously successful. In tandem with this effort, we sponsored a conference on Maya Deren at San Francisco State University that attracted a wide range of scholars, including four graduate students completing dissertations on Deren (two from the United States and one each from Sweden and Germany). Annette Michelson gave the keynote address.

Maya Deren and the American Avant-Garde grows out of this conference. The contents include several papers that have been revised and rewritten but that were first given at the conference. The essays by Lucy Fischer, Maureen Turim, Catherine Soussloff, and Jane Wodening Brakhage and the tribute by Barbara Hammer are ones I solicited to round out the volume and to provide additional perspectives.

This volume reflects new thinking on a legendary figure. The hiatus in scholarship on Deren has allowed scholars to return to her work with fresh eyes and to identify new themes and issues. The degree of interest in Deren in relation to questions of gender politics and lesbian, or bisexual, identity is one vivid example of this process. The reexamination of her work on Voudoun ritual, Haitian culture, possession, and collectivity in light of her own seldom-discussed book *Divine Horsemen: The Living Gods of Haiti;* her still unassembled Haitian footage; and further developments in ethnographic filmmaking also afford new insight into Deren's later work, which many saw at the time as a deviation from her commitment to a new American independent cinema. Fresh eyes are also cast on her extraordinary *An Anagram of Ideas of Art, Form and Film,* a contribution to film theory and the philosophy of art that ranks as one of the most significant reflections on the nature and responsibilities of art and film yet written.

Deren's neglect over the last several decades is not solely the result of the incomplete status of *The Legend of Maya Deren* project. At least five other factors contributed: 1) the rise of a Beat and improvisational sensibility within a large sector of independent cinema—championed by Jonas Mekas—that was at strict odds with Deren's insistence on classicism (leading to her denunciation of surrealism and documentary film alike, the one as self-indulgent, the other as inartistic), 2) the prominence of "structural film" within the American avant-garde of the 1960s and 1970s that stressed formal rather than mythic qualities and that rendered her Haitian work all but irrelevant, 3) the ascendance of *cinéma vérité* at the time of her death in the 1960s further negated her Haitian work, with its lack of a story line, "crisis structure," and synchronous sound, 4) the rise of academic film studies in the 1970s, complete with an arsenal of theoretical tools and critical methodologies (poststructuralism, semiotics, psychoanalysis) to which Deren, unlike Eisenstein or Godard, seemed to make no significant contribution, and 5) Deren's masked feminist perspective, one that went largely unrecognized. Like Cindy Sherman's today, Deren's critique of women's position in society and women's representation in the media was not always perceived as a central element in her work. Deren's early reception hinged on elements of autobiography and introspection, formalism, mythopoetics, and "eternal" human dilemmas; these all fell into disfavor as film studies grew into an academic discipline in the 1970s. Her predominantly unacknowledged preoccupation with more historically specific issues of gender, identity, and subjectivity remained unexplored. For those in search of rigorous theoretical models of a feminist film aesthetic, Deren's example seemed to contribute but slightly. Highly influential feminist writers like Claire Johnston and Laura Mulvey ignored Deren entirely in their search for pioneering feminist filmmakers.

We can now see these factors as limiting conditions with their own historical boundaries. They no longer shape our perception of Deren as forcefully as they once did. For filmmakers and scholars seeking new formal models, alternative approaches to issues of gender and identity, and distinctive experimental and ethnographic practices, Deren is once again a figure of considerable importance. Catherine Russell's *Experimental Ethnography: The Work of Film in the Age of Video* (Durham: Duke University Press, 1999) and the exhibition entitled *Inverted Odysseys: Claude Cahun, Maya Deren, Cindy Sherman*, published as a catalogue of the same name and edited by Shelley Rice (Cambridge: M.I.T. Press, 1999), are prime examples of the type of renewed interest in Deren that shifts the previous grounds of discussion significantly.

It is possible to summarize some of the radical transformations that Maya Deren sought to inspire: 1) in film form, which for her possesses both an inviolate link to questions of ethics and responsibility and a fundamental obligation to reshape the realist elements comprising it in ways that alter or transfigure them; 2) in our understanding of techniques that work to modify our perception, sensibility, and self-conception in historically and culturally distinct ways (a position that has yet to be compared extensively to Walter Benjamin's pronouncements on this topic); 3) in alternative film practices, for which her exemplary acts of self-promotion, distribution, and exhibition served as a vivid model; 4) in our understanding of the woman artist as a figure distinct from but in no wise less than the prevailing model of the male artist; and 5) in our regard for the self, or subject, with her efforts to understand hysteria, trance, and ritual as socially situated acts of collective association rather than as personal dysfunction. Each of these gestures went against the grain of dominant practices; each incurred resistance and misunderstanding. Each remains an emblem of Deren's extraordinary willingness to transgress boundaries and reformulate their contours.

Meshes of the Afternoon is reputedly the most widely shown experimental film in American cinema, and perhaps in all cinema. The enigmatic structure, dreamlike quest, and allegorical complexity, along with its loose affinity with both film noir and domestic melodrama, make *Meshes* an ideal film for posing questions of film form and social meaning. *Meshes* and her other films—*At Land, Ritual in Transfigured Time, Meditation on Violence, A Study in Choreography for the Camera, The Very Eye of Night,* and *Divine Horseman* (even though it is a posthumous assembly of some of her Haitian footage)—are routinely shown in a wide variety of film courses from general introductions and film histories to courses on women and film, the American avant-garde, ethnographic film, and experimental cinema. The frequency with which Maya Deren's name and work figure in any serious attempt to explore the possibilities of cinema and the historical rise of the American independent film makes the lack of written material on her all the more frustrating. This collection seeks to address the need for critical essays that will help locate Deren's work and stimulate further thought on this exceptional figure.

The Contents of *Maya Deren and the American Avant-Garde:* The Essays

The contributors to this volume have addressed a wide range of topics, from innovative readings of some of Deren's classic films to alternative perspectives and frameworks within which to understand Deren's historical situations and overall contribution.

Annette Michelson's revised keynote address, "Poetics and Savage Thought: About *Anagram*," traces Deren's singular influence on the American avant-garde. Michelson sketches out some of Deren's historical ties with and position within the avant-garde of her day before examining Deren's confrontation with the derisive responses of fellow panelists Dylan Thomas and Arthur Miller at the symposium "Poetry and the Film." Michelson then elaborates on the model of cinema for which Deren argued. Using *An Anagram* as a reference point, she traces the distinctive qualities of Deren's call for a poetics of cinema. Her poetics are likened to Sergei Eisenstein's arguments for bold experimentation, reference to other arts, and a sense of ethical or political commitment through a comparison of his unfinished *Que Viva Mexico!* and Deren's never-completed Haitian film project.

In "The Modernist Poetics of Maya Deren," Renata Jackson focuses squarely on Deren's single most important piece of writing on aesthetic theory and social practice, *An Anagram of Ideas on Art, Form and Film*. Jackson attends to Deren's thoughts about science and art, written in the shadow of Hiroshima and Nagasaki, and traces many of Deren's arguments back to her M.A. thesis on French symbolist poetry. Jackson provides valuable contextual references to Henri Bergson and Gestalt psychology for Deren's specific form of modernism. Deren stresses form as the primary source of moral perspective, emotional effect, and cognitive meaning. Form proves more powerful than any act of explanation or interpretation. Jackson also explores the multiple reasons why this formative essay has been so long neglected and gives considerable indication of why close attention is amply rewarded.

In "The Ethics of Form: Structure and Gender in Maya Deren's Challenge to the Cinema," Maureen Turim takes up the uses of form as the means by which Deren seeks to replicate the effects of ritual in nonindustrial societies. Form embodies an ethical stance, and for Deren that stance owes allegiance to some entity larger than the individual psyche. This perspective derives from an ethical sense of art as a therapeutic and restorative practice rather than as a by-product of individual genius. Deren's view of art put her at odds not only with her surrealist predecessors but with her abstract expressionist contemporaries. Turim examines the path Deren proposed in relation to contemporary debates about the nature of art. She gives particular attention to Deren's relationships to another key figure in the rise of the American avant-garde,

Jonas Mekas, and to the ramifications of Deren's status as a woman artist for women filmmakers who have come later. Catherine Soussloff's "Maya Deren Herself" contributes another important perspective to our understanding of the person and the legend. Soussloff takes up the complex issue of the "woman artist" in a period before feminism and links this question of the gendered artist to the act of naming the artist. The name of the artist stands for the mark of a distinctive individuality that qualifiers like "woman" tend to reduce by subcategorizing. How can we understand the particular political and aesthetic challenges that confront the woman artist who, although acutely aware of the issue of gender, must articulate this awareness in terms uninformed by the feminist film theory that would follow several decades later? Soussloff gives this question a strongly historical grounding and suggests that, in large measure, the answer lies in returning to a careful analysis of Deren's work, especially in terms of the role of self-portraiture within it. Soussloff also suggestively compares Deren's efforts to those of Cindy Sherman, whose work also addresses issues of female subjectivity in ways that go across the grain of the "woman artist" as a predetermined category. Like Sherman, Deren demonstrates how specific elements and strategies in her films such as subjectivity and self-portraiture invite a feminist response that has been slower to arrive than we might expect.

"Aesthetic Agencies in Flux: Talley Beatty, Maya Deren, and the Modern Dance Tradition in 'Study in Choreography for Camera'" by Mark Franko locates Deren's work in relation to the modern dance tradition and its racial inflections. Deren herself had trained as a dancer and worked for noted dancer Katherine Dunham, but this aspect of her life and work has received minimal attention. Franko further enriches his essay by addressing the complicating factor of Talley Beatty's status as an African American dancer, recruited by Deren to perform as the solo dancer for this film. Franko contrasts two dances, Martha Graham's *Lamentation* and Beatty's own *Mourner's Bench*, to show how the same themes receive vividly different treatments: Beatty resisted the tendency toward universal symbolism found in Graham. Rather, he based his work on concrete historical references such as slavery. Franko then links Deren's film to her ongoing concerns about ritual and depersonalization while also indicating how Beatty's presence as a black male dancer adds a racial dimension to our reception of these issues.

Ute Holl's "Moving the Dancers' Souls" begins with the famous dispute between Maya Deren and Anaïs Nin that followed Nin's performance in *Ritual in Transfigured Time.* She uses this incident, pivoting as it does around realism, performance, and the poetic transfigurations of which cinema is capable, to explore Deren's overall aesthetic position. While doing so Holl makes use of her original research on the psychoanalytic training of Deren's father, Dr. Solomon Derenkowsky, at the Psychoneurological Institute of Moscow (where Wladimir Bechterew and Hugo Münsterberg were among the faculty). Holl demonstrates how Dr. Derenkowsky's training bears a significant relation to Deren's later understanding of ritual, hysteria, and possession as therapeutic, collective practices. Holl's essay provides a unique angle on Deren's work. Deren herself rejected, throughout the 1940s and 1950s, the standard psychoanalytic interpretations of artists and their work. She also rejected surrealist cinema as an influence—the usual, attempted link of Deren to Europe, a link, if present, clearly mediated by Alexander Hammid. Holl associates Deren with the distinct psychoanalytic and social theories of her father and his Russian colleagues and suggests levels and forms of influence that have previously gone unrecognized.

Jane Brakhage Wodening, former wife of Stan Brakhage, had direct acquaintance with Maya Deren. Her essay is one of the three chapters that comprise her exquisite, limited edition of memories, stories, and legends, *from The Book of Legends* (New York: Granary Books, 1989; reprint, London: Invisible Books, 1993). The other two chapters recount similar tales about Joseph Cornell and Charles Olson. Wodening draws on first- and secondhand accounts to present this more intimate portrait of the artist. That she propels Deren into the realm of the legendary attests to the power Maya Deren's extraordinary figure exerted on those around her, complementing Ute Holl's more analytic discussion of Deren's relation to Anaïs Nin.

Lucy Fischer's "The Eye for Magic: Maya and Méliès" pursues a seldom acknowledged parallelism between Deren and Georges Méliès. Many of the comparisons used by critics to analyze Deren's films are ones Deren herself opposed. For example, she rejected any influence from or affinity with the surrealist cinema of Buñuel, Dalí, Ray, and Cocteau, despite numerous striking parallels between their work and her own; she dismissed the documentary and ethnographic film for its lack of art, even though her Haitian footage drew from the ethnographic filmmaking efforts of Gregory Bateson and Margaret Mead, among others, and she refused to see film form as a formalist or structural end in itself, despite the formal elegance of her work. Fischer's essay explores a tradition and orientation Deren did herself acknowledge: magic. Fischer traces the vicissitudes of the "trick film" from the early work of Méliès and demonstrates how this type of film magic informs Deren's films and contributed to her overall aesthetic. In doing so, Fischer suggests an affinity between early cinema and a later modernist avant-garde that has received far less attention than it warrants.

Taking up another neglected dimension of Deren's work, Moira Sullivan's "Maya Deren's Ethnographic Representation of Ritual and Myth in Haiti" relies on primary-source research in the Maya Deren archive in Boston and at Anthology Film Archives in New York. Sullivan examines Deren's gradually emerging theories of crosscultural representation. Her early association with African American dancer Katherine Dunham, who was herself trained in anthropology and was a student of Haitian culture, and her continuing contact with Gregory Bateson, Margaret Mead, Joseph Campbell, and Melville Herskovits (Dunham's mentor at the University of Chicago) form a rich nexus from which Deren developed her own, original theories on Voudoun ritual, possession ceremonies, and social harmony. Sullivan refers to Deren's unedited Haitian footage and contrasts it with the only publicly circulating version of this footage, *Divine Horsemen*, a work compiled by others after her death. Sullivan shows how Deren's direction was at odds with this finished product. Her theories of "choreography for the camera" bear exceptional fruit for crosscultural understanding through her insistence on finding a way to retain the rhythm, movement, and continuity of dance within each shot without resorting to the static, "objective" camera style favored by Margaret Mead as the proper form for visual anthropology.

In "Seeing Double(s): Reading Deren Bisexually," Maria Pramaggiore starts with the famous still image of Maya Deren peering through a window from *Meshes of the Afternoon* and uses it to launch an exploration of issues of identification and desire in Deren's films. Pramaggiore elaborates a bisexual film aesthetic and argues for Deren's inclusion within such an aesthetic. Each of Deren's narrative films (*Meshes of the Afternoon, At Land*, and *Ritual in Transfigured Time*) becomes the target of a revisionist reading identifying complex patterns of desire that cannot be accommodated by heterosexual, feminist, or explicitly lesbian analyses. Pramaggiore provides us with a provocative framework for analysis that also implicitly demonstrates another reason why Deren's work fits uneasily within the paradigms of early feminist film theory and, hence, for her relative neglect.

Barbara Hammer's "Maya Deren and Me" exemplifies the forms of continuity and influence that Maureen Turim suggests have been at work since the 1950s by offering a personal account of the relationship between Deren's films and her own. Hammer's discovery of a bold, if not transgressive, woman filmmaker in a film history class dominated by male artists proved decisive in her own choice of career and in the specific films she has made. Hammer describes some of her projects and the relation they bear to specific strategies in the work of Deren. Echoing the claims of Annette Michelson, Hammer affirms that the model Deren provided as activist and advocate, promoter and polemicist, as well as artist and theorist has defined a distinctive position for the independent filmmaker ever since.

Barbara Hammer offers us an instructive example of how one artist learns from another in terms that are less transcendentally inspired than historically rooted. Deren's formal innovations remain, for Hammer, inseparable from both the explorations of gendered subjectivity in her work and her confrontations with sexist stereotyping in her life. The vivid sense of a social and artistic connectedness that must be discovered, asserted, and perpetuated, against all odds, attests to the fragility of efforts that go against the prevailing grain and to the explosive power of Deren's own creative accomplishments. This book stands as a testimony to the continuation of Deren's transformative achievement.

Notes

1. This introduction is a revised version of the program note I prepared for a film series of work by Deren and other artists at the San Francisco Museum of Modern Art, "Maya Deren: Her Radical Aspirations and Influences in the Film Avant-garde" (April 12–May 19, 1996), which was co-organized by me and Robert R. Riley, former SFMOMA curator of media arts. I am grateful to the museum for granting permission for the republication of the original material here.

2. The publisher, Anthology Film Archives, has announced plans for the second volume to appear in 2002.

1A · ·
· · ·
· · ·

Annette Michelson

Poetics and Savage Thought

About *Anagram*

I

[O]n its own ground, within its own terms of debate, rationalism sees the cinema as the dissolving agent of absolute rules and fixed definitions. For visual representation, given fresh life through an accustomed cinematic spectatorship, tends to introduce or re-introduce its higher realism within the most static verbal concepts through multiple truths subject to constant variation—even to the point of contradiction, because they are alive. **–Jean Epstein**

The four decades following World War II saw the emergence of an American cinema of independent persuasion and production, distinguished by its range (extending from documentary to narrative and lyric forms), its internationally recognized quality, and its accompanying theoretical literature. Within the larger landscape of our culture, significantly altered and enriched by this development, Maya Deren stands as an especially salient figure, the pioneer who located and defined the issues, options, and contradictions of filmmaking as an artistic practice. In its formulation of aesthetic principles and social tasks, Deren's career as filmmaker, writer, and organizer epitomizes, in a clear and prescient manner, those tensions, central and unresolved, that continue to inform the relations between art and technology, first- and third-world cultures, and the tasks and predicaments of the woman artist.

Thinking of Maya Deren, I begin, as I often have in the past, with an image that documents and emblematizes her project, her role, and the

21

manner in which Deren laid the groundwork for the theorization of an American cinema of independent persuasion and production, one of a deeply transgressive nature. By the latter I have in mind the multiple challenge launched by three generations of filmmakers in defiance of the established codes of industrially produced cinema, the conventions of professionalism, and the constraints of censorship.

A full-length study of Deren would seek to place her within the cultural production of her time, that of the twenty years following World War II. Deren's film work, when casually surveyed, offers evidence of her presence within the intellectual milieus of New York and Los Angeles. John Cage, Anaïs Nin, and Erick Hawkins, to name only a few, were chosen as collaborators in her major films. And her writings demonstrate her familiarity with the poetry, choreography, and music of the period's avantgarde. Her theorization of a cinematic grammar demands, as I shall claim, to be analyzed in relation to the linguistic model then being developed by Roman Jakobson.

The extensive documentation now available informs us of Deren's political commitments in her student days at Smith College, the University of Syracuse, and New York University.[1] It was, arguably, that same impulse that spurred her to action as theorist, polemicist, propagandist, and animator of the early collective efforts among independent filmmakers in this country. If, in fact, these developments assumed the dynamism of a "movement," it was in large part due to Deren's ability to articulate and promote these efforts, to act as spokeswoman for the filmmaker as artist within our culture. Her example, her influence, her concrete programs were to define a model of filmmaking practice for several generations of workers in that field, and it is in terms of that model— rather than through formal influences or morphological parallels—that we can locate and assess the nature and the quality of her contribution to the larger culture of our time.

To do this, I return, then, to a photograph, a group picture made some four decades ago at Cinema 16, a pioneer film society dedicated to the presentation to New York audiences of work by artists of the American avant-garde. The particular occasion here documented was a symposium held in October 1953, "Poetry and the Film." The proceedings, published in somewhat abridged form in Jonas Mekas's review, *Film Culture*, constitute a document of high interest.[2] Rereading them now, one is startled by an intensity and level of exchange among working artists to which we are no longer accustomed. The scene is that of the early 1950s, and here, gathered by Amos Vogel, the director of Cinema 16, in addition to Deren, are its players. Parker Tyler, a poet and film critic already distinguished, had been actively involved, during their wartime exile in New York, with the surrealists. Another member of this group is Willard Maas, filmmaker. The others are Arthur Miller, then the white hope of a certain native theatrical realism, and Dylan Thomas, poet and a frequently visiting star performer of that period. These latter two are undoubtedly there to represent, respectively, prose and poetry. With Maas acting as chairman or moderator, cinema and poesis are most strongly represented by Deren herself.

This occasion unites not only varying conceptions of film but also deeply contradictory notions as to what the nature of such an occasion might be, antithetical presuppositions about the conventions of possible discourse on film. And inscribed within it is the clear evidence of the status of a woman as independent filmmaker—one doubly marginalized and exposed to the lordly contempt affected by intellectuals for seriousness in film and for the female subject as theoretician. Thomas's coarse and derisive wit, his grandstanding joviality are thus directed against the seriousness of a woman filmmaker's attempt to define the subject about which they might profitably converse.

Miller, whose discourse is less narcissistic and more interesting than Thomas's, has obviously given somewhat more thought to the topic at hand, and there is, near the end, one remarkable moment when he suddenly declares, "I think that it would be profitable to speak about the special nature of any film, of the fact of images unwinding off a machine. Until that's understood, and I don't know that it's understood (I have some theories about it myself), we can't begin to create on a methodical basis,

Figure 3. Cinema 16 Symposium, "Poetry and the Film," October 28, 1953. *Left to right:* Dylan Thomas, Arthur Miller, Willard Maas, Parker Tyler, Amos Vogel, and Maya Deren. Courtesy of Amos Vogel.

an aesthetic for that film. We don't understand the psychological meaning of images—any image—coming off a machine. There are basic problems, it seems to me, that could be discussed here."[3]

These remarks are apparently offered as an antidote to what Miller obviously considers to be the questionable rhetoric of Deren's poetics, but that challenge and its invocation of "basic problems" will, of course, nevertheless later come to figure in subsequent attempts at an aesthetic and an ontology of cinema undertaken by American independents and their European colleagues through the reexamination—twenty years later, as their movement develops—of the materiality, the conditions and empirical contingencies of filmmaking and exhibition. The theoretical literature of this postwar cinematic avant-garde remains, to this day, virgin territory for investigation and analysis. Elaborated quite outside the precincts of academia, the theory and practice of Brakhage, Sharits, Frampton, Kubelka, Le Grice, and Gidal, among others, we may now see as an extraordinarily powerful and proleptic corpus of what one might term *une pensée sauvage*, the product of a brilliant *bricolage* accomplished within the general framework of a modernist aesthetic. It is as such that I shall consider Deren's major theoretical text, *An Anagram of Ideas on Art, Form and Film* (*Anagram* hereafter), provided here after page 267.[4]

II

[P]recisely because film, like language, serves a wide variety of needs, the triumphs which it achieves in one capacity must not be permitted to obscure its failure in another. **–Maya Deren**

What was it that Deren was on this occasion proposing? And what did it signify for those who followed in her wake?

Deren spoke for a cinema of poetry and a poetics of cinema, representing an approach to experience as distinguished from that of the "drama." Elaborating and further focusing on this question, which had already engaged a tradition of film-theoretical debate around the issue of medium specificity, she now presents a new set of terms for its consideration, describing her approach as "vertical" in structure, as

an investigation of a situation, in that it probes the ramifications of the moment, and is concerned with its qualities and its depth, so that you have poetry concerned, in a sense, not with what is occurring but with what it feels like or what it means. A poem, to my mind, creates visible or auditory form for something that is invisible, which is the feeling or the emotion or the metaphysical content of the statement. Now, it may also include action, but its attack is what I would call the vertical attack, and this may be a little bit clearer if you will contrast it to what I would call the horizontal attack, to drama which is concerned with the development, let's say, within a very small situation from feeling to feeling.[5]

She continues with a consideration of the relation in Shakespeare's work of the lyric to dramatic form, allowing for the possibilities of varied combinations. "You can have operas where the 'horizontal' development is virtually unimportant—the plots are very silly but they serve as an excuse for stringing together a number of arias that are essentially lyric statements. Lieder are, in singing, comparable to the lyric poem, and you can see that all sorts of combinations would be possible."[6]

Deren is on this occasion arguing passionately and prophetically for something fundamental: a recognition *for* cinema, *in* cinema, of the duality of linguistic structure, that very duality that Jakobson was to propose, through his study of aphasia, as the metonymic and metaphoric modes, on which contemporary film theory eventually builds.[7] The subsequent development within academic cinema studies of the syntagmatic chain as the principal axis of film analysis and scholarship was indeed to strengthen and confirm the hegemony of the heavily coded narrative structure within both industrial film production and academic film theory. (Bazin's defense of the metonymic mode as the epiphanic celebration of the world's flesh would, of course, work toward a confirmation of this structure.)

It was against this hegemony and in validation of a commitment to the substitutive metaphor as an essential constructive element that Deren spoke, and the set of formal strategies entailed by this position and deeply grounded in montage was to generate an entire rethinking, not only of composition and production, but, eventually, of distribution, exhibition, and reception as well.

Deren's intervention at Cinema 16 was by no means her first effort at a *Defense and Illustration of a Poetic Cinema*. It stands, nonetheless, as a dramatic moment of crystallization in the theorization of the New American Cinema, that of the period following World War II. It spoke to her contemporary independents and to the next two generations of filmmakers with a force that can be compared only to the early manifestoes and theoretical texts of Eisenstein. Indeed, we must read her work as re-opening, within the context of postwar America, questions posed by the direction, shape, and scale of Eisenstein's project, which had by that time acquired canonical status within the history of cinema.[8]

What, most generally and strongly, might impel one to make such a claim? The sense of a constant and intimate articulation of theory with practice, a relentless concern with systematization, the determination to ground innovative practice in theory. And, of course, the manner in which both practice and theory stand in a relation of fruitful, unresolved ten-sion, at variance with those of industrial production in her time. Tracing the development of Deren's work and of her role, one discerns a logic that solicits comparison, in some detail, with that of Eisenstein in the con-struction of a New Cinema—in their insistence on the grounding of this cinema in a solid basis of theory, in their reference to other disciplines and forms of artistic practice. Of major importance as well was their grounding in theatrical (and choreographic) movement and gesture, their adventurous forays into other cultures, their interest in ritual, and the manner in which their production is crowned by ambitious and uncom-pleted ethnographic projects—Eisenstein's in Mexico, Deren's in Haiti. To the consideration of those projects I shall return.

I want, however, at this point to stress their common desire for a sys-tematicity that could provide the solid basis and legitimation of their rad-ically innovative practices. Eisenstein's theory and practice are, as we know, marked, like Deren's, from the first by the contrasting strains of a desire for systematicity and for an organicity of structure. And there is ultimately a sense in which the theoretical productivity of both may have been, in part at least, stimulated by and compensated for by the frustra-tions encountered in practice.

Anagram, Deren's major text of 1946, forms an early, ambitious, and nearly definitive statement of her poetics. More than this, it sets the tone and largely defines the terms of what came to be the movement of the New American Cinema for the four decades following the war. *Anagram* is, in fact, the unprecedented attempt, within the United States, on the part of a twenty-six-year-old woman, to propose an ontology, an aesthetic, and an ethos of cinema. Although its density and scope defy the possibility of complete analysis within the constraints of a single essay, I shall want, nonetheless, to convey something of the text's general contours and, in passing, something of its points of convergence with the work of European theorists.

Deren's table of contents for this discursive text ("Contents of Anagram") is itself presented as informed with the dynamic play of horizontal and vertical axes in violation of univocal linearity. Central not only to her poetics, such play will become the primary line of attack for succeeding generations of the American avant-garde in their struggle against the hegemony of narrative codes and conventions. *Anagram* is a concrete, visual form of presentation, offered together with the following introductory explanation of her strategy:

> An anagram is a combination of letters in such a relationship that each and every one is simultaneously an element in more than one linear series. This simultaneity is real, and independent of the fact that it is usually perceived in succession. Each element of an anagram is so related to the whole that no one of them may be changed without affecting its series and so affecting the whole. And, conversely, the whole is so related to every part that whether one reads horizontally, vertically, diagonally or even in reverse, the logic of the whole is not disrupted, but remains intact.[9]

Deren's triple project is, as a close reading of the text reveals, the construction of an ethos (in the three texts of column A), a general aesthetic (elaborated in the three texts of column B), and a cinematic ontology (adumbrated in column C). And all three sections are informed by a critical analysis of developments in contemporary film production seen within a general sociopolitical context. One notes, however, that the project of an ontology is fused and, to some extent, confused with an aesthetic, itself presented as a poetics.

It was, as noted above, in 1946—that is to say, in the climate of malaise created by Hiroshima—that Deren undertook this project of theorization. The cinema of the American avant-garde has been frequently accused of apoliticism. This is, of course, a wholly unjust accusation, as an attentive review of the work of Brakhage, Sharits, Baillie, and Connor, among others, reveals. The movement that was to come to full maturity in the late 1960s was founded by a woman who opened her onto-aesthetic text by an analysis of the American citizenry's passive response to the deployment of the atom bomb. She sees this as an extension of the nation's sense of its inevitable domination by a science and technology that escape comprehension or control, domination by the industrial and military complex that was shortly to emerge in the "reconversion" period after 1945. Her analysis of what she characterizes as "the schizoid nature" of the social formation within modernity is posited in terms that recall T. S. Eliot's observations on "the dissociation of sensibility," whose origins both Eliot and Deren locate in the seventeenth century—an epistemological break that Europeans will more readily identify with the advent of Cartesianism.[10]

It is this analysis that generates Deren's ethos, expressed in her conviction that it was the artist's role, even morally incumbent on the artist, to confront and address the forces threatening a generalized *anomie*, to address them in one's art, "not literally, of course, but imaginatively." For Deren, artistic practice is, then, the most powerful antidote to what she sees as an atrophy of consciousness.

And it is, curiously and interestingly enough, in the name of the struggle against this *anomie* that she launches her project with an attack on realism and on the "romantic realism" of surrealism. She appears to have in mind the figurative pictorialism through which surrealism was largely represented and known by the time of her writing. She rejects, moreover, what she terms surrealism's ecstatic elimination of the "functions of consciousness and intelligence."[11]

It is in the alignment of these two factors that we can see something of the contradictions that inform her categorical rejection of surrealism.

Breton had early on marked out two possible paths for the movement's development of painting. The first, adumbrated in a tribute to Cézanne, proposed the locus of signification in compositional form—the "metaphysics" that transpired through the folds of a curtain within a painted portrait. The second path was that of the graphic elaboration and illustration of the iconography of dreams. It was that second path—taken by Dalí, Tanguy, Ernst, and Matta—that she condemned. What Deren did not perceive and understand, however, was the extent to which a free, gestural play, as in the work of André Masson (sanctioned by a tradition of experimentation in automatic production), was to play a role in the maturation of American painting. We do well to remember that Deren's theory and practice are exactly contemporary with the development of abstract expressionism—with the work of Pollock, Rothko, Kline, de Kooning, and Motherwell. Deren's strategy, involving the rejection of both unconscious processes as operative in artistic production and the primacy of the mimetic-figurative, was aimed at the establishment of a cinematic specificity and at the institution of the filmmaker as "artist," a status that is repetitively, indeed, obsessively invoked on every occasion of presentation of her work, in both theory and practice.

Anagram, presented as an ontology of cinema, offers, rather, an aesthetic and an ethos. Deren sees the aesthetic as predominantly moral in essence. Her critique of contemporary documentary cinema proceeds from the observation that "they stand on moral grounds which are ostensibly impregnable. Yet it is my belief, and I think that I am not alone in this, that the documentaries of World War II illuminate precisely how such a failure of form is a failure of morals, even when it results from nothing more intentionally instructive than incompetency, or the creative lethargy of the 'achieved' professional craftsman. Surely, the human tragedy of the war requires of those who presume to commemorate it— film-maker, writer, painter—a personal creative effort somehow commensurate in profundity and stature."[12]

The "commensurate effort" of documentation is defined throughout Deren's discourse in terms of a resolutely modernist tradition, founded on a crisis of the referent. It is a crisis that enjoins the artist to take part in what Deren, in the idiom of her time, calls "the renunciation of the natural frame of reference." This renunciation is not, she says, an escape from "the labor of truth."[13] On the contrary, it places on the artist "the entire responsibility for creating a logic as dynamic, integrated and compelling as those in which nature abounds." Deren eventually takes care, however, to reassure her reader: "Everything which I have said in criticism of film may create an image of severe austerity and asceticism. On the contrary, you may find me many evenings in the motion-picture theater, sharing with the other sleepers (for nothing so resembles sleep), the selected dream without responsibilities."[14] One notes the allusion to a signal work of the time, Delmore Schwartz's early story, "In Dreams Begin Responsibilities," which commences with a vision of his parents presented as if on a film screen.[15] Deren came to insist that above all, "it must never be forgotten" what film owes to D. W. Griffith and Mack Sennett, to Murnau and Pabst, Méliès and Delluc, Stiller and Eisenstein.[16] And she will express her "deep affection for those films which raised personalities to almost a super-natural stature and created, briefly, a mythology of gods of the first magnitude whose mere presence lent to the most undistinguished events a divine grandeur and intensity—Theda Bara, Mary Pickford, Gish, Valentino, Fairbanks and the early Garbo, Dietrich, Harlow and Crawford."[17]

Deren's critique of the documentary film is, one notes, supplemented by her strictures concerning the abstract film, which she sees not merely as derivative of painting, but for the most part as animated painting.[18] Arguing for the priority of the imagination, she clings, nonetheless, to a conception of cinema as defined by the indexical iconicity of what she terms "elements of reality." This principle is, in fact, fundamental to the aesthetic that she presents as an ontology; it is, one presumes, a cinema that would offer, as no other medium can, "real toads in imaginary gardens." It was, however, her close and most seminal colleague, Stan Brakhage, who would define entirely new dimensions of visual abstraction in the service of a mythopoetic cinema.[19]

Filmic abstraction would require, as Deren has it, a *temporal* abstraction or composition.[20] It is for this reason that she nominates Duchamp's single cinematic work as an interesting and exceptional venture, astutely exempting it from her critical judgment of both abstract and surrealist-inspired film. For *Anemic Cinema* "occupies, like the rest of his work, a unique position."[21] And her analysis of this work remained for another three decades the only serious attempt to account for what has long appeared an anomalous object, a spanner thrown into the works of film history.

> Although it uses geometric forms, it is not an abstract film, but perhaps the only "optical pun" in existence. The time which he causes one of his spirals to revolve in the screen effects an optical metamorphosis; the cone appears first concave, then convex, and in the more complicated spirals, both concave and convex and then inverted. It is time, therefore, which creates these optical puns which are the visual equivalents, in *Anemic Cinema* for instance, of the inserted phrases which also revolve and, in doing so, disclose the verbal "sense."[22]

Deren's analysis of the dissociation of sensibility, its consequences, and the burden now placed on the artist has led her to a critique of the aesthetic and ethos of art as expression: the manner in which the artist now often tends, as she puts it, to work out of compulsions of individual distress. This critique no doubt informs her sympathy for Duchamp's enterprise as a whole. She goes on to propose other possible modes and functions of artistic production. Having rejected the role of unconscious processes in artistic production, she now displaces it, situating it on the level of the larger, general social formation. "Art must at least comprehend the large facts of the total culture and, at best, extend them imaginatively."[23] And she now invokes the role of a *collective unconscious* within " the deep recesses of our cultural memory, the release of a procession of indistinct figures wearing the masks of Africa, or the Orient, the hoods of the chorus or the innocence of the child-virgin . . . the faces always concealed, or veiled by stylization—moving in formal patterns of ritual and destiny."[24]

It is the importance of ritual (invoked against both the "confessional" quality of surrealism and the compulsive narcissism of expressionism) for a *contemporary* art that she ingeniously argues. It is thus not the expression of individual subjectivity, but rather "the application of . . . individual talent to the moral problems which have been the concern of man's relationship with deity, and the evidence of that privileged communication."[25] Interestingly enough, however, neither ritual nor those states of possession, with which Deren is concerned, are invoked as revelatory of a transcendental signifier. For she remarks that man cannot presume to knowledge of divine omniscience and power. Her view of individual subjectivity and its aesthetic expression is, in fact consonant with that offered by T. S. Eliot's "Tradition and the Individual Talent," a text which had, by the time of Deren's writing, achieved canonical status within Anglo-American debates on criticism and aesthetics.[26] Arguing for the crucial role of tradition as a sense of the past in truly dialectical relation to the present, Eliot had launched his attack on the valuation of "personality":

> The point of view which I am struggling to attack is perhaps related to the metaphysical theory of the substantial unity of the soul; for my meaning is, that the poet has, not a "personality" to express, but a particular medium, in which impression and experience combine in peculiar and unexpected ways. . . .[27] One error, in fact, of eccentricity in poetry is to seek for new human emotions to express; and in this search for novelty in the wrong place it discovers the perverse. . . . Poetry is not a turning loose of emotion, but an escape from emotion; it is not the expression of personality, but an escape from personality.[28]

Armed thus with the support of a symbolist-derived aesthetic that had been the object of her academic studies, Deren then develops the manner in which ritual treats the human subject, not as the generator of dramatic action, but as a somewhat depersonalized element in a dramatic whole. The subject is thus *enlarged* beyond the personal dimension and freed from the limits and narrow constraints of personality. She goes on to argue that "he becomes part of a dynamic whole which, like all such creative relationships, in turn, endows its parts with a measure of its larger meaning."[29]

We may then claim that ritual here performs for Deren the role that the epic form did for Eisenstein. And we may further and profitably compare this statement with Eisenstein's realization from his contact with oriental theater that

> when a common cultural heritage and conducting agent exist,
> it is perfectly possible to communicate by means of those general,
> emotionally charged complex units, lacking the sharp individualiza-
> tion of a precise, private, conceptual order. And this may, further-
> more, act to enlarge the sphere of communication. It is interesting
> to note that this method has the advantage of a generalized evidence
> conferred by the symbol; it may sacrifice a certain intellectual sharp-
> ness and precision, but it became, for that very reason, the means
> of communication between untold numbers of people in the East.

For Deren, ritual will provide the model for creation of form and effect through "conscious manipulation," through elimination of what she terms "spontaneous compulsions of expression" and "realistic representation." And it is this that brings ritualistic form into a relation to "modern science"—a relation far closer than that of the naturalism which has claimed science as its ground.

Eisenstein, in the course of his own sustained investigation of the links between artistic practice and scientific research, had remarked on the way in which "at present, we can say that the scientific systems of the Chinese are based not on principles of abstract thought, but on those of sensual thinking. Or, in other terms, that Chinese science is constructed not on the model of scientific systems but in the image of the work of art."

III

Life depends, above all, on the path which leads from the Dionysian forest to the ruins of the classical theater. This must not be merely stated, but repeated with the obstinacy of faith. It is insofar as existence avoids the presence of the tragic that it becomes trivial and ludicrous. And it is insofar as it participates in a sacred terror that it is human. It may be that this paradox is too extreme and difficult to sustain; it is, nonetheless, as essential to life as blood. **–Georges Bataille**

Three great ruins mark the landscape of film history—documentary projects all, incomplete, fragmentary, undertaken by major figures at variance with the systems of industrial film production and dominant practice. Eisenstein, Deren, and Welles essayed a turn from those systems to ethnographic projects and to alternative modes of production (involving, for Eisenstein and Deren, private patronage) to provide the condition for the working confrontation with foreign cultures. And this confrontation would confirm the problematic nature of their relations both to their own cultures and to those of their alternate arenas of enterprise. Like Eisenstein, who had turned to Mexico from his disastrous experience as the visiting artist-revolutionary summoned and dismissed by the American film industry, Deren approached her work in Haiti with the euphoric eagerness of discovery.[30] And like Eisenstein, she knew that she must "permit the culture and the myth to emerge gradually in its own terms and its own form." And she was later to speak of the felt necessity, upon her encounter with the seductions of Haitian culture, for a "discretion," balanced by "a sense of human bond which I did not fully understand until my first return to the United States." She then continues, in a passage that reads like a blow-by-blow description of Eisenstein's journey through America in 1930:

> At that moment I became freshly aware of a situation to which I had grown inured and oblivious: that in a modern industrial culture the artists constitute, in fact, an "ethnic group," subject to the full "native" treatment. We too are exhibited as touristic curiosities on Monday, extolled as culture on Tuesday, denounced as immoral and

unsanitary on Wednesday, reinstated for scientific study Thursday, feasted for some obscurely stylish reason Friday, forgotten Saturday, revisited as picturesque Sunday. We too are misrepresented by professional appreciators and subjected to spiritual imperialism. . . . My own ordeal as an "artist-native" in an industrial culture made it impossible for me to be guilty of similar effronteries towards the Haitian peasants.[31]

From their ethnographically inspired projects, both filmmakers gained access to a dimension of experience that was undoubtedly decisive in their later undertakings: a glimpse, widely sought but denied to many of their generation, of the meaning of community in its most absorbing and fulfilling instance, of collective enterprise grounded in the mythic. One may, in fact, see both as fellows in a program defined by the group of intellectuals gathered in the 1930s around Bataille, who defined their aims as follows:

The precise object of the projected activity may be termed a sacred sociology insofar as it implies the study of social existence in all its manifestations in which the active presence of the sacred appears. It thus proposes to establish points of convergence between the basic and driving impulses of individual psychology and the directional structures that command social organization and direct its revolutions.

Deren had come to the theory and practice of film with preparation of a sort unique in her American lineage: that of her Marxist studies and involvement in the Trotskyist youth movement.[32] These experiences had undoubtedly stimulated a sense of community and predisposed her to shared goals and collective experience. They also provided a context and stimulus for the rejection of Hollywood's native pragmatism and her claim that industrial production's lack of creativity derived from its lack of a theoretical dimension, and for the theorization of her own practice.

Deren had from the first envisaged a cinema recharged, as it were, with the energy of dance. Speaking of *Ritual in Transfigured Time*, whose open-

ing sequence offers an exercise in variational form distilled from the ki-
netics of the social convention of the cocktail party, she accurately describes it as a dance film, but more particularly as one whose continuity
is established and sustained not by the performer, but by the emotional
integrity of the movement itself, independent of its performer, by continuity of movement between disparate individuals so identified, in which
the cinematic unity is a statement of common motivation shared by the
individual elements.[33]

Studying in 1947 the footage of performance shot in Bali by Bateson
and Mead, Deren sees with a sense of mounting excitement the sacred
rites performed therein as totalizing in their design, their integrity supported by the compelling necessity of every detail; they offer the aesthetic
distillation of obsession.[34] She seizes on the relation of accident to design, the attitude toward costume and disrobing, the distancing of theatrical effects, the elimination of transitions within Balinese performance
structure. She establishes, in fact, an inventory of what was later to become the idiom of modernist performance. Reading Balinese performance as a social text, she discovers another instance of the complex integrity of form that she has already observed locally, in children's games
played on the streets of New York. Considering both such games and that
of chess as secularized forms of ritual, she observes in configurations such
as that of hopscotch an element of the "inviolable." She insists, moreover, on the centrality of that inviolability to the issue of formal autonomy. Its prestige, she says, is contingent on satisfaction of the form itself
as authority, and that form may still be completely independent of our
fundamental relation to actuality.

One recalls the reaction, a decade and a half earlier, of Artaud to the
performances of Balinese dancers at the Colonial Exposition of 1931.[35]
(A detailed comparative study of their respective analyses would doubt-
less yield interesting results.) In the two texts that set forth the deeply
revelatory nature of this event, Artaud sees Balinese performance as exemplary. This experience will work to shape his call for a radical recast-
ing of Western performance as the condition of possibility for a "meta-

physical" theater. He declares that among principal sources of pleasure offered by the Balinese theater are the seamlessness of the whole, the actors' supremely skilled and spiritually informed articulation of an established system of gestures and movements, and the sense that these powerful signs were the fruit of a deep and subtle study such that they had lost none of their power over the passing centuries.

Deren's analysis of the Balinese material is propaedeutic to the development of a specific project of her own, to be composed of three ritual forms: children's games, Balinese performance, and Haitian Voudoun. "I wish to build the film, using the variations between them to contrapuntally create the harmony, the basic equivalence of the idea of form common to them all."

And Eisenstein's project? The interweaving of historical periods of Mexican history and culture into a unity, threads to be laid side by side in the *montagiste* tradition. Or, in his words,

> Striped and violently contrasting are the history and culture in Mexico running next to each other and at the same time being centuries away. . . . No plot, no whole story would run through this Serape without being false or artificial. And we took the contrasting independence of its violent colors as the motif for construction of our film, six episodes following each other—different in character, different in people, different in animals, trees and flowers. And still held together by the unity of the weave—a rhythmic and musical construction and an unrolling of the Mexican spirit and character.[36]

IV

Every possession has a theatrical aspect. –**Alfred Métraux**

Deren had not come unprepared to the study of specifically Haitian ritual, for she had produced, in 1942, well before her first journey to Haiti, the paper "Religious Possession in Dancing," published as the first install-

ment of an article with special reference to Haitian ritual.[37] In this conscientiously researched paper, Deren boldly sets forth a number of the
issues that are to dominate later debates in ethnographic theory, including the relation of possession to the nosology of hysteria. Concerned with
establishing the distinction between the two, Deren does so in terms that
are characteristically shy of psychoanalytic theory and its terminology.
Like Alfred Métraux, who, in his study of Haitian Voudoun, was to devote a section to the theatrical aspect of possession, she gives no consideration to Freud's illuminating rapprochement of the hysteric and the
actor.[38]

Métraux does, however, consider that,

> Possession being closely linked with dancing, it is also thought
> of in terms of a spirit "dancing in the head of his horse." It is also
> an invasion of the body. . . . The symptoms of the opening phase
> of trance are clearly psychopathological. They conform, exactly, in
> their main features to the stock clinical conception of hysteria. . . .
> The preliminary phase can soon end. Every possession has a the-
> atrical aspect. This is at once apparent in the general concern for
> disguise. . . . Unlike an hysteric who shows his own misery and
> desires by means of a symptom—which is an entirely personal
> form of expression—the man who is ritually possessed must corre-
> spond to the traditional conception of some mythical personage.
> The hysterics of long ago who thought themselves the victims of
> devils, also certainly drew the devilish part of their personality from
> the folklore in which they lived, but they were subject to influences
> not entirely comparable to those felt by the possessed in Haiti.[39]

The dividing line is that which marks off the individual from the communal, the pathological from the social. Thus, having stated that "psychologists invariably characterize hysteria by an emancipation of a system of ideas as the result of the retraction of cerebral consciousness,"
Deren, in similar fashion, stresses the role of the hysterical subject's personal conflict: "In a possessed Haitian, the process is parallel, but remains
distinct from hysteria by virtue of the social frame of reference. For al-

though drum rhythms emancipate a system of ideas, that system is not the product of individual development; it is a culturally formalized system, so deeply rooted in the sub-conscious by long tradition that although it requires emotional emancipation from the inhibitions of the cortex, it manifests itself in socially prescribed terms."[40]

Despite one's impression, as noted, of the parallels and similarities between the approaches of Deren and Eisenstein to the ethnographic, one is bound to recognize that they differ in an important respect. Deren's, elaborated in postwar America, is one from which historicity is gradually excised. Having set forth her *Anagram* in full consciousness of the critical historical context of her project, she appears to have become convinced, nonetheless, that "the ritualistic form reflects . . . the conviction that such ideas are best advanced when they are abstracted from the immediate conditions of reality and incorporated into a contrived, created whole, stylized in terms of the utmost effectiveness." And it is with especial interest that we realize that it is precisely with the attempt to bring history within the compass of her project that her enterprise begins to founder. Scrupulous observer that she is, Deren begins, as she penetrates Haitian culture, to realize that she is dealing with a form that defies the boundaries of her onto-esthetic. It is with the realization that Haitian dance was not, in itself, a dance form but part of something larger, a "mythological ritual," that she begins to perceive the "total integrity of cultural form" and its distinctive elements "which eventually led me to look for the possible interpolation of another culture, to investigate the history of the Spanish and Indian period of the islands, and finally, the determination of the Indian influences."[41]

This would lead, as one might have expected, to an assessment of the complex dialectic of power relations among white men, Indians, and blacks that subtends the rituals of Voudoun. And it was the full recognition and acknowledgment of the culture's integrity and of the complex historical processes inscribed within it that seems to have precipitated her acknowledgment of defeat and the eventual abandonment of the project. The humility and poignancy of this acknowledgment offer testimony

Figure 4. Film still from Maya Deren's Haitian footage (no date). By claiming a socially therapeutic function for possession rituals, Deren distinguishes Voudoun dance and trance from the social pathologies of hysteria in Western societies. Courtesy of Anthology Film Archive.

to her rapture of discovery and intensity of involvement in the experience of community in ritual and myth. We can, in fact, conclude that by this point of her trajectory, the linguistic model operative in her theorization begins to replace that of ritual. It is recast as a central architectonic element of a modernism that advocates the concreteness and autonomy of the work of art, extending to that of the autotelic sign. In section 3 of *Anagram*, she had ventured a theorization of the filmic signifier in the following terms:

I do not intend to exclude the process of generalization; these are ripples spreading from images that can encompass the richness of many moments. But to generalize from a specific image is not the same as to understand it as a symbol for that general concept. When an image induces a generalization and gives rise to a notion or idea, it bears towards that emotion or idea the same relationship which an exemplary demonstration bears to some chemical principle; and that is entirely different from the relationship between that principle and the written chemical formula by which it is symbolized. <u>In the first case the principle functions actively; in the second case its action is symbolically described in lieu of the action itself.</u> An understanding of this distinction seems to me to be of primary importance.[42]

Artistic practice must be grounded in this realization, and it "must at least comprehend the large acts of an industrial culture and extend them imaginatively. . . . The history of art is the history of man and of his universe and of the moral relationship between them. Whatever the instrument, the artist sought to re-create the abstract, invisible forces and relationships of the cosmos."[43]

It is this large project, informed by a consciousness of the history of science and technology and of their pervasive roles, that haunts her work as a tireless animator of the independent film movement. Her predecessor in this vision was, of course, Jean Epstein, whose *L'Intelligence d'une machine* she notes as a recently received and, although not as yet wholly read, distinctively interesting theoretical enterprise, free of the banalities of film history.[44]

And it is the scope and import of this large project that distinguishes Deren's work from that of her contemporaries and successors—with one notable exception. For there is, in fact, a sense in which when reflecting on the four decades of American independent cinema as a *movement*, one may see it as bounded by the work of its founder, Maya Deren, and that of the late Hollis Frampton. It was Frampton—poet, cineaste, and theoretician—who would assume the strenuous and seminal role marked out by Deren, that of mediator in the difficult and delicate negotiation of the marriage of poesis and mathesis, a union as scandalous and difficult in our culture as that sanctified by William Blake between heaven and hell.

Notes

1. See VèVè A. Clark, Millicent Hodson, and Catrina Neiman, *The Legend of Maya Deren: A Documentary Biography and Collected Works*. Vol. 1, pt. 1, *Signatures*, and pt. 2, *Chambers* (New York: Anthology Film Archives/Film Culture, 1988).

2. See "Poetry and Film: A Symposium with Maya Deren, Arthur Miller, Dylan Thomas, Parker Tyler, Chairman, Willard Maas. Organized by Amos Vogel" (October 28, 1953), in *The Film Culture Reader*, ed. P. Adams Sitney (New York: Praeger, 1970), pp. 171–86.

3. Ibid., p. 177.

4. Maya Deren, *An Anagram of Ideas on Art, Form and Film* (New York: Alicat Book Shop Press, 1946). Reprinted in *The Legend of Maya Deren: A Documentary Biography and Collected Works*, vol. 1, pt. 2, ed. VèVè A. Clark, Millicent Hodson, and Catrina Neiman (New York: Anthology Film Archives, 1988), pp. 560–603, and here, following page 267.

5. "Poetry and the Film," p. 174

6. Ibid., p. 174.

7. See Roman Jakobson, "Two Aspects of Language and Two Types of Aphasic Disturbance," in *Language in Literature* (Cambridge, MA: Belknap, 1987), pp. 98–113.

8. Deren, in considering the lineage of cinema's innovators, takes care to credit her compatriots. "Above all it must never be forgotten that film owes at least as much to D. W. Griffith and Mack Sennett as to Murnau and Pabst of Germany, Méliès and Delluc of France, Stiller of Sweden and Eisenstein of Russia." She adds, on the basis of what appears to be a limited knowledge of Eisenstein's oeuvre: "At the risk of seeming heretical, I feel that although 'Potemkin' has sequences that are extremely impressive (Eisenstein is nothing if not impressive, ponderously so), for sheer profundity of impact and for an intensely poetic concept of film, I find nothing there to equal various sequences in the much less publicized works of Dovzhenko, such as 'Frontier' or 'Ivan.'" See *Anagram*, pp. 44–45.

9. Ibid, preface to *Anagram*.

10. See Deren's historical account of this issue in section IA of *Anagram*, pp. 7–10.

11. Ibid., p. 8.

12. Deren, *Anagram*, p. 37. Deren's acute and extensive diagnosis of the political and moral dilemmas confronting the scientific and artistic communities of the post-war period is informed with the knowledge gained during her period as student activist within the Trotskyist segment of the American Left known as the Young People's Socialist League. This period of activity, researched with the assistance of Hal Draper, a comrade of that time, is abundantly documented in *The Legend of Maya Deren*, vol. 1, pt. 1, pp. 243–87.

13. Deren, *Anagram*, p. 23.

14. Ibid., p. 44.

15. See Delmore Schwartz, *In Dreams Begin Responsibilities and Other Stories*, edited and with an introduction by James Atlas (New York: New Directions, 1978). Schwartz's title is in turn a quotation of the saying, cited by Yeats as derived from "an old play" and offered as epigraph to his volume of poems entitled *Responsibilities*, of 1914.

16. Deren, *Anagram*, pp. 44–45.

17. Ibid., p. 50.

18. Ibid., p. 45.

19. The canonical account of this development is to be found in P. Adams Sitney, *Visionary Film: The American Avant-Garde* (New York: Oxford University Press, 1974), pp. 211–65. See also Stan Brakhage, *Metaphors on Vision* (New York: Film Culture, 1963).

20. "To abstract in film terms would require an abstraction in time as well as in space; but in abstract films time is not itself manipulated. . . . For an action to take place in time is not at all the same as for an action to be created by the exercise of time." Deren, *Anagram*, p. 45.

21. Ibid., p. 45.

22. Ibid., pp. 47–48.

23. Ibid., p. 16.

24. Ibid., p. 18.

25. Ibid., p. 20.

26. Thus Eliot: "Tradition . . . involves, in the first place, the historical sense . . . and the historical sense involves a perception not only of the pastness of the past, but of its presence. . . . This historical sense, which is a sense of the timeless as well as of the temporal and of the timeless and of the temporal together, is what makes a writer traditional. And it is at the same time what makes a writer most acutely conscious of his place in time, of his contemporaneity. See T. S. Eliot, *The Sacred Wood* (London: Metheun, 1920), p. 49.

27. Ibid., p. 56.

28. Ibid., pp. 57–58.

29. These considerations, developed throughout *Anagram*, are laid out in Deren's *Outline Guide* and *Program Notes* prepared by her "for the use of those who introduce the films and who may lead the discussion following them." See *The Legend of Maya Deren*, vol. 1, pt. 2, pp. 626–29.

30. Eisenstein's experience within the American film industry is chronicled in Ivor Montagu, *With Eisenstein in Hollywood* (New York: International Publishers, 1967). The Mexican project is amply documented in Sergei Eisenstein and Upton Sinclair, *The Making and Unmaking of "Que Viva Mexico!"* ed. Harry M. Geduld and Ronald Gottesman (Bloomington and London: Indiana University Press, 1970). See also Sergei Eisenstein, "Letters from Mexico," *October*, no. 14 (fall 1980): 55–64.

31. Maya Deren, *Divine Horsemen: The Living Gods of Haiti* (New York: McPherson, 1970), pp. 7–8.

32. For detailed consideration of this aspect of Deren's activity and its intensification during her student days at the University of Syracuse, see *Legend*, vol. 1, pt. 1, pp. xx-xxii, 186–345.

33. See Deren's notes for the opening sequence in *Legend*, vol. 1, pt. 2, pp. 452–53. Her meditation on cinematic temporality leads her to affirm, as Jean Epstein and Dziga Vertov had previously done, that "slow motion is the microscope of time." For her published presentation of *Ritual in Transfigured Time*, see pp. 457–62.

34. The journal in which she recorded her analysis of this footage is reproduced *in extenso* in *October*, no. 14, pp. 21–46.

35. In Antonin Artaud, *The Theatre and its Double* (London and New York: Calder and Boyars, 1958); see "On the Balinese Theatre," pp. 53–67, and "Oriental and Occidental Theatre," pp. 68–74.

36. This description of Eisenstein's Mexican project, extracted from correspondence with Upton Sinclair, is included in S. M. Eisenstein, *Que Viva Mexico* (London: Vision, 1952), p. 10. For the fullest account of this entire episode, see Eisenstein and Sinclair, *The Making and Unmaking of "Que Viva Mexico!"*

37. This text is reproduced in Deren, *Legend*, vol. 1, pt. 2, pp. 480–97.

38. This relation is elaborated on in *Psychoanalysis and Religious Origins*, a text of 1919 in which Freud postulates that if psychoanalysis "has hit upon a truth it must apply equally to normal human events and even the highest achievements of the human spirit must bear a demonstrable relation to the factors found in pathology . . . it was evident that the forms assumed by the different neuroses echoed the highest achievements of the human spirit."

39. See Alfred Métraux, *Voodoo in Haiti*, trans. Hugo Charteris, introduction by Sidney W. Mintz (New York: Schocken, 1972), pp. 120–21.

40. Deren, "Religious Possession in Dancing," in *The Legend of Maya Deren*, vol. 1, pt. 1, p. 592.

41. Deren, *Divine Horsemen*, pp. 10–11.

42. Ibid., p. 27.

43. Ibid., p. 27

44. Ibid., p. 47.

5

Renata Jackson

The Modernist Poetics of Maya Deren

Maya Deren's writings on the art of the motion picture, like those of other early film theorists such as Rudolf Arnheim, André Bazin, Jean Epstein, Sergei Eisenstein, or Dziga Vertov, to name just a few, fall within the tradition of modernist film theory and abide by its core assumption of medium-specificity: the two-pronged belief that art forms are differentiated from one another by virtue of their distinctive formal or structural capabilities, and that there is a direct connection between these structural characteristics and each art form's "proper" expressive realm. Modernist film theory has over the years been referred to alternatively as classical or essentialist—the latter term used rather pejoratively to emphasize the ontological character of the theorists' assertions. As Noël Carroll explains in *Philosophical Problems of Classical Film Theory*, for these early theorists, "The special subject matter of each medium supposedly follows from its nature."[1] Carroll goes on to tell us that the idea of medium-specificity intertwines a presupposition of uniqueness with an assumption of excellence: aesthetic essentialists (taking their lead from the eighteenth-century German philosopher Gotthold Ephraim Lessing and his *Laocoön: An Essay Upon the Limits of Painting and Poetry*) presuppose that each art form is fated for a singular purpose (thus the isolation of each medium's distinctive capabilities) and from this further assume that these distinct abilities are therefore not

Figure 5. *Study in Choreography for Camera* (1945). Courtesy of Catrina Neiman.

only what the art form can do best, but also what it must do to be true to the medium.

One problem, of course, is that these sorts of prescriptive and restrictive pronouncements about a medium's appropriate realm tend to look on each art form as a "highly specialized tool" whose form delimits function; another problem is that indeed many art forms have overlapping abilities—such as narration—so how is one to decide to which art form (epic poetry? prose? theater? film?) the function properly belongs?[2] Maya Deren's film theory, for example, indeed champions as distinctive the capabilities of the film medium (the manipulation of space and time via various camera speeds and editorial choices) and counterposes these abilities to the structural characteristics of other art forms.[3] She often argues her points in purist terms of aesthetic integrity; that is, she insists that film is primarily a visual medium and therefore that film art must communicate through its imagery, not through theatrical or literary dialogue.[4] And she privileges historical precedent as a means of distinguishing one art form's "essential" expressive means from another: for example, since dance and theater already employ the movement of bodies through space, then film artists, Deren tells us, must create new types of motion that can exist only in filmic representation.[5] Thus she sets forth a very circumscribed mode of film practice in the name of "true" film art: "The form proper of film is, for me, accomplished only when the elements, whatever their original context, are related according to the special character of the instrument of film itself—the camera and the editing—so that the reality which emerges is a new one—one which only film can achieve and which could not be accomplished by the exercize [*sic*] of any other instrument."[6]

While Carroll thoroughly critiques the logical flaws of medium-specificity, he does briefly mention its "beneficial side effects": it inspired scrupulously close formal analysis, in opposition to an earlier "tendency to reduce all the arts to a common denominator," and it "enhanc[ed] our understanding of film."[7] Nevertheless, after reading Carroll, one may come away with a sense of classical film theory as irredeemably wrongheaded. With the essentialist project already so dissected, its limitations already pointed out, and its "benefits" minimized, one might ask why take the time to explore Deren's film theory, if it too is rooted in the assumptions of the specificity thesis? The answer is that the lasting value, which must not be downplayed, of Deren's and the other early theorists' work is precisely in their having increased our comprehension and appreciation of the cinema through the imaginative insights they afford us: Arnheim's formalist aesthetic, for instance, or Bazin's realist aesthetic, Epstein's concept of *photogénie*, Eisenstein's dialectical montage, Vertov's theory of intervals. Maya Deren gives us an aesthetic of experimental or avant-garde film practice as well as the metaphors of "horizontal" and "vertical" film form.

Deren continually honed the language she used to express her particular film aesthetics. In the preface to *An Anagram of Ideas on Art, Form and Film,* for instance, she wrote that after *Meshes of the Afternoon* (1943) was finished, she believed "the function of film . . . was to create experience—in this case a semi-psychological reality."[8] After making *At Land* (1944), however, she began to feel that the primary function of film was to manipulate the time and space of reality. After *A Study in Choreography for the Camera* (1945), she retained her emphasis on space-time manipulation but added that the resultant image should maintain a "visual integrity, which would create a dramatic necessity of itself," meaning that the space-time of the action must be created through filmic means rather than be a recording of a preexisting theatrical or literary drama.[9] After her fourth film, *Ritual in Transfigured Time* (1945–1946), and by the summer of 1946 as she was writing *Anagram,* she insisted on the importance of all the considerations mentioned above but maintained that "special attention must be given to the creative possibilities of Time, and that the form as a whole should be ritualistic."[10] In other words, although the film artist must take advantage of the medium's special ability to creatively manipulate movement, these space-time manipulations must not be used to make a film form solely for the purpose of self-expression; rather, like the shaman or artist in "primitive society," the film artist must engage in a more selfless goal of creating depersonalized art objects whose design and function, like that of ritual forms, is to assist others in comprehending their contemporary social conditions.[11]

Despite Deren's stated conviction that film form should be ritualistic, however, and despite the fact that ritual form receives high critical praise over all the other art forms she discusses in *Anagram* (surrealism, realism, naturalism, modern primitivism), in "The Art of Film" chapters of this text neither the word "ritual" nor the term "ritualistic film-form" is ever mentioned. Even where a discussion of ritual form does appear—it is introduced in the last paragraph of the last chapter in column A, "The Nature of Forms," and is the main subject of the following (first) chapter within column B, "The Forms of Art"—Deren proposes the term rather tentatively, admitting that its anthropological use with regard to "primitive" cultures, as well as the fact that rites and ritual art forms are generally of anonymous design, may inhibit an acceptance of the term "ritualistic" in relation to the creation of consciously designed contemporary art forms.[12] Both these factors—Deren's hesitance about the term and its absence from "The Art of Film"—provide us with clues that, in the long run, Deren drew the metaphors for her film aesthetics from elsewhere.

Deren continued to use the word "ritual" in reference to only two of her films. One is, of course, *Ritual in Transfigured Time*, which she always described as ritualistic both in form and content.[13] The other is a project she alternately called a "visual fugue" or "cross-cultural counterpoint"— a nonnarrative film she initially hoped to make by juxtaposing images of secular and religious rituals.[14] By mid-1949, however, Deren not only abandoned this film idea of counterposed rituals (Balinese and Haitian religious rituals intercut with secular rituals of New York City children at play), but she also shifted from a filmic application of the term "ritual form" to a use of it almost exclusively with regard to actual religious practice.

While we do not find any insistence on the proper form of film art as "ritualistic" in any of her writings after 1949, the subject of ritual forms and performance, particularly with regard to Haitian Voudoun, continued to be of supreme interest to Deren throughout her life. She made four trips to Haiti to learn about their rites and customs and to film Voudoun ceremonial dances; she wrote a well-received book-length ethnographic study, *Divine Horsemen: The Living Gods of Haiti*[15]; and during the late 1940s and 1950s, when she was not lecturing about film as an art form or working on her experimental films, she spent much of her time writing, lecturing, and appearing on television and radio programs as a self-proclaimed advocate for Voudoun, attempting to redress the general misperception of it as "voodoo," hocus-pocus, or black magic.[16]

Deren's involvement with Haitian culture is a fascinating topic that I have elsewhere given extended consideration.[17] My focus here, however, is on her film theory. If Deren rejected the "ritual" metaphor, using it neither to describe the proper form for film art nor as an umbrella term for her own films, then what terms does she use, and from what sources do her aesthetics arise?

As early as October 1946, Deren replaces "ritualistic" with the descriptive term "classicist," insisting that her own creative method (and by implication, the proper method for creating any true work of film art) consists in reasoned (purposeful and conscious) attention to order and form, in contradistinction to that of the romantic's flights of fancy or the surrealist's appeals to the unconscious.[18] Through the late 1940s to 1950, Deren continues to describe her works as classicist, but by the early 1950s she begins to call all her films "choreographies for camera," "chamber films," or "cine-poems," while also emphasizing the medium's ability to manipulate the temporal dimension above all else.[19] Deren thus informs her lecture audiences that the uniqueness of the cinema lies in its being

a time-form, and [therefore] it is really rather more closely related to music and dance than it is to any of the spatial forms, the plastic forms. Now it's been thought that because you see it on a two-dimensional surface which is approximately the size and shape of a canvas . . . that it is somehow in the area of the plastic arts. This is not true, because it is not the way anything is at a given moment that

is important in film, it is what it is doing, how it is becoming;
in other words, it is its composition over time, rather than within
space, which is important. In this sense, as I say, structurally it
is much more comparable to the time-forms, including poetry.[20]

Film—like the art forms of dance, music, and poetry—deals with rhythm
or cadence, which necessarily involves movement or change over time,
what Deren expresses in very Bergsonian terms as "becoming." She sees
her films in particular as "choreographies for camera" because she does
not simply record staged dance movements but creates new movements
out of the quadruple interactions of the dancers' motions, her camera
movements, various recording speeds, and her editorial choices.[21] They
are "chamber films," because, like the compositions for a small ensemble of musical instruments (for example, a flute trio or a string quartet),
Deren's films too are modest in size but demonstrate the "virtuoso" capabilities of the motion picture instrument.[22]

Deren was an avid aficionado of classical music, and although not a
professional dancer, she was self-assured of her skill as an amateur, so we
can see from where arise her analogies to chamber music and dance. But
from where does Deren's conception of poetic film structure emerge?
Furthermore, how does it coincide with her general aesthetics as she expresses them in *Anagram* and elsewhere? Indeed, there is a snug fit, and
so it is to Deren's theory and its sources that I now turn.

A Humanist Ethics and Aesthetics

Deren wrote *An Anagram of Ideas on Art, Form and Film* the year after
World War II ended, and thus, in the wake of the war and the dropping
of the bomb, it is not surprising to find the text permeated by her appeals to moral probity:

> At the moment, it has become fashionable, among all the self-
> appointed mentors of public conscience, to bemoan the inertia
> of the people towards the atom bomb, and to chastize [*sic*] this

complacency with elaborate attitudes of righteous indignation, or pompous didacticism, or despair and silence. But inertia is, precisely, not a reaction—wrong or right;—it is the sheer persistence of an attitude already firmly habitual. The almost casual acceptance of the use of atomic energy is, if anything, testimony to man's complete adjustment to science; for him, it is merely the most recent in a long series of achievements, some of which, like electricity and the radio, have had far more the quality of miracle.[23]

Deren's statement here, while sarcastically critical of anyone's nonchalance toward the atom bomb ("merely the most recent" of scientific advancements, a device she soon thereafter likens, in size and destructive force, to the forbidden apple from the Tree of Knowledge in the Garden of Eden) is not, as one might initially think, a call to turn away from technology and back to nature.[24] On the contrary, her point is that the inventions of modern science are so commonplace in the middle of the twentieth century that most people fail to give them a second thought. But this attitude is unacceptable, for either the artist or the scientist: the advancements of the twentieth century must neither be neglected nor ignored. For the scientist this responsibility entails being mindful of the moral responsibility that accompanies the ability to wield a power so vast that it could "bring the world to an end."[25] For the artist, as we shall see shortly, the great moral obligation is to use one's conscious faculties in combination with modern art instruments in order to create artworks that help us make sense of our lives.[26]

The atomic bomb aside, Deren sees most of the nineteenth and twentieth centuries' innovations and discoveries (the telephone, radio, airplane, the theory of relativity, and of course the invention of the cinema) as positive achievements—the products of "Man's mind, his consciousness, [which] is the greatest triumph of nature."[27] Deren believes the exercise of conscious faculties is not just the purview of science, however; it is also that of the artist. And it is from the conscious mind that the contemporary artist must draw if he or she is to comprehend a reality so pervaded by technology. This exercise of conscious control is thus not merely an artistic choice but unquestionably also an ethical one. Given her views on this matter, one can understand Deren's harsh criticism of the surrealist artists, whose appeals to *un*conscious faculties attempt "to achieve, and end by only simulating, [what] can be accomplished in full reality, by the atom bomb."[28] In other words, for Deren, a dependence on the chaotic outpourings of the unconscious (the preferred method of the surrealists) prevents the artist from succeeding at either of his or her charges: rejecting conscious control is tantamount to obliterating what makes us human, and relying on the operations of chance cannot help us understand the complexities of the modern world.

In *Anagram* Deren lays out her own cosmography through a brief overview of the philosophical and scientific advancements that were ignited in the seventeenth century. She writes of a gradual shift in Western thought from humankind as god fearing (with the concomitant belief that actions in the world are determined by the will of a supreme being) to humankind as fearing no one and nothing (believing instead that actions in the world can be explained through the logic of science).[29] Deren finds that the outcome of this shift toward greater faith in the powers of scientific observation, discovery, and prediction had two interrelated and quite major consequences: it usurped the centrality of an all-knowing, all-powerful deity and thereby transformed the heretofore obligatory moral relationship between human beings and a supreme being: "Only when [mankind] relinquished his concept of divine consciousness did he confront the choice of either developing his own and accepting all the moral responsibilities previously dispensated by divinity, or of merging with inconscient nature and enjoying the luxurious irresponsibility of being one of its more complex phenomena."[30]

That is, if we are not answerable to an absolute moral code under the jurisdiction of the divine, then moral behavior is open either to adoption or rejection. In the fashion of a Kantian categorical imperative, Deren insists there is only one choice to make: with intellectual/creative consciousness comes one's moral obligation toward all of humankind to use this ability wisely. Rejection of consciousness is akin to rejection of an ethical code, and thus tantamount to reducing oneself to an amoral organism, surely more complex in structure but in fact no greater than the flora and fauna of the amoral natural world.

As we can see from the foregoing discussion, Deren believes that aesthetic issues are inseparable from the concerns of ethics. Aesthetics for Deren are not merely formal choices, but the conscious expression of human values embodied in material form: "For the serious artist the esthetic problem of form is, essentially, and simultaneously, a moral problem. Nothing can account for the devoted dedication of the giants of human history to art form save the understanding that, for them, the moral and esthetic problems were one and the same: that the form of a work of art is the physical manifestation of its moral structure."[31]

In other words, as she expressed metaphorically a number of years later, "a work of art is skin for an idea."[32] But not only does the work of art make immaterial concepts apprehensible to the senses; it must also "illuminate certain ethical or moral principles" as well as *comprehend the large facts of its total culture, and, at best, extend them imaginatively*"[33]—by which she means that an artist must exhibit an awareness of his or her contemporary social conditions and must then endeavor to clarify these conditions through the creative work of art. The artist's role is thus as an elucidator of the human condition, and his or her work of art can succeed at this responsibility only if it *"involves a conscious manipulation of its material from an intensely motivated point of view."*[34] Nothing must be left to chance or unconscious operations, nor may the artist ignore the discoveries and inventions of the twentieth century. Any artwork that does so is inevitably both a creative failure and culturally irrelevant.[35]

To succeed at these tasks, the film artist for Deren must take advantage of the motion picture medium's twin "instruments of discovery and invention" (the camera and the editing bench) in order to fashion the recorded material into an aesthetic whole that has "a filmic integrity and logic."[36] That is, a film artist must not imitate reality on film but rather must transform the material world by playing with the capabilities of the medium to manipulate space, time, and movement (through slow motion, reverse motion, or the editing of disparate locations to fabricate a seemingly continuous action, and so on), and thereby *add* something new to the world: an aesthetic object whose spatial and temporal dimensions can exist only in filmic representation.

True to the character of modernist or essentialist film theory, Deren's rhetoric (and mine, of course, in imitating the character of hers) consists in descriptions of what a particular art form *can* do—often in very celebratory tones—intermixed with equally emphatic dicta regarding what, in the name of aesthetic integrity, the artist *must* do, along with either explicitly or implicitly stated stylistic preferences. Deren's film theory is in fact a clarion call to action for the film artist, as is evident from the exuberant content and tone of the final paragraph of *Anagram:*

> The history of art is the history of man and of his universe and
> of the moral relationship between them. Whatever the instrument,
> the artist sought to re-create the abstract, invisible forces and rela-
> tionships of the cosmos, in the intimate, immediate forms of his art,
> where the problems might be experienced and perhaps be resolved
> in miniature. It is not presumptuous to suggest that cinema, as an art
> instrument especially capable of recreating relativistic relationships
> on a plane of intimate experience, is of profound importance. It
> stands, today, in the great need of the creative contributions of
> whomsoever respects the fabulous potentialities of its destiny.[37]

Since for Deren the major responsibility of the artist has historically been the illumination of the human condition, filmmakers too are therefore obliged to take on the moral mantle of their predecessors and use this new medium to create, on the small scale of film production, art objects that manipulate space and time in order to help us understand a world within which the inventions of the radio and airplane, as well as Einstein's discovery of relativity, have indelibly altered our long-held conceptions of time and space: "And so, ready or not, willing or not, we must come to comprehend, with full responsibility, the world which we have now created."[38] Film aesthetics for Deren are thus inextricably linked to issues of ethics and education. But how is Deren's mode of creative film production to achieve this moral purpose?

In *Anagram* Deren states but does not directly explain her connection between creative or experimental film production and moral effectivity. However, in a shorter essay entitled "Creating Movies with a New Dimension: Time," completed also in August 1946 and published that December, she makes more explicit a relation between the generative power of the creative work of film art and its moral value:

> The desire to discover and to experience something new is responsible for growth and development in the individual, progress in civilization. And so it seems to me that a labor which results in something created, to add to the sum total of the world, is infinitely more valuable than a labor devoted to the reproduction of something already familiar. Thus, the fact that the motion picture camera is capable of creating new relationships between time and space, different from those of any other medium, is what has led me to this emphasis upon the temporal considerations of film-making. But remember—whatever the technique, it must serve the form as a whole, it must be appropriate to the theme and to the logic of its development, rather than a display of method designed to impress other movie makers.[39]

This passage actually answers not just the question of *how* the filmmaker is to achieve his or her moral purpose—it also provides a clue to Deren's thoughts on *why* the film artist is so morally obligated, by implying a connection between creative activity and human progress. The probable source for Deren's linking of these two phenomena may be found in T. E. Hulme's commentary on Henri Bergson's *Creative Evolution*. Although there are no records among Deren's papers of her having read Bergson in the original, it is clear both from *Anagram* and her master's thesis on symbolist and imagist poetry that she read *Speculations*, a collection of essays by Hulme, an aesthetician who was involved with the imagists and who also translated Bergson.[40] In "The Philosophy of In-

tensive Manifolds," Hulme explicates a number of the French philosopher's concepts:

> The most familiar part of Bergson . . . comes in his account of
> evolution. . . .
>
> In life you do appear to get continuous evolution and creation.
> Bergson suggests then that the only theory which will fit the facts
> of evolution is to suppose that it is produced by a kind of *impulse*
> which is something akin to the creative activity we find in our own
> mind and which, inserted in matter, has, following out this creative
> activity, gradually achieved the result we see in evolution. . . .
>
> One can get at a picture of the course of evolution in this way:
> It is as if a current of consciousness flowed down into matter as into
> a tunnel, and, making efforts to advance on every side, digs galleries,
> most of which are stopped by a rock which is too hard, but which
> in one direction at least has broken through the rock and back into
> life again once more. This direction is the line of evolution resulting
> in man.[41]

Bergson sees evolution (the phenomenon of changes in inorganic and
organic matter) as caused by a metaphysical "impulse," that is, a natural
and vital urge or tendency infused into physical matter that motivates it
toward change. Hulme explains Bergson's understanding of evolutionary development by analogy to a creative impulse in human beings (evolution is "something akin to the creative activity we find in our own
mind"). A link between this creative evolutionary impulse and human development is then not far behind, for he likens the flow of evolution to
"a current of consciousness" through organic matter, eventually "resulting in man." This last comparison between evolution and human consciousness shifts from analogical to causal relation. Deren makes a similar causal statement when, in "Creating Movies with a New Dimension,"
she relates intellectual and creative activity to human progress (the "desire to discover and to experience something new" results in "growth and
development in the individual, progress in civilization"). The kind of

modernist art that Deren advocates (that which "add[s] to the sum total of the world" rather than represents it) therefore inherently has the capacity to enable human beings' further development. For Deren (who believes that consciousness "is the greatest triumph of nature"), such an activity indeed serves the artist's moral obligation to illuminate the human condition.[42] It is little wonder then that Deren tells aspiring film artists that they must not make films whose point is a self-aggrandizing show of technical expertise ("designed to impress other movie makers"). Rather, they must have in mind a theme to communicate, and they must use the motion picture medium to create a film form comprising new space-time relations through which that theme can be embodied and discerned, thereby enabling others to learn and grow from their experience of it.

Many of Deren's pronouncements on art and ethics are not only adapted from Hulme on Bergson but also from the aesthetics of New Criticism, which itself was influenced by the writings of Hulme and, among others, Matthew Arnold, F. R. Leavis, I. A. Richards, and the American transplants to England T. S. Eliot and Ezra Pound. For these men, the purpose of literary art was to educate society and to communicate moral values; the romanticism of late-eighteenth- and nineteenth-century literature—particularly its poetry—wrongly emphasized individualism, an escape from real-world conditions, and maudlin sentimentality. Thus what was needed was a return to the classicist tradition of reasoned thinking, attention to order and form, and a use of language that was not vague but concrete and experiential.[43] One can clearly hear these notions echoing throughout *Anagram*, particularly in Deren's assertion that a true work of literary art or a visual art-object "creates experience": "*the distinction of art is that it is neither simply an expression, of pain, for example, nor an impression of pain but is itself a form which creates pain* (or whatever its emotional intent)."[44] In other words, true art is the embodiment of an idea or emotion which, like a hypodermic needle, is powerful enough to inject that idea into or affect directly the reader/observer.[45]

In *Anagram* Deren refers to this directly communicative form as a verbal or visual "image."[46] The sources for Deren's understanding of this term can be found by reading her master's thesis, "The Influence of the French Symbolist School on Anglo-American Poetry," which reveals her great admiration for modern poets such as Richard Aldington, F. S. Flint, Hilda Doolittle, and especially Pound and Eliot. These and other Anglo-American writers, save Eliot, became known as the imagist school—poets whose style was in part a sympathetic extension of the French symbolists' use of *vers libre* and who believed in the poet's ability to synthesize emotional content with form.[47]

Eliot, while not an imagist per se, nevertheless published some of his poems in their periodicals and similarly advocated free verse, a turn away from the romanticist to the classicist tradition, and a conception of good poetry as effecting "direct communication with the nerves."[48] Pound too links poetic form with emotional effect: it is the rhythm or cadence of the words in free verse that "corresponds exactly to the emotion or shade of emotion to be expressed."[49] Furthermore, for Pound, who coined the term "imagism" but who credited his inspiration to Hulme's use of the concept, "a work of art is the honest reproduction of a concrete image."[50] In the March 1913 journal *Poetry*, Pound defines his understanding of this last word: "An 'Image' is that which presents an intellectual and emotional complex in an instant of time."[51]

In her master's thesis, Deren cites this as well as other definitions of an "image,"[52] but it is clearly Pound's conception, with only slight variation, that she adopts in *Anagram:* "A work of art is an emotional and intellectual complex whose logic is its whole form."[53]

Deren's adaptation of her literary mentors' aesthetics to the art of film provides her with two very important things: an established aesthetic paradigm through which she argues for film's legitimate status as an art form and a conceptual term—the "image"—which is for obvious reasons easily applicable to the visual medium of film. For Deren, proper film form (the creative manipulation of space-time via the camera and editing bench) *is* already an "image" in Pound's sense and a work of art in hers:

a consciously constructed form that concretizes ideas or emotions and generates them directly in the mind of the perceiver.

Hand in hand with the New Critics' and the imagists' assertions about directly communicative poetry was their belief in intrinsic meaning, which was to be found by engaging in rigorous analysis—what I. A. Richards called the "rather intricate navigation" through every facet of the text itself, dissected line by line so the critic could evaluate how its particular features worked or did not work successfully across the poem as a whole.[54] But while Deren herself performed this type of close analysis on the poetry of the symbolist and imagist movements when she wrote her master's thesis in the late 1930s, as a filmmaker in the mid-1940s she insisted that "a dis-sectional analysis of a work of art fails, in the act of dismemberment, to comprehend the very inter-active dynamics which give it life. Such an analysis cannot substitute, and may even inhibit, the experience itself, which only an unprejudiced receptivity, free of personal requirements and preconceptions, can invite."[55] From where does this attitude against analysis emerge? And, if not by analysis, how is one to interpret or understand a work of art? Deren's thinking on these issues may be traced by turning again to Hulme's writing on Bergson.

In "The Philosophy of Intensive Manifolds," Hulme explicates Bergson's distinction between two faculties of mind: intellect and intuition.[56] Bergson aligns the former with the rational mind and the activities of scientific analysis that endeavor to explain, say, a complex phenomenon by breaking it down into its components and examining its parts.[57] Such an analysis, writes Hulme, yields an "extensive manifold," which he defines by appealing to the etymology of "explanation": just as the Latin *ex plane* means "the opening out of things on a plane surface," an "extensive manifold" (for example, a mathematical model or a diagram) is similarly an "unfolding" out into space of the elements comprising the phenomenon under study.[58] In contrast and in addition to this method of comprehension by rational intellect, Bergson proposes intuition.[59] Hulme tells us that intuition for Bergson is the manner by which we grasp certain complex phenomena, such as the human mind or evolution, which cannot properly be understood through the methods of scientific analysis.[60] Hulme refers to such a complex as an "intensive manifold," that is, a whole whose parts are so interrelated that it cannot be understood by taking it apart, for the very act of disentangling its components results in a qualitative distortion. One comprehends the intensive manifold therefore not by intellectual (spatial or extensive) analysis, but rather through one's experience of it, for experience and intuition in Bergson's philosophical schema are continua as indivisible as real Time (duration).[61]

In *Anagram*, Deren does not directly reference this particular essay or these ideas by Bergson and Hulme, but Hulme's explication of an "intensive manifold" as a complex whole comprising interpenetrating and indivisible parts dovetails perfectly with the rhetoric of part-whole relations in Gestalt theory—which she does specifically mention. The creative work of art is thus an

> "emergent whole" (I borrow the term from Gestalt psychology) in which the parts are so dynamically related as to produce something new which is unpredictable from a knowledge of the parts. It is this process [of the artist's conscious rearrangement of elements] which makes possible the idea of economy in art, for the whole which here emerges transcends, in meaning, the sum total of the parts. The effort of the artist is towards the creation of a logic in which two and two may make five, or, preferably, fifteen; when this is achieved, two can no longer be understood as simply two. This five, or this fifteen—the resultant idea or emotion—is therefore *a function of the total relationships, the form of the work* (which is independent of the form of reality by which it may have been inspired). It is this which Flaubert had reference to in stating that "L'idee n'existe qu'en vertu de sa forme."[62]

Both a Gestalt view of part-whole relations and Bergson's concept of an intensive manifold are complemented by Flaubert's assertion that meaning is inextricably linked to form. For Deren, who believes that aesthetics and ethics are one, the meaning or moral purpose of a work of film art (its ability to enable the perceiver to learn and grow) also resides in the form itself. Therefore we can understand that Deren's objection to "dis-sectional analysis" comes not just from the invested ego of the intentionalist but from her belief in indivisible artistic wholes whose "dismemberment" leads both to a blocked aesthetic experience for the viewer and a failure for the artist to achieve his or her moral goals. How then can the misinterpretation of a complex art form be obviated? By giving oneself over to it, by one's "unprejudiced receptivity," it can thus be grasped as a whole through Bergsonian intuition.[63]

Deren's Modernist Poetics

Given Deren's academic background in literature, her understanding of Bergson's metaphysics, and her adoption of the imagists' tenets, one can see why poetry is afforded rather different treatment in *Anagram:*

> Just as the verbal logics of a poem are composed of the relationships established through syntax, assonance, rhyme, and other such verbal methods, so in film there are processes of filmic relationships which derive from the instrument and the elements of its manipulations.[64]
>
> To the form [of film art] as a whole, such techniques [those of spatiotemporal manipulation through shooting and editing] contribute an economy of statement comparable to poetry, where the inspired juxtaposition of a few words can create a complex which far transcends them.[65]

Thus it is the creative filmmaker and the talented poet both who take advantage of the tools of their respective media and, as true artists, recombine their specific raw materials into new and imaginative wholes whose meanings exceed that of their individual components.

While throughout "The Art of Film" chapters of *Anagram* Deren warns the filmmaker against borrowing inappropriately from the methods of any other art form, she clearly describes as comparable filmic and poetic creativity. If, after such a wholesale dismissal, Deren nevertheless finds filmic spatiotemporal and audio manipulations akin to poetic strategies, then she is not simply condoning shared methods between the poet and film artist but is in fact implying that a filmic adaptation of the methods of poetry is the only proper means of creating film art. We can therefore more clearly understand her criticisms in *Anagram* of Hollywood cinema (which borrows narrative from literature and theater), abstract film (which imitates painting), or the documentary (which in Deren's view must not be considered an art form, since its task is to represent reality rather than to create new forms).[66] True film *art* does not consist of linear narratives, animated paintings, or documentary realism; for Deren it must be the result of more poetic approaches.

It is not in *Anagram*, however, that Deren fully explains her ideas about poetic structure. Rather, her most elaborate articulation of it can be found in the transcript of the 1953 "Poetry and the Film" symposium in which she participated, along with Willard Maas, Arthur Miller, Dylan Thomas, and Parker Tyler:

> Poetry, to my mind, is an approach to experience. . . . The distinction of poetry is its construction (what I mean by a "poetic structure"), and the poetic construct arises from the fact, if you will, that it is a "vertical" investigation of a situation, in that it probes the ramifications of the moment, and is concerned with its qualities and its depth, so that you have poetry concerned, in a sense, not with what is occurring but with what it feels like or what it means. A poem, to my mind, creates visible or auditory forms for something that is invisible, which is the feeling, or the emotion, or the metaphysical content of the movement. Now it also may include action, but its attack is what I would call the "vertical" attack, and this may be a little bit clearer if you will contrast it to what I would call the "horizontal" attack of drama, which is concerned with the development, let's say, within a very small situation from feeling to feeling. Perhaps it would be made most clear if you take a Shakespearean work that combines the two movements. In Shakespeare, you have

the drama moving forward on a "horizontal" plane of development, of one circumstance—one action—leading to another, and this delineates the character. Every once [in] a while, however, he arrives at a point of the action where he wants to illuminate the meaning [of] *this* moment of drama, and, at that moment, he builds a pyramid or investigates it "vertically," if you will, so that you have a "horizontal" development with periodic "vertical" investigations, which are the poems, which are the monologues.[67]

One way of understanding this reference to "vertical" and "horizontal" structures, as Annette Michelson points out in "Film and the Radical Aspiration," is to see them as Deren's means of "positing disjunctiveness against linearity, claiming for film the strategic polarity of discourse which Jakobson . . . proposed in the metonymic and metaphoric modes."[68] That is, Deren's distinction between the "vertical investigation" of poetry versus the "horizontal attack" of narrative could be seen as similar in some ways to linguist Roman Jakobson's distinction between the paradigmatic and syntagmatic axes of language. Whereas the paradigmatic axis involves the consideration of permissible word substitutions (the choices of which are based upon qualitative similarities between the concepts that the words stand for), the syntagmatic axis involves consideration of the succession of words, or linear word combinations (the choices of which are based upon rules of grammar). Jakobson further aligns the paradigmatic axis with the poetic figure of metaphor and the syntagmatic with metonymy, which he considers a trope of prose.[69] Jakobson's alignment of metonymy with prose may seem odd, since of course metonymy is a poetic figure as well, but Jakobson himself is being figurative by ascribing these labels to the two interrelated operations of language, whether in prose or poetry: that of relations made by similarity and substitution (metaphor) and that of relations made by combination and context (metonymy).

An additional way of seeing Deren's notion of "vertical" structure is through the poetics of Pound, at least from the period of his involvement with the imagists. When Deren describes poetic construction as an "investigation of a situation," a structure that "probes the ramifications of the moment," we can hear in her rhetoric the sympathetic vibrations of Pound's definition of a poetic image: "that which presents an intellectual and emotional complex in an instant of time." When she says that a poem "creates visible or auditory forms" for invisible thoughts or feelings, she, like Eliot or Hulme, sees poetic language as concretized ideas or emotions. Furthermore, we can hear in Deren the metaphysics of Bergson via Hulme and the distinction between intensive and extensive manifolds. Recall that an intensive manifold is a complex structure understood intuitively through one's experience of it and that experience is not an analyzable (spatial) phenomenon but rather (like Time or Bergsonian duration) is indivisible. For Deren, dramatic narrative or "horizontal" structure is concerned with the linkage of actions or events and, like an extensive manifold, is understood through its unfolding across space, while "vertical" poetic structure "is an approach to experience," concerned with what a particular moment or situation means or how it feels, grasped over time.

Although Deren's ideas about "vertical" and "horizontal" structures were not well received by some of her copanelists, let alone the audience at this 1953 symposium (Dylan Thomas and Arthur Miller were particularly condescending, rude, and dismissive), anyone familiar with the film theory of Gilles Deleuze from thirty-some years later can see in his Bergsonian analysis of the cinematic "movement-image" and the "time-image" a comparable distinction between "horizontal" and "vertical" filmic structures.[70] For Deleuze, classical narrative cinema consists in the "movement-image" and emphasizes the development of actions across space. Conversely, much of modernist cinema, in Deleuze's view, presents "direct" images of time. What he means by this rather abstract notion is that, instead of privileging the construction of rational dramatic space-time (as in classical film), many filmmakers of modern cinema either do away entirely with or greatly subordinate space-time continuities and a steady flow of action to spatiotemporal disjunctions and/or a slower, more contemplative pace (say, the collapsed distinction between past and present in Resnais's films, for example, or Antonioni's empty spaces, or Ozu's extended moments of inaction). Deleuze's point is that this type of filmmaking has opened up the cinema to the temporal phenomenon of *thought*.[71] Deren's metaphor of "vertical" structure similarly implies a lyrical form less concerned with exterior (spatial) actions than with interior (temporal) experiences.

Indeed, Deren's insistence on a more poetic or "vertical" structure for film anticipates the feminist call in the 1970s for an alternative to the stylized realism of classical narrative cinema. It would well describe Chantal Akerman's *Jeanne Dielman, 23 Quai du Commerce, 1080 Bruxelles* (1975), in which the strain of a woman's imprisonment within a life of mundane routine is conveyed cinematically by exceedingly long takes that follow many of her activities in real time. Though various housekeeping chores are repeated either partially or in full, this film is not about action but about endurance.[72] "Vertical" form is metaphorically descriptive also of Yvonne Rainer's essay film *Journeys from Berlin/1971* (1979), in which the multilayered and complex mix of sound track, printed text, and imagery splits our focus and attention. For example, we hear the off-screen sounds of a man and woman conversing as they prepare a meal, while on screen we see printed text explaining the political history of Germany, beginning with 1953. At times we see a repeated tracking shot across objects (which vary from one shot to the next) on a mantelpiece, while we hear the man and woman discussing the political revolutionaries Emma Goldman, Vera Figner, and Ulrike Meinhof. Or we see and hear the sync-sound imagery of two women sitting around a table as one teaches the other to play the recorder, while also on the sound track we hear another woman describe the frustration she experienced when called upon to serve jury duty. If classical cinema is metaphorically seen as "horizontal" and homophonic (the visuals illustrating a single, unified narrative line; the voice track providing a simple, synchronous accompaniment to the visuals; musical scoring added to enhance emotional effect), then the multiple discourses and simultaneous presence of competing audio, printed text, and images in *Journeys from Berlin* present many "vertical" moments of highly dissonant polyphony.

In its fracturing of unified, linear narrative, Sally Potter's *Thriller* (1979), too, is more "vertical" in form. Taking the finale of *La Bohème* as its starting point—with a deceased Mimi asking "who killed me and why?"—*Thriller* re-presents the story of *La Bohème* and Mimi's death through performed song, still photographs, freeze-frames, and moving images of dance. The story is told repeatedly, but from the woman's voice and point of view, which switches from third person, to first-person singular, to first-person plural—a varied vocal and visual perspective that continually and self-consciously questions and revises the very narrative in which she is involved. Finally, the predetermined ending of *La Bohème* is overturned: Mimi survives. Potter's film presents (literally and figuratively) a "vertical investigation of a situation": the questioning and rewriting of the oft-repeated dramatic line of romantic fiction in which a woman, as the object of a man's desire, inevitably dies.[73]

Over the years, Maya Deren may have exchanged one descriptive term for another when referring to her own films or film art in general, but she always conceived of art, poetry, and "proper" film form in terms borrowed from the humanism of the New Critics, the antiromanticist rhetoric of Hulme and Eliot, the poetics of Pound and the imagists, the part-whole relations of Gestalt theory, and Bergson's metaphysics. If in this essay I have slipped back and forth between discussing Deren's labels for her own films and for "true" film art, it is because the two were inseparable for her, in no way different from, say, Sergei Eisenstein's citing various sequences in *Battleship Potemkin* (1925) or *October* (1928) as exemplary of dialectical montage.[74] One way of assessing the enduring value of any of the modernist filmmaker-theorists' terms, however, is in finding their applicability beyond just the filmmaker's own work. Thus, just as Epstein's concept of *photogénie* furnishes us with a concise word for the beauty of subtle cinematic movement and Eisenstein's "dialectical montage" provides a term through which to discuss ideational infer-

ence through editing, so do "horizontal attack" and "vertical investigation" give us metaphors for discussing various qualitative differences, in
form and subject, between films that foreground narrative, spectacle, and
action, and those that challenge the structural conventions of classical
narrative and emphasize ideas, issues, mood, and tone.

Notes

1. Noël Carroll, *Philosophical Problems of Classical Film Theory* (Princeton: Princeton University Press, 1988), p. 84. Carroll devotes chapters to Arnheim, Bazin, and
V. F. Perkins, and he extends his critique to others in the classical canon as well. He
does not, however, make any reference to Deren or her theoretical work.

2. Ibid., pp. 83, 86.

3. Maya Deren, *An Anagram of Ideas on Art, Form and Film* (New York: Alicat
Book Shop Press, 1946), pp. 37–43.

4. Ibid., pp. 30–31, 41, 49.

5. Ibid., p. 48.

6. Ibid., pp. 39–40. By "elements" and "original context," Deren means the individual shots and the real-world referents that have been recorded on them.

7. Carroll, pp. 81, 91.

8. Deren, preface to *Anagram*.

9. Ibid.

10. Ibid.

11. Ibid., 19–20.

12. Ibid., 17, 19–20.

13. Ritualist in form because rituals consist in repeated patterns, and Deren creates repetition of movement through the choreography and her editorial means; she
feels the film is ritualist in content because its theme (a widow's transformation into
a bride) is about a life transition, as are many rituals. See, for example, her Premiere
Program for *Ritual and Ordeal*, 1 June 1946, the Poetry Center, YM & YWHA, New
York; reprinted in VèVè A. Clark, Millicent Hodson, and Catrina Neiman, *The Legend of Maya Deren: A Documentary Biography and Collected Works*, vol. 1, pt. 2, *Chambers (1942–1947)* (New York: Anthology Film Archives/Film Culture, 1988), pp.
460–61, at 461; hereafter any references to this text will be cited as *LC*. (Deren changed
"ordeal" to "transfigured time" within a matter a months.) See also Deren, "Ritual in
Transfigured Time," *Dance Magazine* (December 1946); reprinted in *LC*, p. 459. And
see her "Art of the Moving Picture" brochure (c. 1960), in box 23, folder 54, Maya
Deren Collection, Special Collections Section, Mugar Library, Boston University
(hereafter any references to materials from Deren's papers housed at Boston Univer-

sity will be cited as "Maya Deren Collection"). The "Art of the Moving Picture" brochure was a promotional flyer for Maya Deren Films (her film distribution company) and her lectures on film as an art form.

14. For her writings on this film project, see Deren, "Film in Progress. Thematic Statement. Application for the Renewal of a [Guggenheim] Fellowship for Creative Work in the Field of Motion-Pictures" (February 1947); reprinted in *Film Culture* 39 (Winter 1965): 15. See also Maya Deren, New York City, to Gregory Bateson, New York, 9 December 1946; printed in *October* 14 (Fall 1980): 16–17. (Deren had been taking a class from anthropologist Bateson and was corresponding with him about her ideas for this film, for which he and Margaret Mead donated over twenty thousand feet of footage they had shot in Bali.) And see Maya Deren, Port-au-Prince, to Henry Allen Moe, New York City, 21 January 1948; originals in the archives of the J. S. Guggenheim Memorial Foundation (Moe was then the secretary general of the Foundation); a carbon copy of this letter is housed in Steele box 6, folder 10, Maya Deren Collection.

15. See Deren, *Divine Horsemen: The Living Gods of Haiti* (New York: Thames and Hudson, 1953). A reprinted version by Dell Publishing in 1970 retitled the book as *Divine Horsemen: The Voodoo Gods of Haiti*. In 1983, McPherson & Company reprinted the text under its original title.

16. See box 4, folder 20, Maya Deren Collection, for (auto)biographical documents listing programs (such as CBS's *Vanity Fair* in 1950 and *Night Beat* in 1957) on which she or excerpts of her Haitian footage appeared. See Deren's publicity material for "Art of the Moving Picture" (c. 1960), which includes promotional copy for a lecture-demonstration on Haitian Voudoun (box 23, folder 55); Deren often lectured with Teiji Ito, her companion and, later, third husband, who would demonstrate Haitian drumbeats. See, for example, "Voices of Haiti—Studio Visit: Maya Deren Teiji Ito," *Zig Zag: Monthly of the New York Enthusiasts* 11, no. 6 (December 1956), box 26, folder 46, Maya Deren Collection. See the transcript of Deren's radio interview with Alma Dettinger for WQXR, 19 January 1949 (Maya Deren file, Anthology Film Archives), her interview with Dave Garroway for NBC radio, 5 June 1953 (Maya Deren file, Anthology Film Archives), and the transcript for her television interview with Mike Wallace on *Night Beat*, 30 May 1957 (Steele box 2, folder 35, Maya Deren Collection), for the way in which Deren spoke about Voudoun as a legitimate religion. See also the letter Deren wrote to WBC Productions regarding her appearance in May of 1961 on *PM East*; this scathing diatribe (addressed only to Mr.—[name left blank]) lambastes those involved with this program for having punctuated her taped interview with "musical interludes . . . shoddy, banal, tin-pan alley lyrics about voodoo and witchcraft," which undermined Deren's purpose "to establish at least respect if not belief in other peoples' religion" (a carbon copy of this letter is housed in Steele box 3, folder 10, Maya Deren Collection).

17. See chapter 4 of my dissertation, "Voices of Maya Deren: Theme and Variation" (Ph.D. diss., New York University, 1998), pp. 178–226.

18. Deren, "Films in the Classicist Tradition," October 1946 Screening Program; reprinted in *LC*, pp. 398–401, at 399. On whether Deren's claims can be upheld, regarding a distinction between her films and the character of romanticism or surrealism, see P. Adams Sitney, *Visionary Film: The American Avant-Garde 1943–1978*, 2d ed. (New York: Oxford University Press, 1979), pp. 3–46. For an argument against Sitney, see Patricia Mellencamp, *Indiscretions: Avant-Garde Film, Video, and Feminism* (Bloomington: Indiana University Press, 1990), pp. 17–35. Mellencamp takes *Visionary Film* to task in general and also makes an important distinction in tone between *Meshes* and the quintessential surrealist film *Un Chien Andalou:* whereas the surrealist film is parodic, Deren's is "deadly serious." I believe this difference in tone can be equally applied to Deren's other two oneiric narratives, *At Land* and *Ritual in Transfigured Time.*

19. Once she begins to refer to her films as "choreographies," Deren also renames *A Study in Choreography for the Camera* as *Pas de Deux*. See, for example, the Dimensions, Inc., rental catalogue (Autumn 1951, unpaginated) (box 26, folder 31, Maya Deren Collection), as well as the "Art of the Moving Picture" brochure from around 1960. Dimensions, Inc., was a Seattle, Washington, company that Deren used for distribution for a number of months in late 1951 to early 1952, before reverting back to self-distribution. In this catalogue, Deren singles out *Pas de Deux* and *Meditation on Violence* (1948) as the choreographies for camera, but in the later "Art of the Moving Picture" brochure she makes no such distinction among her six films. Deren's program notes for screenings of all six of her films scheduled at the Bleeker Street Cinema in February 1961 and at the Living Theater in March of that year are entitled "Chamber Films" and subtitled "Choreographies for Camera" (see a reprint of this flyer in *Filmwise* 2 [1962]: 37). At the "Poetry and the Film" symposium in 1953, Deren expresses her conviction that film "by its very nature [is] a poetic medium"; see "Poetry and the Film: A Symposium," *Film Culture Reader,* ed. P. Adams Sitney (New York: Praeger, 1970), pp. 171–86, at 179. In the Dimensions, Inc., rental catalogue, she also describes her films as "CINE-POEMS . . . *neither to entertain nor to instruct, but to BE that experience which is poetry*" (italics, capitalized emphasis, and ellipses all hers). She continues to use similar rhetoric ten years later in her "Art of the Moving Picture" brochure, when she expresses her hope that her films will "create a mythological, poetic experience" for the viewer.

20. Deren, Smith lecture (1961), p. 22; transcript in box 19, folder 1, Maya Deren Collection. For additional places in which Deren compares film to other time forms, see also the transcripts of her Yale lecture (1949) and her Cleveland lecture (1951), both in box 19, folders 2 and 3, Maya Deren Collection. The Cleveland lecture was also reprinted as "New Directions in Film Art," *Film Culture* 29 (Summer 1963): 64–68.

21. For Deren's explanation of her "choreographies for camera" metaphor, see her "Art of the Moving Picture" brochure; see also her flyer for a February 1955 screening of three of her films at the Centre d'Art of the Haitian American Institute, in box 26, folder 38, Maya Deren Collection; and see Maya Deren, New York City, to Cecile Starr of the American Federation of Film Societies, 7 August 1956 (carbon copy of this letter is in box 29, folder 15, Maya Deren Collection).

22. For Deren's explanation of her "chamber film" metaphor, see her "Movie Journal" column, *Village Voice* 25 (August 1960); reprinted in *Film Culture* 39 (Winter 1965): 54; or her Smith lecture (1961), pp. 6–7.

23. Deren, *Anagram*, p. 7.

24. Ibid.

25. Ibid., p. 52.

26. Ibid., pp. 17, 52.

27. Ibid., p. 9.

28. Ibid., p. 10.

29. Ibid., p. 8. Deren divides this shift into four parts, starting from the belief in a supernatural power as absolute and causative ("the reason why a stone fell was because God willed that it do so") to a belief that the world functions according to various divinely created natural laws ("The reason why a stone fell, now, was because such action was of its divine nature") to attributing a rational character to the workings of the cosmos and its divine authority ("Milton wrote that it was more 'reasonable' for the earth to revolve in the heavens than for the immense heavens to revolve their bulk around the earth") to, finally, a greater reliance on the explanatory strength of science and logic in understanding causes and effects in the universe. Deren's understanding of this shift and her expression of it in *Anagram* are condensed from one of her graduate school research papers entitled "Reason, or the Dyadic Relativity of the Seventeenth Century and its Development Toward Modern Triadic Relativity in Science, Philosophy and Ethics." A copy of this sixty-page typed term paper is housed in box 5, folder 5D, Maya Deren Collection.

30. Ibid., p. 9.

31. Ibid., p. 37.

32. Deren, Smith lecture (1961), p. 52.

33. Deren, *Anagram*, pp. 16, 27–28; italics hers.

34. Ibid., p. 33; italics hers.

35. Ibid., p. 16.

36. Ibid., pp. 46, 48.

37. Ibid., p. 52.

38. Ibid.

39. Idem, "Creating Movies with a New Dimension: Time," *Popular Photography* (December 1946): 130–32, 134 passim; reprinted in *LC*, pp. 612–16, at 615–16.

40. See "The Influence of the French Symbolist School on Anglo-American Po-

etry" (M.A. thesis, Smith College, 1939), in box 5, Maya Deren Collection. (Here-after this manuscript will be cited as "The Influence"). In *Anagram*, Deren cites Hulme on the subject of abstraction in "primitive" art (p. 15); although she does not name the essay, she takes his ideas from "Modern Art and its Philosophy," in T. E. Hulme, *Speculations*, ed. Herbert Read (London: Routledge & Kegan Paul, 1924), pp. 73–109.

41. Hulme, "The Philosophy of Intensive Manifolds," *Speculations*, pp. 201, 203–4, 210–11; italics his.

42. Deren, *Anagram*, p. 9.

43. These views are expressed explicitly in Hulme's essays "Modern Art and Its Philosophy" and "Romanticism and Classicism, in *Speculations*, pp. 75–109, 113–40; as well as in his "Lecture on Modern Poetry" and "Notes on Language and Style," in *Further Speculations*, ed. Sam Hynes (Lincoln: University of Nebraska Press, 1962), pp. 67–76, 77–100 ("Notes on Language and Style" was probably available to Deren in its earlier published version in 1929). See also T. S. Eliot, "Tradition and the Indi-vidual Talent" (1920), reprinted in *The American Tradition in Literature*, 3d ed., vol. 2, ed. Sculley Bradley, Richmond Croom Bailey, and E. Hudson Long (New York: Nor-ton, 1967), pp. 1269–76. See also I. A. Richards, *Practical Criticism* (New York: Har-court Brace, 1929; reprint, London: Routledge & Kegan Paul, 1954) or F. R. Leavis, *Revaluation: Tradition and Development in English Poetry* (London: Chatto & Windus, 1936). Eliot's essay is cited in Deren's thesis and clearly influences much of her aes-thetics. I do not know if she read the specific texts I mention by Leavis or Richards, but her rhetoric against interpretation via "personal context" and for "unprejudiced receptivity" (see *Anagram*, pp. 24–25) is consonant with theirs. The *Legend* compil-ers do note that she had read Matthew Arnold's *Culture and Anarchy* (1875; reprint, New York: Macmillan, 1925) while studying at the Ecole Internationale in Geneva; see *LC*, pp. 657–58 n64. And while she was working toward her master's degree in literature at Smith College, Deren wrote a term paper entitled "Classicism in the Pe-riod of Nineteenth Century Romanticism, with Special Reference to Landor, Arnold and Swinburne," so clearly she was familiar with a number of Arnold's other works. A copy of this term paper is housed in box 5 of the Maya Deren Collection. For an excellent summary of the New Critics, their influences, and their worldview, see Terry Eagleton, *Literary Theory: An Introduction* (Minneapolis: University of Minnesota Press, 1983), pp. 17–53.

44. Deren, *Anagram*, p. 17; italics hers.

45. I do not use the term "hypodermic needle" unwittingly. Deren and her lit-erary mentors' belief in directly communicative art and poetry in fact closely re-sembles the mass media theory of the 1930s—the "hypodermic needle" or "bullet" theory that suggested the media "injected" attitudes into the public and thereby di-rectly affected its beliefs and behavior. Just as this hypothesis ignored the individual as an active "receiver" bringing his or her own cultural, political, and economic back-ground into play in response to media information, so New Criticism made no al-

lowances for social or historical context, let alone active and/or resistant readership and reception.

46. Deren, *Anagram*, p. 27.

47. Imagism was a short-lived movement that spanned the years roughly from 1909 to 1917, beginning quite informally around weekly café discussions organized by Hulme in London's Soho. Hulme left the club early on to pursue other endeavors (translating some of the works of Bergson, for example), but the group was subsequently led by Pound until 1914, at which point he shifted his attention to vorticism. The continued existence of the movement was aided by the organizational work of Amy Lowell, whose publishing connections enabled the printing of the three annual imagist anthologies between 1915 and 1917. The list of imagist poets varies depending on whom you read, but generally includes (among a few others in addition to Aldington, H. D., Flint, and Pound) John Gould Fletcher, D. H. Lawrence, and Amy Lowell. Deren's claim regarding the symbolists' influence on Hulme, Pound, Eliot, and other poets, especially those of the imagist school, is corroborated by other authors as well. See, for example, René Taupin, *L'Influence du Symbolisme Français sur La Poésie Américaine (de 1910 à 1920)* (Paris: Librairie Ancienne Honoré Champion, 1929); the introduction by editor Sam Hynes to Hulme's *Further Speculations;* and J. B. Harmer, *Victory in Limbo: Imagism 1908–1917* (New York: St. Martin's Press, 1975).

48. Eliot quoted in Eagleton, p. 41; see also Deren, "The Influence," pp. 50, 133–57; and especially T. S. Eliot, "Tradition and the Individual Talent," pp. 1269–76. In her thesis Deren refers to Eliot as "perhaps the major English Symbolist" who exerted enormous influence upon other American and British poets of the teens onward. And of course it is Eliot's essay and his preferred aesthetics to which Deren alludes in her October 1946 screening program entitled "Films in the Classicist Tradition."

49. Pound, from *Pavannes and Divisions*, quoted in Deren, "The Influence," p. 123.

50. Pound quoted in Harmer, pp. 176, 214n35. Hulme wrote that the best poetic language "is an entirely physical thing, a real clay before me, moulded, an image"; see Hulme, "Notes on Language and Style," in *Further Speculations*, pp. 81–82.

51. Cited in Deren, "The Influence," p. 82; and also in Harmer, p. 165.

52. Hulme's notion of a "physical thing," as if present to him, for example, or F. S. Flint's explanation of it as "the resonant heart of an exquisite moment." See Deren, "The Influence," pp. 73, 81.

53. Deren, *Anagram*, p. 25. "Logic" here for Deren implies the artwork's consciously intended and inherent meaning.

54. See Richards, *Practical Criticism*, p. 11.

55. Deren, *Anagram*, p. 25.

56. Hulme, "The Philosophy of Intensive Manifolds," pp. 173–214.

57. Ibid., p. 177.

58. Ibid.

59. Ibid., pp. 174–75.

60. Ibid., pp. 179, 188, 204. Bergson's is clearly a metaphysics. His rejection of rational analysis for phenomena as complex as evolution or the human mind is of a piece with his vehement objection to any scientific attempts at comprehending movement (changes over space-time) or Time (duration) by dividing them up into segments.

61. Ibid., pp. 180–81, 187, 197.

62. Deren, *Anagram*, p. 24; italics hers. Flaubert's phrase translates as "an idea does not exist but by virtue of its form." Her understanding of Gestalt theory is indeed accurate. See Kurt Koffka, *Principles of Gestalt Psychology* (New York: Harcourt, Brace and Company, 1935), p. 176: "We could solve no problem of organization by solving it for each point separately, one after the other; the solution had to come for the whole. Thus we see how the problem of significance is closely bound up with the problem of the relation between the whole and its parts. It has been said: The whole is more than the sum of its parts. It is more correct to say that the whole is something else than the sum of its parts, because summing is a meaningless procedure, whereas the whole-part relationship is meaningful." Deren had studied with Koffka during her master's program at Smith, and his *Principles* was one of the textbooks for the course.

63. Deren implies the possibility of just such an intuitive understanding by the audiences of her own films, when she tells Alma Dettinger that "one confuses the amount one has understood with one's ability to tell it over again." See the transcript of Deren's radio interview with Alma Dettinger for WQXR, 19 January 1949, p. 1 (Maya Deren file, Anthology Film Archives).

64. Deren, *Anagram*, p. 48.

65. Ibid., p. 51.

66. Ibid., pp. 31–41, 44–46. My summary here is far too brief; for a more nuanced analysis of Deren's critique of Hollywood, which fails for her on moral grounds as well, or of her extended and scathing critique of documentary film, which she limits greatly (and impossibly) to the "*objective, impartial rendition of an otherwise obscure or remote reality*" (*Anagram*, p. 33; emphasis hers), see my "Filmmaker/Theorist as Film Critic," in chapter 3, "Voices of Maya Deren," pp. 129–49.

67. Deren, from "Poetry and the Film: A Symposium," *Film Culture Reader*, pp. 173–74.

68. Annette Michelson, "Film and the Radical Aspiration," in *Film Theory and Criticism*, 2d ed., ed. Gerald Mast and Marshall Cohen (New York: Oxford University Press, 1979), pp. 617–35, at 632. This edition of Michelson's essay is an expanded version of the paper she delivered at the New York Film Festival in 1966. The earlier version was printed in *Film Culture* 42 (Fall 1966) and reprinted in Sitney's *Film Culture Reader*, pp. 404–21. However, only the Mast and Cohen expanded version contains the passages on the "Poetry and the Film" symposium.

69. See Roman Jakobson, "Two Aspects of Language and Two Types of Aphasic

Disturbances" (1956), in *On Language*, ed. Linda R. Waugh and Monique Monville-Burston (Cambridge: Harvard University Press, 1990), pp. 115–33. This idea of paradigmatic and syntagmatic choices is of course also discussed in the film semiotics of Christian Metz; see his *Film Language*, trans. Michael Taylor (Chicago: University of Chicago Press, 1974).

70. See Gilles Deleuze, *Cinema 1: The Movement-Image*, trans. Hugh Tomlinson and Barbara Habberjam (Minneapolis: University of Minnesota Press, 1986) and *Cinema 2: The Time-Image*, trans. Hugh Tomlinson and Robert Galeta (Minneapolis: University of Minnesota Press, 1989).

71. See especially Deleuze, *Cinema 2*, pp. 204–15.

72. Or, as Ivone Margulies aptly writes, "the defamiliarizing effect of duration." See Margulies, *Nothing Happens: Chantal Akerman's Hyperrealist Everyday* (Durham: Duke University Press, 1996), p. 73 (pp. 65–99 provide an especially detailed analysis of this feminist film and how it challenges classical narrative cinema on many levels).

73. I thank Women Make Movies for loaning me a copy of this wonderful film.

74. See, of course, Eisenstein's essay "A Dialectical Approach to Film Form" (1929), in *Film Form: Essays in Film Theory*, ed. and trans. Jay Leyda (New York: Harcourt, Brace & World, Inc., 1949), pp. 45–63.

2A

Maureen Turim

The Ethics of Form

Structure and Gender in Maya Deren's Challenge to the Cinema

"For the serious artist the esthetic problem of form is, essentially, and simultaneously a moral problem . . . the form of a work of art is the physical manifestation of its moral structure."[1] The morality of form to which
Maya Deren refers in the above quote is a puzzling notion. It is form without formalism, form as a value, not simply in itself, but in its function as
an ethos. This valuation of form has to do with the weight Deren places
on structure as defining a process of audience engagement. For her, form
in art provides the equivalent of ritual in nonindustrialized cultures. If
art were to play an equivalent function in American culture of the years
1943 to 1961, the years during which Deren sought to have an impact
on the directions taken by the U.S. cinematic avant-garde, it would do
so by engaging form in new ways.

What does Deren mean by form? For her, form constitutes those structures that take advantage of cinematic specificity and that mold reality
through artifice. Form elicits and even demands an attentive and thoughtful spectator. The form in which Deren put her faith structures rhythms
and intervals, within and between shots and sequences. It is consonant
with much of contructivist art making. Care of composition yields
weighted, planned schemas within the image; image-to-image relationships are equally carefully wrought, seeking poetic resonances of repetition and variation, patterning that build conceptually across a work.

Yet a quite different impulse informed the very period in U.S. art during which Deren worked; the belief in improvisation and the directly

expressive gesture that characterizes U.S. abstract expressionism was at odds with aspects of the emphasis on form in Deren. Jazz and improvisitory theater too constructed performance as a unique instance of expression governed by the moment and the flow of creative impulses rather than the score. Deren herself articulated the opposition: "Accustomed as we are to the idea of a work of art as an expression of the artist, it is perhaps difficult to imagine what other possible function it could perform. But once the question is posed, the deep recesses of our cultural memory release a procession of indistinct figures wearing the masks of Africa or the Orient, the hoods of the chorus or the innocence of the child virgin . . . the faces always concealed or veiled by stylization—moving in formal patterns of ritual and destiny."[2] She contrasts form to both "feverish narcissism" and "naturalism." In her opposition, she not only attacks works that trace the expression of selfhood, sensitivity, intensity, and individualism of the artist, but she also attacks mimesis when it molds itself as naturalism. She posits an "essential amorality of a natural form."[3] In this essay, I will look at how Deren's notion of form constitutes the kernel of her innovation, the source of one of her conflicts with other currents of filmmaking and film theory operating at the time, and the means by which she prefigures both structuralist and feminist tendencies in filmmaking in the U.S. avant-garde. First, then, let us take a look at the controversial historical question of Deren as innovator, a question both preliminary and central to understanding how her position on form fits into a history of avant-gardes.

As Christopher Horak's anthology on the first avant-garde, *Lovers of Cinema: The First American Film Avant-garde 1919–1945*, makes clear, Deren's work has been seen erroneously as the first manifestation of a U.S. filmic avant-garde by historians such as Arthur Knight and P. Adams Sitney.[4] Cecile Starr summarized the prevalent assumptions of Knight and Sitney in her "Maya: The Mother of the Avant Garde Film" and added to it a feminist appreciation of Deren's gender by focusing on the "mothering" of an artistic practice at a historical juncture in which feminists began rediscovering the historical contribution of women artists.[5] When Starr writes, *"Meshes of the Afternoon* set the tone of the American Avant Garde film for a decade and linked the movement to the older European Avant Garde Films of Cocteau and Bunuel,"[6] she celebrates a link between Deren and European surrealism and poetic symbolism, eclipsing precisely the first American filmic avant-garde that contemporary historians are currently reestablishing.[7] Starr lauds a link that others had cited to Deren's deficit; the debt to European precedents would in the minds of detractors undercut any claims to originality. All these arguments center on issues of originality, influence, and lineage, issues more important to art historical disciplinarity than to the functioning of films and art theoretically.

In several ways, the writings of Lauren Rabinowitz attempt to disentangle this knotty question of originality, innovation, and precedents. Rabinowitz contributes a significant chapter to Horak's volume that establishes Mary Ellen Bute's key role within an earlier avant-garde.[8] According to Rabinowitz, the historical view of Maya Deren as the first significant woman avant-garde filmmaker needs to be seen in a larger historical context, and through a lens that understands how Deren drew attention to herself through appearances in front of the camera and on the stage of an avant-garde scene, beyond the films themselves.[9] While we might note that Deren initially refrained from even identifying herself as the lead in *Meshes* (there is no screen credit for acting) and could at times construct her artist-persona in the self-effacing terms that her emphasis on ritual and group dynamics demanded, Rabinowitz has a point here. Deren laid the basis, intentionally or not, of her legend to which the two-part volume *The Legend of Maya Deren* attests. Yet Rabinowitz further argues in her book *Points of Resistance: Women, Power and Politics in the New York Avant-garde Cinema 1943–71*, that while Deren should be seen in the context of such contemporaries as Marie Menken, her attempts "to unify practices among filmmaking, organization administration [*sic*], and public discourse" make her stand out as a filmmaker playing a defining role in female participation and expression within the American avant-garde cinema.[10]

Let me suggest that while historians in the late sixties and seventies drew an image of Deren as the first woman to play a leading role, this role is one that women repeatedly play in the arts, of being at once a token woman, a salon organizer, and even a scapegoat for those who differ with their positions or resent a female competing for a position of power. Annette Michelson, in comparing Germaine Dulac, the French filmmaker whose career in the twenties and thirties avant-garde included the struggle with Antonin Artaud over their collaborative project, *La Coquille et la Clergie* (The Seashell and the Clergyman), to Deren points out the parallels in the way their gender seems to have conditioned the reception of these female innovators as film theorists.[11]

Deren's innovation was to draw broadly and creatively on the European avant-garde, not just the surrealist and poetic symbolist movements but the constructivist ones as well, not simply to repeat, but to reinscribe poetically, her difference, as American, as woman, as theorist informed by dance and an "amateur" anthropology that presages the subdiscipline of visual anthropology. When speaking of form, she is not afraid to evoke the term "classicist" which she defines as "a controlled manipulation of any or all elements into a form which will transcend and transfigure them."[12]

Deren was also a passionate figure who hinted at herself as lover, as fierce dreamer. So despite her insistence on the formal structuring of expression, this passionate persona of the artist tied her to both the surrealist and the abstract expressionist movement, to the function they assigned the artist, even as she drew sharp lines of distinction in the theory and analysis of their practice.

If current poststructuralist stances welcome a renewed place for historical accuracy yet move beyond a fixation on origins, perhaps a more productive way to approach Deren is to speak of innovative spurs, movements that launch new energies. It is in this sense that one understands why Deren's work inspired historians at one point in history to claim Deren as the avant-garde's filmic foremother: no *simple* mistake here of flawed research and historical perspective, since this claim can be read symptomatically as an effort to mark significance. Not first, not even first woman, Deren still represents a significant reinvigoration, an amalgam of the forces of modernity in artistic expression inspired by the pre-modern, the ancient, and the primitive, as a celebration of collective affectivity and the ritual participation in communities.

This strategy, modernity inflected with lessons drawn from cultural memory, clearly presented in her writings, affects the ordering of her films and puts her at odds with some of her contemporaries in the avant-garde film movement. Elsewhere I have discussed how Deren's concern with formal compositional values clashed with views held by Jonas Mekas, who was emerging as another leading figure in diverse roles as critic, filmmaker, and organizer.[13] Here I would like to revisit this debate for the perspective it offers on Deren's concern with structure. Mekas at first pejoratively dismissed Deren, by then one of the elder spokeswomen of avant-garde cinema. He termed her works "intellectual formalism" that resulted from "mechanical creation, without enough emotional content" and claimed that her "supposed depth" is "artificial." An exchange between Deren and Mekas in the *Village Voice* between July 1960 and June 1961 has Deren refusing Mekas's casting of her on the side of orthodoxy and artistic law and order as traditionally defined. Films that Mekas called early examples of personal cinema, such as Alfred Leslie and Robert Frank's *Pull My Daisy* and John Cassavetes's *Shadows*, Deren claimed were in fact "more orthodox in structure and style" in their use of "semi-documentary structure" than were her own films.[14] Part of what emerges in this debate is the role of immediacy as a critical value for Mekas, but beyond this, the debate between Deren and Mekas is interesting, because it implicitly raises issues of the gendered subject: both what happens to the notion of the personal cinema when the person behind the camera is a woman and what happens to the representation of the other (and by extension the world) within that which is offered as the personal vision of the self. In this same article he claimed that

If the man, the most frequent protagonist of American film poems is presented as an unreal frustrated dreamer, the woman here is usually

robbed of both her true spirituality and her unashamed carnality.
She is a white-dressed, unearthly, elusive symbol flowing dreamily
along seashores (or sea-bottom) through bushes and upon hills
(Deren, Harrington, Markopoulos, Broughton, Hugo and so
forth).[15]

To see Deren's female imagery this way involves a misreading of the
complex permutations these figures undergo in her films. Though we may
find Deren's females occasionally in placements that correspond to
Mekas's descriptions, they are never simply fixed there, robbed of "both
spirituality and carnality." One might describe as "white-dressed, unearthly" the image of the young woman (Rita Christiani) holding a flower,
floating in negative through the vertical axis of the frame in *Rituals in
Transfigured Time*. Similarly, the beached mermaid images in *Meshes of the
Afternoon* and *At Land* (which I will examine in some detail shortly) correspond in some way to Mekas's description of heroines flowing "dreamily along seashores (or sea-bottom)." Yet each of these images is but an
element in a complex weave of transformations; textual structure makes
these representations assume different shapes.

Certainly the reconsideration of Deren's work by feminist film theory has indicated what Mekas's formulation of the personal cinema could
not see—that which distinguishes her women protagonists from those
of her male counterparts. If the personal was primarily a historically
bound male perspective whose myths, heroics, and metaphors were conditioned by the consciousness of the male artists who sought to equate
the camera with their own subjective eye, Deren infuses the personal with
her experience as a woman. She then arranges the force of experience
into a form that evokes connections to shared cultural experience, to the
inheritance that is the legacy of ritual. It is this emphasis on the relationship between drawing on emotional experience and insisting on formal structuration to which we will return repeatedly in tracing how feminist filmmakers who came later can be seen as inspired by Deren: the
notion of autobiography and female space was a great influence and in-

spiration for women filmmakers in particular. In conjunction, her insistence on form as it relates to dance, movement, and ritual will provide a complex legacy for the feminist filmmaking to follow.

What emerges in the Mekas-Deren exchange is a debate between the random and the ordered—Deren is a precursor of a more structural approach to film at a time when expressionist and improvisitory tendencies are seen as closer to freedom. Her fight with Mekas was over film structure as much as anything else. Looking at examples from her films, we can see how her work uses form to embody her ethics, how her practice coincides with her theory.

Deren recommends conceiving of "chamber films" analogous to musical compositions for chamber ensembles in contrast to full-scale orchestral symphonies (the musical reference here is to classicism, too). In doing so, she is drawing an analogy that not only echoes her championing the "amateur" film over the large-budget film produced by the industry but also advocates compositional order. Evident throughout Deren's writings is a sense that spontaneity is only a component in a process of art making that according to her should be governed by concepts and composed in highly articulated forms. In one of her exchanges with Mekas, published on June 1, 1961, Deren says:

> Jonas Mekas undertook to choose me as representative spokesman for the opposition to the improvised "catch as catch can and I hope the camera caught something" school of filming by quoting my reference to such artists as "amateur burglars." . . .
>
> The implication is that since I am against amateur burglary I am therefore on the side of orthodoxy and artistic law and order as traditionally defined. Actually, Mr. Mekas himself has praised my own films for leaving behind the "epic picture (form like the novel) . . . "
>
> Moreover, my criticism of the amateur burglar was that he was not a good thief! I am for the real bank robber, who gets down in the deep vaults. "The creative artist must be willing to rob his own bank . . . ," which takes "time, planning and a great deal of self-

knowledge if one is to come out with more than what the teller has
on hand from recent deposits, . . ."

To accomplish such a great bank robbery, I maintained, one must
start with a concept.[16]

Deren's economic metaphors of robbery switch her usually positive use
of the word "amateur" to a negative connotation in her disdain for "amateur burglars." The passage gives us insight into how strong a concept
"art" remains for Deren; her interest is not in any random gathering of
images, but rather in a noncommercial venture by the artist who shapes
the events, metaphors, and spatiotemporal configurations she projects
onto the screen.

Using Deren's own metaphor, we can say that by tunneling deep in
her own vault, Deren committed "grand larceny" in making her first film,
Meshes of the Afternoon (1943). For what she has robbed from the cache
of her own resources is a film that is at once a home movie (a biography
inside the home, inside the artist's mind, inside the unconscious) and a
formally realized work of art, whose innovative spatiotemporal ordering
transformed its audiences' concept of film. The film is "located" in the
artist/protagonist's home in the Hollywood hills, a home she shared with
her husband, Alexander Hammid, who plays her husband in the film and
codirected. With these biographical elements of the home movie, Deren
meshes a wide range of ideas on memory and the psyche, repetition and
variation, spatial and temporal cognition. The concepts include ones that
subtend the process of structuration: parapraxis, game structure, ritual,
the divided and multiple self, the self in relationship to other, and the
death drive and murderous impulses.

Parapraxis, the psychoanalytic term for the traces of failed actions, gov-
erns numerous events in the film: a key falls beyond the reach of a hand
down the front stairs of the house, a phone is found off the hook, a record
player is turning relentlessly beyond the borders of its inscribed musical
information, a knife falls from where it is precariously poised on a loaf
of bread. These sorts of parapraxes occur in everyday life. While for-

getting to hang up a phone may be a purely random act of forgetfulness, a chance occurrence, theories of parapraxis signal us to pay attention to such instances as insistences of the unconscious. They tell us of some as yet undetermined causal factor. The action fails because of an unexpressed desire or conflict. If objects in *Meshes* fall down or trip up, they do so across carefully edited frames, creating a visual rhythm that the female protagonist watches with a gaze that implies her interiority, as if these events in her house were somehow a part of her, as one might look at figuration in one's own dreams. Parapraxis belongs, after all, to the order of the symptom, as a trace of the unconscious. It is an indication of some unconscious force that can seemingly only take this disguised form of expression.

There is, however, no single, simple key to Deren's image riddles; the key has already fallen away in the first "act" (the return to home, the climb up the external stairs) and besides, Deren's writing in section 3B of *An Anagram* cautions against a traditional psychoanalytical reading, a static interpretation of symbols suggested by the objects in this film.[17] What seems to worry her here is a one-to-one deciphering that can account neither for transformative energies nor for structure. Instead, she creatively mobilizes the same concepts as psychoanalysis, seeking not illustration, but creative play, mystery, and awe.

Looking at these elements displaced throughout the film reminds one of those childhood image games such as "what's wrong with this picture?" in which one searches a drawing to find the lamp rendered upside down, or a doll replacing the bird in the cage. This element, shared with game playing and ludic structures, is a central concept providing order in Deren's work. In *Ritual in Transfigured Time*, the game that gives birth to a stunning sequence of images in the film's third section is "statue maker"; a lead player twirls the other players around, swinging them by a single hand, then lets go, throwing each out into space until they (playing along) arrest their movement in a poignant still pose, an action sculpture that bears the trace of the spin. In the film this childhood game becomes a dance, as the male lead dancer spins the others, the women, off into a trajectory that halts in a freeze-frame lingering on their stopped-motion pose. Inherent in this transformation of game to dance is the underlying tension of a nascent desire within potential relationships spun through the gazes, gestures, and poses of the players/dancers. The male spinner (Frank Westbrook) directs his female statues into a spatial chance operation, but evidence in the script shows that nothing here is left to chance, as all was diagrammed in detail in the planning stages. Here the insistence on a formal strategy that structures even games of chance separates Deren from earlier art movements, such as Dada, and her contemporaries' improvisitory inclinations.

At an earlier stage in planning, another game was to have ended the film in a segment entitled "The Child at Play" when it was planned as a longer eight-part film called *Ritual and Ordeal;* lacking the detail of other parts of the script, we are given simply indications of a dispute between a girl and a boy in which she knocks down his blocks, setting off the animation of various toys—"marbles roll in."[18] The toys are catalogued in the script: "dolls, spiral, chair, spelling blocks, Clara's father's doll, Masks from Wally, Masks from Tei-ko, Wooden beads, flying bird, Jack-in-the-box, balloons, John Meyer's puppet." Yet exactly how we get from this scene to the ominous final indication of the "Death Fall"—remains somewhat mysterious, since the intervening shots are uncharacteristically vague, though staircases and windows figure here. One is tempted to take this unfinished game as a puzzle fragment of some autobiographical trace from childhood (especially as I read it as a woman remembering her girlhood with an older brother); in many ways it reiterates the tensions linked to gazes and violence echoed in falling and animate objects at work in *Meshes* and *At Land,* locating this tension at the heart of child's play.

Figures 6–8. *Ritual in Transfigured Time* (1946). In the film this childhood game becomes a dance, as the male lead dancer spins the others, the women, off into a trajectory that halts in a freeze-frame lingering on their stopped-motion pose. Figure 7 depicts Frank Westbrook and Rita Christiani; figure 8 depicts Westbrook and Maya Deren. Figures 6 and 7 courtesy of Anthology Film Archive. Figure 8 courtesy of Catrina Neiman.

6

7

8

Cat's cradle, the game of geometric transformations of a string loop whose rule is not to disturb the hidden order of the lacing as one passes the loop from player to player, was to have structured another film, never completed, bearing the name *Witch's Cradle*. From evidence in the script and outtakes, Deren juxtaposes the child's game with direct references to the surrealist game in this film in a strategy to document Marcel Duchamp and the Art of the Century gallery.[19] To choose games of child-hood not as simply a reference but as the basis of ordering a filmic se-quence is to tap profoundly the structures of risk and win, venture and gain, struggle and pleasure that a game entails. For Deren games are not so much chance operations but ludic structures, puzzles whose fit orders one's life. She writes:

> Certain of children's games can be regarded as the ultimate in orig-inal, secular ritual. Often they are created by the players themselves, but even when they are "learned," the tradition is not so much an inviolable authority for the form as it is a suggestion which may be modified, elaborated, combined with others, etc. What is important is that while the tradition is easily violable, the form, once estab-lished in its immediate terms, is as rigidly executed as if it had an exterior, traditional obligation.[20]

Deren uses childhood games as a way of linking her art to rituals that all of us have experienced innocently but invested in deeply. These games from childhood become her way of linking the modern audience to the ritual participation in art she seeks as antidote to a modernity hollow of meaningful ritual. For if ritual holds a key place in Deren's conception of the morality of form, it is part of her drive to counteract alienation. There are very serious stakes in these games, reminiscent of the phrase "what's at stake in women's struggles."

If the childhood game "what's wrong with this picture?" informs *Meshes*, the film only suggests an answer—the hint of a domestic disorder beyond that concerning objects. The unspoken trouble that seemingly gives rise to the disturbed imagery resides in a woman's relationship to

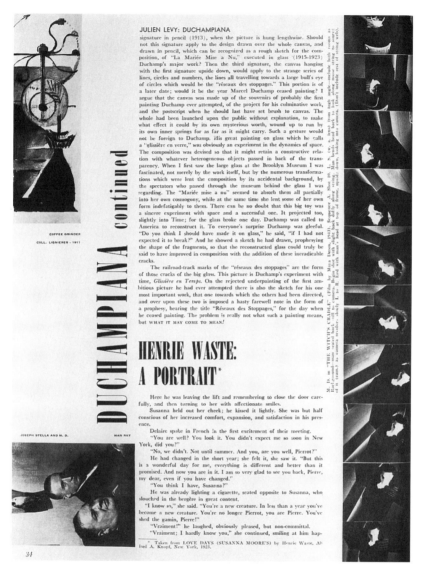

Figure 9. *Witch's Cradle* (unfinished film, 1943). Deren's selected frames from this sequence became an illustration two years later in an issue of *View* magazine (March 1945) devoted to "Duchampiana." The term "witch's cradle" may refer to a training saddle for apprentice witches, a Voudoun-like effigy used to torment someone, or a stage in the game of cat's cradle. Courtesy of Catherine Soussloff.

the other, to her various selves, to the mirrored, hooded figure who ever so enigmatically seems to predict a brush with death. The objects are all animate, transformational; a man becomes a hooded figure with a mirror face, the figure disappears around the edge of the path, a key becomes a word, issuing from the artist's mouth, a key becomes a knife, as does a flower. Transformations of this order suggest a transmographicatory power rather than a fixing of symbols. This power of transformation concerns shifting energies, such as an anger toward the other that can be later experienced as aggression taken out against the self.

All these objects are shifters in a traversal of spaces and a multiplicity of positions, fragmentations, and transformations that appear to be seeking a *location* for domestic violence. Is it the dream of the man or the woman, is it an act performed by the woman that shatters the man/mirror of her self? Or is she drowned already as she sits dreaming on the easy chair in her living room? These suspended questions reside in this house as unresolved enigmas; the sequence around the table in which the woman multiplies into four incarnations of her self (what Deren termed the "conference scene") asks these questions in a manner that evokes the splitting of the subject.

In this sequence (shots 100–114), the woman multiplies into four incarnations of her self, and then like the ritual of an African trial-by-fire, each woman touches the key until for one of them it does not flip upside down as itself but becomes a knife. Such references to rituals, like the references to games, are another of the "external" ordering patterns that Deren seeks to incorporate into her work. We will return to the complex structuring role that ritual has for Deren shortly; for now let us note that as an external reference it floats in meaning but supplies a definitive sense of shot sequence to this conference scene. The order and even the rhythm of the shots follow from expectations of sequence and conclusion once one adopts the pattern of trial (object placed in hand) proposed by the ritual. Expectations lead us around the circle, until the transformation called for by the roulette game of elimination plays itself out. The resolution that completes the sequence is punctuated by the Ito score

Figure 10. *Meshes of the Afternoon* (1943). The central character, doubled, en route to her multiplication into four incarnations. Courtesy of Catrina Neiman.

added to the film in 1961. Providing resolution in the sense of completing this segment, it also initiates elements of the next sequence; there is never any complete resolution within the fragment in Deren's films. Each part introduces elements that will be reworked by the next interval or segment.

In *Meshes*, several possibilities coexist, enmesh, so that no one interpretation can dominate this film of the home, of the female self, of the artist's eye. The resolution of form in *Meshes* begs for close formal attentiveness, for the ending on the beached mermaid is one that is suggestively not terminal, despite the death imagery. Let us note in contrast Hollywood's propensity for drowning its misfits in the Pacific *(Humoresque, A Star Is Born, Interiors)*; the form death takes here is quite different. In *Meshes* the sea doesn't cover, and therefore claim, its corpse. The image of a death draped in seaweed, seated on her own living room's easy chair is hardly a simply convenient or guilty capitulation to narrative closure. It is a careful substitution for an ending that we suspect from the outset but are never allowed to possess as ending: the wakening of the dreaming woman whose eyes first closed when she stroked her body on the chair. This dreamer never wakes up to the lover's kiss simply to end the film. Instead that awakening, that fairy-tale kiss, is earlier inscribed in the middle of her dream, as but an initiator of exactly that violent reaction that will lead to the image of the beached mermaid. The violence, the knife thrown at the man's face, which only succeeds in shattering a mirror, connects the bedroom to the seashore as site of death. The shattering of the mirror allows the sea to emerge from underneath and triggers the jump cut to the beachfront traces of mirror shards and seaweed that eventually become metonymically linked to the mermaid as a subjective pan reveals these fragments first scattered in the living room before reaching the shot of the beached mermaid in her chair.

The beached mermaid sits in the house, just as she dreamt in it earlier. The house space is magical, imbued with the force of a restless and unsettled female artistic imagination: its architecture includes an infinite staircase, a second-story window that one can leap into from the outside, a picture window that becomes a telescopic tunnel into the space of dreams. In Deren's astute use of filmic intervals, of sequences that link rhythmically and poetically, the tropes won't rest, the film won't end, the key is falling still.

Maya Deren gives us her vision of a home movie as a gift to a future generation of filmmakers. Many women filmmakers since Deren have made their own versions of home movies, the autobiography of the relationship between artist and lover, artist and home. In fact this legacy extends back into literature, to Charlotte Perkins Gilman's *The Yellow Wallpaper* and Virginia Woolf's *To the Lighthouse* and into painting, to Frida Kahlo's images of her bedroom, garden, and her relationship with Diego Rivera. The home and the relationship are fertile grounds for the woman artist, whose intensity of associations often releases imagery bespeaking an angry rush of pain. *Meshes* is Deren's most direct expression of that pain.

Yet her image of the beached mermaid, whose suicide or death haunts the living room and confronts the lover at the end of the film, surfaces in another film, *At Land*, where it takes on the form of a quest, an abstract climbing. The ascendant rhythms of *At Land*'s quest merge with images of a chess game with surrealist implications that we will look at in a moment; then the quest falls back toward the sea. Rising and falling action is given a cyclical structure here, a mythic quest structure whose classic heritage gives way to deft abbreviation and abstraction. In the tradition of symbolist poetry in its drive toward minimalism, as in the work of Stephane Mallarmé, *At Land* transfers to film a form of imagery that flourishes in the cinematic potential for visual transformations and change. She has found an action language in a filmic expression in which each new act is registered by her female protagonist, Deren herself, as wide-eyed witness. Deren doubles and redoubles sight and vision, seeing and witnessing in relationship to acts that are always surprising. Yet surprising acts occur within a definitive structure of the classical quest cycle. *At Land* seeks to play theoretically with the process of identification between filmmaker, protagonist, and viewer. It does so quite differently than does the more expressionist autobiographical film in which this process is assumed and iterated directly. The autobiographical elements of *At Land* or *Meshes* are never simply presented as experiences or even stories with which we are immediately asked to identify. Here structuration is crucial, as form dissociates embodiment from the natural. We are always aware of the dance of this body moving through space and that time here is figured in transformed form. We are always aware of the signifying processes, even if meanings are always suggestively in an active state of change.

Form's morality leaves open here the questions posed by death, displacement, and anger. *At Land, Meshes,* and *Ritual* construct their rituals around some very violent unconscious drives, ones that reveal death imagery and violence as pivotal to the turns of the symbolist imagery. Chess is, after all, a ritual battle to death and checkmate an intellectual and symbolic annihilation, which the chess piece that falls away out of grasp embodies in the same way as does the key in *Meshes*. These elements may be out of grasp of the film's protagonist, but they are structured within a form that seeks to grasp them by the protagonist's double, the filmmaker. She grasps the open questions of death and violence by structuring them, by poetically posing them as open questions.

Consider how the use of social rituals is treated as a formal device to structure the first two sections of the triptych of sequences that comprise *Ritual*. The first section interlaces two rituals, yarn winding and female conversations, as one woman winds the yarn being held as a loop by the other and we see the animated gestures of a verbal exchange that we do not hear. Skein, loop, thread, ball: the story of this yarn winding dates from the spinning wheel, culturally determined by the domestic-craft manufacture of clothing as female ritual. It is connected to the classical image of fate, to the structure of Homer's *Odyssey*. The conversation is represented by the same rhythms as the arms that hold the skein, dipping first left, then reversing right; the specificity of words, the instance of language is indicated (lips move) but withheld (absent sound). This pattern is repeated in the party greeting ritual that informs the second section, for once again the gestures of conversation make the statement. The absence of particularity here and the alienated wandering of a lone woman through a group suggest that the social ritual in modern form is not the defining participatory ritual of cultural memory but the trace of ritual presented as its alienated form.

Here Deren's formal inscription, drawing on the vital energies of ritualistic cultures of the past, critiques social rituals devoid of such meaningful communal expenditure of spirit in the present. Haunting the social ritual is a triangulation of the female figure, her splitting into fragments wary and uncertain of one another (see figure 21, p. 156). One woman stands ominously gazing from the doorway as the yarn winding occurs. She watches, contemplates, perhaps judges, silently. This gaze on the scene troubles, but of what does this trouble speak? Here the form

Figure 11. *Ritual in Transfigured Time* (1946). The story of yarn-winding dates from the time of the spinning wheel and is connected to the classical image of fate, to the structure of Homer's *Odyssey.* Courtesy of Catrina Neiman.

refuses the motivation of narrational fullness, offering instead the enigma of representational placements. Painting a scene through placement, retaining the mystery of symbolic ordering of the text that refuses to clarify exchanges, psyches, economies, this watching woman is in excess, a supplemental figure who poses as a stand-in for the viewer. What does this conversation, this thread winding signify? What happens when the thread binding a film is conceptual rather than narrative? Thread wind-

ing, weaving, and enmeshing will become metaphors for a textual practice that refuses the binding of a too-clear meaning; what is clear is that
differentiated parts are meant to be seen as part of a construct.

The morality of form asks us to hold onto relationships between parts
and a whole, to work through the gaps as significant, to explore the sup-
plements that may condition the understanding of any new elements. The
"morality of form" can be seen as equivalent to Roland Barthes's notion
in *The Responsibility of Forms*, when in reviewing Jean-Louis Schefer's book
he writes "to ask if painting is a language is *already* an ethical question,
one which requires a mitigated, a censored answer safeguarding the rights
of the creative individual (the artist) and those of a human universality
(society)."[21] Rather than answering this "rigged question," Barthes says
Schefer proposes a new question: "What is the relationship between the
picture and the language inevitably used in order to read—i.e. in order
(implicitly) to write it?"[22] If the connection is constituted as within the
picture itself, as Barthes suggests, then form is where ethics will be worked
out, where "the very practice of the picture is its own theory." Barthes
goes on to say:

> Schefer's discourse reveals not the secret, the truth of this Chess
> Game, but only (and necessarily) the activity by which it is struc-
> tured: the work of the reading (which defines the picture) is radically
> identified with the work of the writing: there is no longer critic, nor
> even a writer talking painting, there is the grammatographer, some-
> one who writes the picture's writing.[23]

This way of examining form as a means of structuring visual tableaus
opens decipherment to a poststructuralist rewriting of all that the struc-
turalists discovered about the play of meanings. This rewriting may reinscribe fundamental notions of structure, of relation, but not as absolutes,
as already known quantities. Barthes here is seconding Schefer's notion
(shared with their contemporary Julia Kristeva) that structuration and
signifying are processes actively and specifically inscribed in form. How
curious for us that the painting in question as Schefer's choice for his

demonstration should be the chess game of Paris Bordone, since its mo-
tifs gain echoes in the very preoccupation with chess that we earlier saw
in Deren's *At Land* and her unfinished film, *Witch's Cradle,* which are
themselves refigurations of the Dada figuration of chess in Hans Richter's
Ghosts Before Breakfast. Chess, after all, inscribes the significance of
differentiated pieces in a position on a game board, a demarcated grid.
Chess becomes an object of metaphorical reinscription by the tableau that
inscribes in newly reconfigured spaces the dispersed statuettes that serve
as elements of this game.

The woman watching over the first segment of *Rituals* (Anaïs Nin) may
be seen as a supplement that infuses the next two parts; can we risk comparison of her to the queen in chess, as even her physiognomy suggests?
We can let her presence disturb us as she stands looking in doorways at
the two other women. We can let her representation suggest how she
poses a problem of speculation, of the third term overseeing the duo that
gives rise in narrative to the thrust of triangulation. We do get a hint of
jealousy, perhaps, of voyeurism in her representation, but these are but
hints within an insistence on her function as the one who watches. She
provokes speculation about the social situation of the forties within a class
of artists on the fringes of middle-class American life. The oblique representation of this woman watching drives the film through to its third
segment, the statue-maker segment, in which she, along with the other
two women, are the beings spun off to transmographize into statues. In
other words, triangulation energizes here, as it does in so many narratives, but the terms of the triangulation are spatial, gestural, and abstract
with only visual hints at characterization and motivation. The social geography of visual representation meets a geometry of form.

There is no doubt that this passionate exploration of form significantly
prefigured and inspired the group of filmmakers emerging in the sixties
and seventies who were themselves increasingly interested in cinematic
construction and filmic structuration. Certainly the highly structural
games of Hollis Frampton's films and the poetic composition of Larry
Gottheim's bear the traces of the same artistic investment in devising im-

ages and intervals of images in which the arrangement of each part articulates concerns and propositions of the other parts, often displaying the type of gaping disjunctions we looked at in *Rituals*. These gaps ask for connections to be made across an articulation of quite different segments, infusing the more classical notion of form with principles of a more modernist poetics and a more contemporary musical theory. Variations need not necessarily follow predictable patterns, as any elements can be threaded as a variant of themselves, the game being precisely how one discerns difference in relation to repetitions and variations.

Yet it is with feminist avant-garde filmmaking that perhaps the resonance of Maya Deren's ethics of form is perhaps most pronounced. Yvonne Rainer and Abigail Child are two quite different filmmakers who come to mind. Rainer's films' use of dancelike movements and tableau poses certainly echo Deren's on numerous other levels as well, but consider how the parts of *Kristina's Talking Pictures, A Film About a Woman Who, Journeys from Berlin/1970,* or even the more narratively grounded *Murder and MURDER* play Deren's game of combining relatively autonomous segments into a mesh through which one structures a film.

The rapidly cut found footage of Abigail Child's films, such as that in *Covert Action,* may seem to emanate from a sensibility quite different from Deren's, but here the sense of development out of formal patterns across their repetitions as well as the exploration of violence underlying the domestic scene can indicate another sense in which a legacy informs. *Covert Action's* images are taken primarily from home movie footage that one eventually understands as the chronicles two men made of their amorous encounters with various women at their vacation house. Mainly the personages are seen cavorting in the backyard, but there are also a number of close-ups, many of them shots of kisses. Child fragments duration of shots to an extreme—some are only a few frames long—then systematically repeats, varies, and interweaves them, matching or contrasting the motion or graphic dominants involved. The frenzied pace is augmented by an autonomous and equally rapid soundtrack montage of musical clips, conversational fragments, random phrases, and periodic announcements.

Montage patterns are the driving mechanism of the film. Once an image fragment is introduced, it is submitted to variations such as a flipping of the frame from left to right, which inverts the graphic elements of the image. Thus a close-up of a woman turning left will be followed by the same shot with the direction of the movement inverted, in a manner that recalls the interval montage of Fernand Léger's *Ballet Méchanique*. However, unlike the topically or spatially oriented series in *Ballet Méchanique* devoted to object types or actions, the series here is even more pronouncedly determined by kinetic or graphic patterns. In *Covert Action* each shot migrates into new montage contexts, becoming a part of many different heterogenously ordered series.

Over the course of a screening, one begins to recognize the shots through their repetitions. One begins to know the image of the woman in the cloche hat and distinguish it from the woman in the fedora, or the one in the bandanna, from the close-up face in soft focus, or the young girl in the Eskimo jacket. The images gradually accrue the weight of referentiality, and we can reconstruct the individual women, the events of each visit. Thus a walk by a stream, acrobatics on a lawn, a game of leapfrog, drinks by the beehive, an embrace on a wicker chair become events through the sum of their fragmented parts, dispersed throughout the body of the film. Women's faces and their bodies, alternately self-aware or captured in unsuspecting innocence, dominate the imagery, creating a swirl of sensuality, of performance for the camera. This ambiguity of the means by which these images were taken (complicity or naive abandon) adds to the violence built by graphic contrasts and fast pace. The sounds accentuate this violence, especially the screams and screeches, and the words comment on it with such intertitles as "He had to be eliminated," "She had to be bitten," "Ending with a rupture of the hypnosis," and "My goal is to disarm my movie." Perhaps one might say that Child is far more fragmented, abstract, and intensely rapidly paced than Deren and stop the comparison at this point of contrast; certainly her film *Mayhem* is more extreme in this regard than is *Covert Action*. Yet if I insist here on an intertextuality with Deren that illuminates both sets of films, it is because *Covert Action* benefits by being seen with *Meshes* and *At Land*, since the female protagonists chart a relationship to space while the female filmmakers play with form. The violence explored in Child is already present in Deren, as I discussed earlier. Feminism can find in both filmmakers an ability to explore violence and the death drive from the perspective of female experience.

With so much of the theorization that surrounded feminist filmmaking initially centered on a questioning of the representation of the female body, of voyeurism, and of identification (when not entirely on issues of discursive content), it is useful now to reexamine the issues of a morality of form. When so much that seemed vitally pressing in earlier arguments has washed ashore lifeless in the wake of much rediscovered pleasures in female sexuality, it is perhaps time to pay more attention to the nuances of a morality of form that is less absolute, more playful, born between ritual and play, borrowing from the classic, from earlier avant-garde traditions, but forging its own rhythms, its own protagonists, its own dance.

Notes

1. Deren, *Anagram*, p. 37.
2. Ibid.
3. Ibid., p. 32.
4. Horak, *Lovers of Cinema*, pp. 3–11.
5. Starr, "Maya: The Mother of the Avant Garde Film," p. 13.
6. Ibid.
7. Alexander Hammid's shared credit with Deren as codirector of *Meshes of the Afternoon* may account for some of the tendency to link this film to the European avant-garde historically. It is also likely that critics were simply responding to a similarity between certain aspects of imagery and montage.
8. Rabinowitz, *Points of Resistance*, pp. 315–34.
9. Ibid. pp. 48–52
10. Ibid. p. 23.
11. Michelson and Bruno, "Women in the Avant-garde," pp. 142–43.
12. Maya Deren, "Program Notes," p. 6
13. Turim, "Reminiscences, Subjectivities, Truths," pp. 200–202.

14. Deren, letters in the *Village Voice*, August 25, 1960 and June 1, 1961. Reprinted in *Film Culture* 39 (1965): 55–56.

15. Jonas Mekas, "The Experimental Film in America." In *Film Culture Reader*, edited by P. Adams Sitney (New York and Washington, D.C.: Praeger, 1970), p. 23.

16. The quotes and italics are in the original. Deren is citing an earlier article she wrote for the *Village Voice* on July 21,1960, and an article by Jonas Mekas, also for the *Village Voice* on March 2, 1961.

17. Deren, *Anagram*, sec. 3B, pp. 26–29.

18. Deren, *Legend of Maya Deren*, pt. 1, pp. 511–13.

19. Ibid., pp. 150–65

20. Maya Deren, "Theme and Form: Thematic Statement," *Film Culture* 39 (Winter 1965): 14.

21. Barthes, *Responsibility of Forms*, p. 150.

22. Ibid., p. 150.

23. Ibid., p. 151.

Works Cited

Barthes, Roland. *The Responsibility of Forms.* Translated by Richard Howard. New York: Hill and Wang, 1985.

Clark, VèVè, Millicent Hodson, and Catrina Neiman. *The Legend of Maya Deren: A Documentary Biography and Collected Works.* Vol. 1, pt. 1. New York: Anthology Film Archives and Film Culture, 1984.

———. *The Legend of Maya Deren: A Documentary Biography and Collected Works—Chambers.* Vol. 1, pt. 2. New York: Anthology Film Archives and Film Culture, 1988.

Deren, Maya. "Program Notes" *Film Culture* 39 (Winter 1965): 6.

———. "Theme and Form: Thematic Statement," *Film Culture* 39 (Winter 1965): 11–17.

———. *An Anagram of Ideas on Art and Form. The Legend of Maya Deren: A Documentary Biography and Collected Works.* Vol. 1, pt. 2. New York: Anthology Film Archives, 1988; and here, following page 267.

Gilman, Charlotte Perkins. *The Yellow Wallpaper and Other Writings.* New York: Bantam Books, 1989.

Horak, Christopher. *Lovers of Cinema: The First American Film Avant-garde 1919–1945.* Madison: University of Wisconsin, 1995.

Michelson, Annette, and Gulianna Bruno. "Women in the Avant-garde: An Interview with Annette Michelson," *Millennium Film Journal* (Fall–Winter 1986–1987): 17/18/19, 141–48.

Rabinowitz, Lauren. *Points of Resistance: Women, Power and Politics in the New York*

Avant-garde Cinema 1943–71. Champaign and Chicago: University of Illinois, 1991.

Starr, Cecile. "Maya: The Mother of the Avant Garde Film." *New York Times,* 2 May 1976, sec. 2, p. 13.

Turim, Maureen. "Childhood Memories and Household Events in the Feminist Avant Garde," *Journal of Film and Video* 38 (1986): 86–92.

———. "Reminiscences, Subjectivities, Truths." In *To Free the Cinema: Jonas Mekas and the New York Underground,* edited by David James. Princeton: Princeton University Press, 1992, 193–212.

Woolf, Virginia. *To the Lighthouse.* New York and London: Harcourt Brace Jovanovich, 1927.

Catherine M. Soussloff

Maya Deren Herself

The "I" with which we speak stands for our identity as subjects in language, but it is the least stable entity in language, since its meaning is purely a function of the moment of utterance. The "I" can shift, and change places because it only ever refers to whoever happens to be using it at the time. **—Jacqueline Rose**

The name: What does one call thus? What does one understand under the name of name? And what occurs when one gives a name? What does one give then? One does not offer a thing, one delivers nothing, and still something comes to be which comes down to giving that which one does not have, as Plotinus said of the Good. What happens, above all, when it is necessary to sur-name [surnommer], renaming there where, precisely, the name comes to be found lacking? What makes the proper name into a sort of sur-name, pseudonym, or cryptonym at once singular and singularly untranslatable? **—Jacques Derrida**

The meaning of "Maya Deren" shifts according to who speaks her name. In the discourse on film, "Maya Deren" occupies two places: one of them apolitical and aestheticizing, the other political and feminist. In the former, Maya Deren is an artist and the origin of an American (mainly male) avant-garde film practice. In the latter, Maya Deren is part of a feminist film canon but before its time. Here Maya Deren is an icon, a model, an inspiration. She is in the canon of "women artists" but not of feminism,

Figure 12. Maya Deren (1942 or 1943). The refraction of light by the glass cylinder produces a cubist effect. It also undercuts the assumption that one viewpoint and a fixed perspective confirm a singular identity. Photographed by Alexander Hammid. Courtesy of Anthology Film Archives.

because she predates its appearance as a political project and she does not do what feminist filmmaking does, that is, draw attention to the problematics of a gendered identity. The first two parts of this essay will explore the historiography of Maya Deren in the discourse on film. The final section will locate Maya Deren's (Eleanora Derenkowsky's) own use of "Maya Deren" in her work and practice. Here Deren's subjectivity will be examined in terms of self-representation in her films.

The History

Begin with *The Legend of Maya Deren: A Documentary Biography and Collected Works* (hereafter referred to as *The Legend*), volume 1, part 1, planned by Millicent Hodson and collaborators in Berkeley and New York between 1973 and 1978 and published in 1984 in New York by Anthology Film Archives under the aegis of Jonas Mekas, to whom the three-volume project is dedicated. Mekas, the curator of the American film avant-garde, presides over this historiography of Maya Deren after, as Hodson writes, a decade of obscurity following her death in 1961.[1] This historiography promotes Deren as the originator of American avant-garde cinema through what came to be known as her "subjective film," *Meshes of the Afternoon* (1943, directed by Maya Deren and Alexander Hammid).[2]

As Lauren Rabinovitz and others have argued, the project of legitimating American independent cinema as an art form, which began in the 1960s, consisted of positioning it in contradistinction to the Hollywood machine. Here Deren's film *Meshes*, made in Hollywood but without the aid of any studio and using a handheld camera, could serve as the ideal marker of independent American cinema. Further, Alexander Hammid brought a European art film genealogy to the collaboration, distancing her films further from American commercial cinema. Their collaboration establishes Deren, and initially Hammid, as the beginning of the U.S. manifestation of European avant-gardism. P. Adams Sitney, for example, opens his discussion of *Meshes* by drawing a parallel to the partnership of Salvador Dalí and Luis Buñuel in *Un Chien Andalou* (1928), although from 1943 Deren consistently denied any surrealistic influence on her films, as he admits.[3]

Feminist critics have long recognized that an essential ingredient to establishing a history of American avant-garde cinema is a canon of *auteurs.* While the concept of *auteur* may be traced to a particular critical and filmmaking practice developed in *Cahiers du Cinema* between 1951 and 1958, that is, after the appearance of Deren's films, it nonetheless affects her historiography, and thus subsequent assessments of her, perhaps more than any other American avant-garde filmmaker, precisely because she is theorized both as originator of the American avant-garde *and* as "woman artist."[4] The concept of the *auteur* in the historiography of the American avant-garde required less a commitment to a certain film practice, as it did in France, than to a notion of the filmmaker as artist.

This emphasis on the individual filmmaker was in perfect harmony with all so-called avant-garde art practices in America beginning in the late 1940s. In the European tradition, the visual artist (particularly painters, sculptors, and architects) had been viewed as an individual creator since the Renaissance.[5] In this tradition, the artist was always understood to be male; the "woman artist" was a marked term and constructed differently in the discourse. In the history of the European avant-garde, which began in the nineteenth century, the individuality of the artist became somewhat compromised as an absolute term because of a history of collaborations and collective beliefs that characterized avant-garde practice. Recently, Michael Leja has argued that the history of the first American avant-garde, the New York School, reflects the tensions between the concept of the individual artist and the pressures for a theory of collectivity in the avant-garde.[6] Another recent study of postwar American art argues "that the isolated artist in his studio was a gendered construct excluding women, a continuation of nineteenth-century romantic traditions which required a freedom from any group identity."[7]

According to Leja, these tensions between collectivity and individuality were never resolved in the historiography of the New York School; indeed they characterize it. But in terms of both the later historiography of avant-garde film and the later concept of the auteur that adheres to it, we could say that these tensions between the two were resolved perhaps because the critical effort to establish a genealogy for American independent cinema came in the 1960s and 1970s, after the earlier discourse on avant-garde art from which it borrowed so much.[8] In this historiographical light, "Maya Deren" resolves the tensions because she symbolized a synthesis between the individual auteur and the filmmaker devoted to collective practices. First, temporally, she represents the originary moment of the birth of the American avant-garde. Second, as Rabinovitz writes: "Her work was no less than consolidating the first cohesive system of cinema as collective artistic activity and practices, thus defining an American avant-garde cinema."[9] Her gender remains the only distortion in this critical picture.

Feminist discourse, beginning with *The Legend*, revisits Deren and proposes a way to resolve this final distortion of gender. She helps to establish the beginnings of a postwar American independent cinema to be sure, but she also serves as a model to the very women who are themselves involved in the production of *The Legend* during the halcyon years of the American feminist movement. Millicent Hodson writes:

> In our work on *The Legend* we have attempted to see the world
> through Deren's eyes and to remember that such situations as
> Barthes describes [in *Mythologies*] were faced daily by any actively
> creative women in our mothers' generation. . . . But to stake your
> identity on your art alone put you in a nether world threatening to
> men and women alike. . . . The self-defined protagonists Deren plays
> in her films project a nascent feminism. These are women seeking
> their own way, creating with every step an iconography of female
> experience.[10]

To summarize this statement: 1) beginning in the 1930s Deren challenges the status quo of gender stratification; 2) she herself is threatened by this challenge (for example, "Throughout her 30's the conflict between woman and artist intensified."); and 3) by 1943 with her first film, *Meshes*, she identifies with and is identified by viewers with her feminist characters.

The historiography of Maya Deren assumes dimensions unlike that of any other filmmaker of the second half of the twentieth century, as *The Legend* reveals, because it responds in form and content to the burden of criticism placed upon it in the early 1970s; a weight, we could say, determined by two separate but interrelated projects—one of them aesthetic, the definition of an American avant-garde cinema, and the other political, the establishment of a place for the "woman artist" in this avant-garde. It is through the figure of Maya Deren that these two projects become interrelated in film history. This is why the legend of Maya Deren is so powerful in the field of film criticism to this day; its beginnings in criticism coincide temporally and discursively both with the project of the definition of the avant-garde and with the project of feminist film criticism.

These dual projects operate in the literature on Deren after the publication of *The Legend* and *Visionary Cinema*, the extremely influential study of American avant-garde film written in 1974 by P. Adams Sitney. Further, as the quotations from *The Legend* indicate, these two powerful strands of critique require the individual and personal presence of the woman called Maya Deren not only behind the camera and at the editing table but also on screen as an active presence. Identical to the historiography of Simone de Beauvoir, another "woman artist" (novelist and philosopher) of the same generation, "the question of subjectivity" (Deren perceived as a speaking subject) and "the question of textuality" (Deren perceived as a body of texts and films) "here overlap completely."[11] The slippage between the "I" and the projected image—or the speaking "I" and the spoken text—appears inherent in the critique of Deren from at least the early 1970s. Later in this essay, I will suggest possible motivations for this characteristic of the discourse on Deren.

Clearly the question "Who was Maya Deren?" looms large in both strands of the critique, particularly in the originary voluminous text of *The Legend*, a compilation of "documents," as they are called by the editors: interviews, oral histories, letters, autobiographical materials, and memoirs. "We cannot apologize to our readers for the amount of material in these pages. That is how Deren lived. What gives motion to it all—the countless documents and the tales told by the documenters—is the chronology of her days and weeks, works and dreams, the rhythm she created in her life."[12] *The Legend* is autobiographical and biographical, documentary and fictional. Like autobiography, it speaks in the first person; it is confessional; it gives testimony to the experience of the individual by articulating experience in terms of both feelings and memory. The reader recognizes these methods of self-representation from countless literary and historical models. Like biography, *The Legend* structures the account of the subject's actions and works chronologically in order to show the development of the individual's creative output through the documentary evidence of letters, personal documents, personal accounts of others, and critical reception of the work. This is the normative model of the biography of the artist that has been operative in Western literature and history since the early modern period. The "woman artist" requires a biography in order to be written into history.

Although there exists in art history no text on a woman artist of dimensions equal to *The Legend*, a comparable project of constructing the histories of individual women artists took place beginning at the same time in the 1970s.[13] In 1971 Linda Nochlin asked in a famous essay, "Why Have There Been No Great Women Artists?"[14] One response from art history was to construct a canon of women artists into which each successive scholarly generation could insert its own pantheon. This canon building, borrowing from a long tradition in the history of art, used the biography of the artist as the primary textual and critical instantiation of the artist in history writing. So, too, the editors of *The Legend* insisted on the genre of the biography as the determining form for their history: "So we have called *The Legend* a documentary biography—*documentary* to underscore our commitment to the original materials, *biography*, to honor the life. *The Legend* is the first biographical project to be published on Maya Deren."[15]

The "Woman Artist," Feminism, and Film Theory

How is Maya Deren located in feminist analytic discourse? As history, *The Legend* depends on the earlier documentary and autobiographical evidence to interpret the meaning and value of its subject and her works but to an extent not usually encountered with the male artist. *The Legend* is merely a symptom, albeit a historicizable one, of a larger phenomenon of art history, the myth of the "woman artist"—one characterized in part by a historiography that stresses the compilation of masses of biographical and autobiographical documents together with the work.[16] Thus, for example, while Toril Moi writes of her project on de Beauvoir at a different historical moment than do the editors of *The Legend*, she too stresses the compilation of numerous and varied "documents": "The intertextual network of fictional, philosophical, autobiographical and epistolary texts that she left us *is* our Simone de Beauvoir. In addition to this, we have all the texts about her: letters, diaries, newspaper interviews and reviews, scholarly studies, films, biographies, personal recollections by friends and enemies—all contribute to the production of the network of images and ideas we recognize as 'Simone de Beauvoir,' and which certainly condition our perception of her texts 'in themselves.' "[17]

While we might well be able to say the same about a male artist, such statements about explicit methods of collection and display of texts do not occur as motivations or justifications for studies of him. The discourse on the male artist is "natural." It builds on the work and life of the artist without anxiety. But the "woman artist" is different. "Artist" is her surname, but she comes before us in the guise of "woman." Traveling as a woman she must produce her papers at the border of the art world to prove she is an artist.

Using the case of de Beauvoir, Moi calls the emphasis on personality, which is the result of the collection of evidence on the life of the woman artist, "depoliticizing."[18] It is an effort, not necessarily conscious, on the part of critics to deny the disturbing potency of the concept "woman artist."

Rather than exploring her difference from the male artist, the excessive documentation sets out to prove her worthy of being regarded in the company of men. The effect is particularly potent for the woman artist, an effect that could be termed, following Barthes, a "strong myth" in which "the political quantum is immediate."[19] The documents then serve an avant-garde historiography to establish Deren as a woman artist within a depoliticized aesthetic discourse: I am not a "woman"; I am an artist. On the other hand, the myth of the woman artist serves a feminist film historiography to establish Deren as a protofeminist icon: I am an artist who is a woman.

The subject "Maya Deren," like "Simone de Beauvoir," functions as an excessively mutable term in the historiography of both the avant-garde and feminism. This characteristic centers in the vacillation between political and aesthetic evaluations of her, but it also occurs in the slippage between discussing characters that Deren portrays and discussing Deren herself. Speaking in the aesthetic discourse of an avant-garde historiography, Sitney coined the term "trance film" for *Meshes* because "the heroine undertakes an interior quest." He continues: "She encounters objects and sights as if they were capable of revealing the erotic mystery of the self."[20] For Sitney, this character and Deren herself are unified and whole. She "embodies the reflective experience, which is emphasized by the consistent imagery of mirrors in the film." On the other hand, Tom Gunning has suggested that *Meshes* seeks a "destruction of the principle of identity" in which the same multiple reflections of Deren in the mirror point to a breakup of the self rather than to a reflection of it.[21]

In another vacillation, Deren's work has been extolled both for its formal qualities as a "primitive" film style and for its appropriation of political topics such as "primitivism." Judith Mayne, speaking in the discourse of a feminist film historiography, interprets "primitive" both politically and aesthetically: first with Deren's preoccupation with the so-called primitive cultures of Bali and Haiti and second with her use of "primitive narration" techniques borrowed from early film and seen in *Meshes.*[22] These are not commensurate categories of analysis. Mayne slips between a characterization of a certain culture and a characterization of early cinema.

As critics have observed, the feminist construction of a canon of women artists performed a valuable political and historical role in the early years of feminism, but it also ensured that the woman artist remained isolated in the context of cultural productions. In the 1940s and 1950s, before the heyday of feminism, artist contemporaries of Deren in New York, such as Lee Krasner and Helen Frankenthaler, resisted being classed separately in exhibits or publicity as "women artists."[23] Deren also refused such a positioning in her public roles. These women sought to be identified as artists, not to be separated as women. As a reaction to the isolation that may have been enhanced by the canon building of the woman artist in the 1970s, artists like Cindy Sherman began, in the early 1980s, to resist the appellation "woman artist" this time by purposefully complicating the assumptions that viewers bring to the depictions of and by women.[24]

A recent essay on Sherman by art historian Amelia Jones suggests that Sherman's work can be particularly useful in the exploration of the "woman artist" in film history, because in her photography Sherman responds in a systematic way to contemporary feminist art theory, providing us with a model of how female subjectivity has been produced in the visual realm during these years and helping to illuminate Deren's position in it.[25] In her research on Sherman's photographs Jones finds two important aspects of feminist film theory that derive from psychoanalysis.

The first begins with Laura Mulvey's essay of 1975 that theorized the male gaze "as signifier for the male other, bound by a symbolic order in which man can live out his fantasies and obsessions . . . by imposing on them the silent image of woman still tied to her place as bearer, not maker, of meaning."[26] In this influential account, images of women *on screen*, for male consumption either as (prohibited) object of desire or fetishized other, remain the subject of interpretation. This aspect of images of women seemed most appropriate for an analysis of Hollywood genres such as film noir and the horror film as well as the role of the Hollywood

13

14

star.[27] Looking for Deren's place in this critique we find an absence, because the critique of the male gaze and female body as aspects of male
fantasy and desire do not extend to Deren's work since she is not a male
(although Hammid is). This feminist critique did not find alternative
models to Hollywood in the film practice of Deren's time. This left Maya
Deren as a nonentity within this critique.[28]

Jones finds that the second psychoanalytic theme in feminist film theory responded to by Sherman relies on Joan Rivière's famous essay
"Womanliness as Maquerade" (1929), in which "the victim exaggerates
the very modes of passivity and object-ness projected onto her via the
male gaze; here, she might be able to open up the closed circuits of desire this eye has attempted to establish via its penetrative thrust through
a kind of restaging of exactly what is expected of her."[29] Beginning with
the series *Untitled Film Stills* Sherman explores intersubjectivity by trying to get at the desire binding artist, subject, and viewer together—most
obviously so in the realm of sexuality and in the genre of portraiture. Here
Jones uses Mary Anne Doane's important work on female spectatorship
and psychoanalysis that understands "masquerade as a type of representation which carries a threat, disarticulating male systems of viewing."[30]
In her later work on the same topic, Doane probes further the use of masquerade in representational technologies in order to rethink a feminine
subjectivity.[31] It is this question, "How does woman see?" that Sherman
explores in her later untitled series of herself in historical masquerade
and in the series of photographs of exploded fragments of vomit and body
parts. With the latter, Jones argues that Sherman "blinds" "the projec-
tive eye," on which classical spectatorship depends, thereby challenging
the idea of an externally defined subject.[32]

Figure 13. Maya Deren (no date). Photographed by Alexander Hammid. Courtesy of
The Legend of Maya Deren Project.
Figure 14. Cindy Sherman. *Untitled Film Still #14* (1978). Photographed by Cindy Sherman. Sherman explores intersubjectivity by trying to get at the desire which binds
artist, subject, and viewer together—most obviously so in the realm of sexuality and
in the genre of portraiture. Courtesy of the artist and Metro Pictures, New York.

The richness of these two aspects of psychoanalytic film theory in the interpretation of Sherman's photographs cannot be denied. While Jones insists that Sherman's response to feminist theory must be historicized, that is, located in the 1970s and 1980s and seen as responding to critical trends of the time, the similarities between the films of Maya Deren and the concerns for subjectivity expressed in Sherman's photographs call for further reflection, not least because feminist film theory, which uses a psychoanalytic approach, has not addressed the issue of female subjectivity in the films of Deren. As the psychoanalytic critic Kaja Silverman has said of feminist discourse from this period: "There is no sense in which the feminist author, like her phallic counterpart, might be constructed in and through discourse—that she might be inseparable from the desire that circulates within her text, investing itself not only in their formal articulation but in recurring diegetic elements."[33]

Deren, Maya. See MAYA DEREN.

How can we locate Maya Deren's own use of "Maya Deren" in her work and practice? The examination of *The Legend* along with Deren's films and their subsequent historiography reveal that Maya Deren sets into play a crisis in subjectivity in film criticism and practice. If this crisis has not been identified until now it is in part because the topic of subjectivity itself is of necessity elusive, most acutely so in the case of the "woman artist." Simplistic formulations such as "artistic intentionality" must be avoided here, for, like Sherman, Deren used "the subject," representations of herself, critically.

The analysis of subjectivity in discourse relies on Emil Benveniste's formulation: " 'Ego' is he who *says* 'ego.' "[34] When Deren cites herself as artist or author, which she does repeatedly in her films and writing, she speaks to herself and to us and is spoken of and by discourse. The preface of *An Anagram on Art, Form and Film* (1946) provides an excellent example of the discursive complexity of Deren's subjectivity. She begins by citing herself in the historical voice, for example, "Any critical statement by an artist which concerns the field of his creative activity," using the third-person category "artist" and the male-gendered pronoun "his."[35] She changes in the next paragraph to the first person and then cites her films by number without naming them: "In my case I have found it necessary, each time, to ignore any of my previous statements. After the first film was completed . . .".[36] Her citations of herself construct a variety of active and passive positions: filmmaker, critic, author, and in the films, actress.

Subjectivity in film, as Silverman has explained, has no prehistory beyond the socially constructed one of a visual and verbal language.[37] Any interiority to the subject in discourse comes through discourse itself, both a limiting and infinite situation. Deren's own writing reveals that her view of the "subject" came very close to this understanding of its constitution. Deren chose the name "anagram" for what had formerly been called "the artist's manifesto." For although the artist's manifesto has a long tradition in the history of the avant-garde, Deren rejects identification with that history.[38] Further, in the very form of *Anagram*, as explained by Deren, she refuses a "linear" model of understanding: "An anagram is a combination of letters in relationship that each and every one is simultaneously an element in more than one linear series. This simultaneity is real, and independent of the fact that it is usually perceived in succession. Each element of an anagram is so related to the whole that no one of them may be changed without affecting its series and so affecting the whole."[39] Deren decries the surrealists for abnegating the agency of consciousness but she also refuses the absolute consciousness that had been theorized by Hegel for art in the *Phenomenology of Spirit*. Deren's artist and her filmmaking were contingent subjects:

Man himself is a natural phenomenon and his activities may be either an extension and an exploitation of himself as a natural phenomenon, or he can dedicate himself to the creative manipulation and transfiguration of all nature, including himself, through the exercise of his conscious, rational powers. . . . The forms of man, furthermore, are much more explicitly and economically determined by the function for which they are intended, even to the point of being limited, in their use, by that intention.[40]

With this view, Deren considered any art form to be responsible, moral, and with a claim to judgment by history.

Linguistic theory agrees with a basic presupposition of psychoanalysis in regard to the subject: "the subject is not conscious of all 'its' thoughts, is not present in all 'its' representations, not even virtually or potentially."[41] In her first serious essay on film, which she wrote in 1945, an essay that was key to her more elaborate formulations in *Anagram* of 1946, Deren insists on the preeminence of the subjectivity of the film-maker's eye that gives meaning to the reading made by the apparatus.[42] This essay appeared as a pamphlet, which Deren distributed as publicity for her films. On one page of the pamphlet she included a statement by George Amberg, curator at the Museum of Modern Art, that specifically addresses the differences between the surrealists and Deren in their approaches to subjectivity:

> Surrealism, however, claims the objective validity of the logically irreconcilable and severs the connecting link between the subjective level of real meaning and the objective level of logical implication. This results in shock effects which destroy confidence in the validity of the world which they create and frustrate the potential participation of the spectator in it. In the films of Maya Deren, however, the images are chained to each other on the level of emotional, visual and logical implication with the same compelling inevitability which governs the development of the underlying subconscious drama. Thus once the spectator surrenders to the logic of her universe, it emerges as consistent, ordered, and, above all, a powerfully convincing reality.[43]

The successful "chaining" together of the images in Deren's films relies on her use of herself in the films, a method that creates a "logic"—the same logic of the subject that we observe in many of Sherman's photographs.

In 1946 Hammid published an essay on film that expresses similar views regarding the potential for identification between the subjectivity of the viewer and the subject of the film:

The film, with its changing visual angle, its capacity for unlimited detail and significant elimination, involves the spectator physically in a magic world in which he seems to be taking personal part. The lens of the camera and its complement, the screen, are endowed with the unique capacity of becoming the very eye of each spectator, or even, as I hope for its development, the inner eye.

When the film-maker has achieved the identification between the camera lens and the eye of the spectator, his basic task is fulfilled: he has established an intimate, direct contact with his audience. He has completed a circuit of communication between his and the specta-tor's mind and heart.[44]

When the analysis of subjectivity encounters the "strong myth" or the marked term of the "woman artist," certain aspects of identity present themselves as excessive or exaggerated in comparison with their occur-rence in the "weaker," more natural myth of the (male) artist. It could be surmised that Deren's own emphasis on subjectivity threatened the "reading" of her films in later historiographies as the product of a de-politicized version of a "woman artist."

In Western tradition, the name of the artist has been the primary marker of his subjectivity. Artists' names signify to an extent incom-mensurate with other beings because they are attached both to objects of value (works of art and films) that circulate geographically and his-torically and to biographies.[45] Pierre Bourdieu has understood the proper name of the artist as the "constant" in the social identity of the bio-graphical subject, particularly in all institutional and official contexts.[46] The historiography of Deren reveals the excessive situation in which the name of the "woman artist" is articulated. The first part of *The Legend* itself is called "Signatures," and its chapter headings adopt names used by Deren up until 1943, the date of her father's death and of her first film. Hodson writes, "It is the story of how Eleanora became Maya that we have documented in Volume One of *The Legend of Maya Deren*."⁴⁷ But as the congruence of a final name and the death of her father indicate, the names betray the contingency of subjectivity of Maya Deren herself and of the "woman artist," as much as they support the chronology of artistic development established by the editors. First, her original surname Derenkowsky was changed to Deren when she emigrated from the Ukraine with her parents in 1922, because her paternal uncle, Louis, had already changed his name in America before their arrival.⁴⁸ She successively took the name of her husbands and often published under those names: Bardacke, Hammid (who himself had been named Hackenschmied, sometimes spelled Hackensmid, until just around the time that Deren changed her first name), and Ito.

But it is Deren's first name that is the subject of discussion by many of those interviewed in *The Legend*, although her multiple names can be explained quite easily by her family background and situation. Like many whose mother tongue is Russian, in her family Eleanora Derenkowsky was called by one or more diminutive. Her mother wrote to her as Elinka. By the time Deren went to college she spoke at least three languages and was known by different names in each one, signing letters in those years with Elinka, Elinor, Eleanora, Elie, and Boots or Bootsie (the nickname she used during some of her adolescent years).

However, the story of her naming at birth as told by her mother to *The Legend* interviewers is most revealing. The naming of the artist is a common trope in artists' biographies, and in many cases it is narrativized in a prominent anecdote.⁴⁹ In such cases, the name of the artist is predictive of and signifies future characteristics of the work of the artist. The story of Deren's naming must have been repeated to Deren and others in earlier years, because it occurs in various recollections published in *The Legend*. Her mother named her Eleanora after Eleanora Duse, the famous dancer. Throughout childhood, as the mother recounts, Eleanora showed a talent for dance, and, of course, she collaborated with modern dancers in her films, most particularly in *A Study in Choreography for Camera* (1945).

But what is clear in the story is the fact that Deren's father, Solomon, had not had any role at all in the naming; indeed, he was conspicuously absent at the time Maya was born. Thus, when Deren took the name Maya immediately after his death in 1943 and when she had finished shooting *Meshes*, she consciously rejected her mother's name for her. With a re-naming, Deren bound herself to another idea of herself and to her father, inasmuch as she took the name her husband Hammid had chosen for her, Maya. At the same time she took the life insurance money left to her by her father and "bought the Bolex she used for all her films."[50] In this way Maya Deren "enacted" an important aspect of the biography of the artist in order to establish herself in another relationship to her world, a relationship that also included herself as filmmaker. We could say that Maya Deren replaced her natural, woman's name, Eleanora, with the "strong" or unnaturalized name of the "woman artist," Maya. In later years, a friend recalled that Deren chose the name because it meant "illusion." Charles Boultenhouse said: "It was very important to her to have changed her name, because the *true* Maya, then, which was always there, really came out. She didn't pay attention to anything very much that happened before that. So she is, literally, an artist, self-created."[51] We can read the name Maya Deren in terms similar to Man Ray, the name taken by the famous surrealist photographer (Emmanuel Rudnitsky or Radnitsky) in part to cover his origins and to mark his practice; "Ray" refers to the light rays that inscribe on film the image viewed. "Maya" covers and comes before the unmarked name, the surname of the father, Deren. At the same time it marks her métier, film, in its ability to make an illusion of reality.

The constancy or naturalization of the name of the artist is marked in its visual instantiation by the self-portrait, a common genre of the representational arts, including photography, since the Renaissance. The self-portrait is a genre that includes both the discrete portrait of the artist *and* the citation of the artist by the artist in paintings belonging to other genres, particularly narrative genres.[52] Cindy Sherman plays with the visual conventions of both the classical self-portrait genre format, the vertically orientated rectangle, and the citational portrait in her photographs. Self-portraits refer to conventions of portraiture such as resemblance and family history, as well as to names and naming, and provide complex commentaries on the topic of the representation of the individual herself.

When Deren began working seriously in the medium of photography, preliminary to her work as a filmmaker, she turned first and most frequently to the classical portrait genre with pictures of her family, her friends, and herself. She called these "experimental portraiture."[53] Her second husband, Hammid, who taught her photography and film, made classical portrait photos of Deren when they first lived together in Hollywood. His film *The Forgotten Village* (1941), made with Herb Kline and finished just before his marriage to Deren, makes use of extensive close-up shots, using the conventions of the classical portrait, of the inhabitants of a Mexican village.[54] Deren used these shots as inspirations in her own photography, as an examination of her photos reproduced in *The Legend* reveal. Classical portrait photos by Hammid of Deren are cited in her first film, *Meshes*. In her early films (before her work on what became *Divine Horsemen*), her portraits and his transpose to the characters of the films, mixing the categories of classical portrait and citational portrait. In many shots in *Meshes* and *At Land* (1944) the lines between portraiture and self-portraiture blur.

This blurring of the primary genres for the representation of the subject provokes commentary on the roles of the characters in the film's narrative and the roles played by Deren and others in life. For example, Deren cites her own group of friends in *Ritual in Transfigured Time* (1946). In *Meshes* and *At Land* Hammid is portrayed, but in later years, after their divorce, she inserts her third husband, Teiji Ito, into her and Hammid's earlier film by including him on the soundtrack of *Meshes*. He also appears in sound and person in *Meditation on Violence* (1948). Deren and her friends don various guises as themselves and characters in her films. Playing characters, they masquerade, foregrounding the issue of subjectivity as Doane has argued. The *doxa* of portraiture maintains that the portrait or representation is fundamentally an instantiation of the individual it portrays. Deren's films blatantly question that assumption; these films simultaneously reinscribe her subjectivity.

In this light, we should regard the extensive use of mirrors in Deren's early films as antimimetic, in contradistinction to the opinions of some influential critics. The mirror has been an essential tool in the technology of self-portraiture in the history of art since the Renaissance. Nevertheless, as an early painting in the genre by the Italian artist Parmagianino reveals, it should not be prized only for its reflective capabilities but also for its distortions. In many cases of the citational self-portrait the mirror is absent, muting the active voice of the subject in order to allow his insertion into the narrative space of the picture. A good example of this absence of the technology of self-representation is Vermeer's famous *A Painter at Work* (Vienna, Kunsthistorisches Museum), where the issue of masquerade is also prominent. Thus, when Deren insists on the mirror and her reflection in it, as she does in *Meshes* and *At Land* or the reflection of others in a mirror, as we find in *Ritual in Transfigured Time*, she activates the subject of the artist by inscribing her within the visual regime of the narrative.

The repetition to excess of self-portraiture in many forms in the work of Deren reveals the strong, unnaturalized myth of the "woman artist." She never gives herself a film credit as "actress." Such repetitions and excesses can be found in other women artists contemporary with Deren—Frieda Kahlo would be a good example. Today the location of the "woman artist's" portrait in her own work can excite what would be seen as excessive responses to subjectivity in the male artist, as Sherman's work and much of the criticism of it reveal. But in Deren's day these citations of the subject were not remarked on except insofar as they were covered over with the male pronoun "he," as when Deren spoke of the artist in *Anagram.* Later, with the beginnings of a history of the American avant-garde film, topics that concerned the "subjectivity" of Maya Deren's films were presented as ungendered, also covered over or avoided. When she emerged as a "woman artist" in *The Legend* her subjectivity became an issue of biography—of her life as she lived it. The films in which she appeared were so many more documents of that life. The status of Deren's work in the historiography reflects the ways in which film history and our culture have been able to speak the prefeminist woman filmmaker. As I have argued, this situation has produced a trap for those who seek a critical view of Deren's films. By relocating her films in their historical moment we may begin to overcome the weight of this historiography. Reading through the temporal and textual distance of that historiography to Deren herself can only disrupt our views of that problematic subject.[55]

Notes

Epigraphs: Jacqueline Rose, "Feminine Sexuality—Jacques Lacan and the école freudienne," in *Sexuality in the Field of Vision* (London: Verso, 1986), 54. See also Stephen Heath, "Difference," *Screen* 19 (Autumn 1978): 97: "The image is at once a position and the effective work of resistance is first and foremost, the emphasis of Ackerman and Mulvey, a matter of transformation of the relations of subjectivity in the production of the enunciation, the movement against the single unity of the subject, the confirmation of the difference." Jacques Derrida, *On the Name*, trans. by Thomas Dutoit (Stanford: Stanford University Press, 1995), xiv.

1. Millicent Hodson, "A Woman Seeing," in *The Legend of Maya Deren: A Documentary Biography and Collected Works*, ed. VèVè A. Clark, Millicent Hodson, and Catrina Neiman, vol. 1, pt. 1 (New York: Anthology Film Archives, 1984), xiv. The statement regarding a decade-long neglect of Deren is belied by Mekas's publication in 1965 in the house organ of Anthology Film Archive of materials that would become part of *The Legend*; see the entire issue of *Film Culture* 39 (Winter 1965). On the influence of Mekas in the project of defining an American avant-garde cinema, see the acknowledgments of P. Adams Sitney, *Visionary Film: The American Avant-Garde* (New York: Oxford University Press, 1974), xi. At the time of the publication of this extremely influential book, Mekas and P. Adams Sitney were the codirectors of the Anthology Film Archive. On the influence of this group on Deren's historiography, see below and Lauren Rabinovitz, *Point of Resistance: Women, Power and Politics in the New York Avant-Garde Cinema 1943–71* (Urbana and Chicago: University of Illinois Press, 1991), 16–19, 24–25.

2. Constance Penley and Janet Bergstrom, "The Avant-Garde Histories and Theories," *Camera Obscura* 19 (Autumn 1978): 120–23.

3. See Sitney, *Visionary Film*, 3, 7, and 10, in which the author delineates Hammid's extensive background prior to his association with Deren as a documentary

filmmaker and cameraman, providing further distance from Hollywood narrative cinema. Hammid does not direct any other films with Deren, although he is involved with them in various ways. His subsequent work in documentary takes a different path from hers.

4. For the clearest historical explanation of the mode of film criticism called *la politique des auteurs*, see the excellent articles by John Hess, "La Politique des auteurs: Part One World View as Aesthetic," *Jump Cut* (May–June 1974): 19–22; "La Politique des auteurs: Part Two Truffaut's Manifesto," *Jump Cut* (July–August 1974): 20–22. On the significance of the concept of *auteur* for the history of women filmmakers, see Penley and Bergstrom, "Avant-Garde Histories and Theories," 122–25; the excellent discussion by Kaja Silverman, *The Acoustic Mirror: The Female Voice in Psychoanalysis and Cinema* (Bloomington and Indianapolis: University of Indiana Press, 1988), particularly 187–234. Rabinovitz, *Point of Resistance*, 15–23; Judith Mayne, *The Woman at the Keyhole: Feminism and Women's Cinema* (Bloomington and Indianapolis: Indiana University Press, 1990), 89–154; Patrice Petro, "Feminism and Film History," *Camera Obscura* 22 (1990): 14–18. All these accounts must be considered partial, because the concept in terms of "the woman artist" or filmmaker has not yet been completely examined or historicized.

5. For a discussion of the individual artist in European art history, see Catherine M. Soussloff, *The Absolute Artist: The Historiography of A Concept* (Minneapolis: University of Minnesota Press, 1997); "Artist," in *The Encyclopedia of Aesthetics*, edited by Michael Kelly (Oxford: Oxford University Press, 1998), 1: 130–35; and "The Aura of Power and Mystery That Surround the Artist," in *Rückkehr des Autors. Zur Erneuerung eines umstrittenen Begriffs*, ed. Fotis Jannidis, Gerhard Lauer, Matias Martinez, and Simone Winko (Tübingen, Germany: Max Niemeyer Verlag, 1999), 481–93.

6. See the important discussion of this historiography by Michael Leja, *Reframing Abstract Expressionism: Subjectivity and Painting in the 1940s* (New Haven and London: Yale University Press, 1993), 18–48.

7. Caroline A. Jones, *Machine in the Studio: Constructing the Postwar American Artist* (Chicago: University of Chicago Press, 1996), 40–41.

8. This argument deserves more elaboration than I can provide here, particularly in the links between New York School painters and sculptors and New York avant-garde filmmakers in the 1950s.

9. Rabinovitz, *Points of Resistance*, 85.

10. Hodson, in *Legend*, vol.1, pt. 1, xi.

11. Toril Moi, *Simone de Beauvoir: The Making of an Intellectual Woman* (Cambridge, Mass., and Oxford: Blackwell, 1994), 5.

12. Hodson, in *Legend*, vol.1, pt. 1, xv.

13. For a good critical overview of this project in art history, see Thalia Gouma-Peterson and Patricia Mathews, "The Feminist Critique of Art History," *Art Bulletin* 69 (September 1987): 326–57.

14. Linda Nochlin, "Why Have There Been No Great Women Artists?" in *Art and Sexual Politics*, ed. Thomas B. Hess and Elizabeth C. Baker (New York and London: Collier Books, 1971).

15. Hodson, in *Legend*, vol.1, pt. 1, xv.

16. See, for example, the monograph on the seventeenth-century painter Artemesia Gentileschi, Mary Garrard, *Artemesia Gentileschi: The Image of the Female Hero in Italian Baroque Art* (Princeton: Princeton University Press, 1989).

17. Moi, *Simone de Beauvoir: The Making*, 4.

18. Toril Moi, *Feminist Theory and Simone de Beauvoir* (Cambridge, Mass., and Oxford, 1990), 27–34. Moi borrows the term "depoliticize" from Roland Barthes, who saw this to be an effect of any myth to "celebrate." Roland Barthes, "Myth Today," in *Mythologies*, trans. Annette Lavers (New York: Farrar, Straus & Giroux, 1972), 142–45, for example: "Now myth always comes under the heading of metalanguage: the depoliticization which it carries out often supervenes against a background which is already naturalized, depoliticized by a general metalanguage which is trained to *celebrate* things, and no longer to '*act* them.'" Bill Nichols and I have discussed the de- politicization of the "woman artist" in the case of Leni Riefenstahl, an interesting comparison to Deren; see Catherine M. Soussloff and Bill Nichols, "Leni Riefenstahl: The Power of the Image," *Discourse* 18 (Spring 1996): 20–44.

19. Barthes, *Myth Today*, 144. Barthes opposes "strong myths and weak myths." The male artist could be called the weak myth, because "the political quality of the object has *faded* like a colour, but the slightest thing can bring back its strength brutally." What brings back the strength of the artist is the "woman artist."

20. Sitney, *Visionary Film*, 11 (and for the following quotation).

21. Tom Gunning, "An Unseen Energy Swallows Space," in *Film Before Griffith*, ed. John L. Fell (Berkeley and London: University of California Press, 1983), 358.

22. Mayne, *Woman at the Keyhole*, 184–91.

23. Jones, *Machine in the Studio*, 40. Anne Wagner's recent book on women artists in the New York art world explores how gender roles in the art world and particularly in marriage affected the lives and careers of Eva Hesse, Lee Krasner, and Georgia O'Keefe; see Anne Middleton Wagner, *Three Artists (Three Women)* (Berkeley and London: University of California Press, 1996). In the cases of Simone de Beauvoir and Maya Deren, it must be assumed that the role of wife (or its prominent absence) as well as that of "woman artist" was an extremely significant factor in their self-perception and in the reception of their work.

24. The most cogent discussion of this strategy in art practice that begins with photography and is later taken up by performance art can be found in Abigail Solomon-Godeau, *Sexual Difference: Both Sides of the Camera*, exhib. cat. (New York: Miriam and Ira De. Wallach Art Gallery, Columbia University, 1988), 5.

25. Amelia Jones, "Tracing the Subject with Cindy Sherman," in *Cindy Sherman*

Retrospective (Chicago: The Museum of Contemporary Art; Los Angeles: The Museum of Contemporary Art, 1997), 33–53.

26. Laura Mulvey quoted in Amelia Jones, *Tracing the Subject*, 35.

27. Judith Mayne implicitly argues a similar position in her discussion of female authorship in film; see Mayne, *Woman at the Keyhole*, 94–98.

28. For example, Mayne, in *Woman at the Keyhole*, 186, holds that Deren should have been more present in the criticism because she was avant-garde, when I would argue that her position in film; historiography prevents her from being the subject of critiques of spectatorship. Rabinovitz also laments the lack of feminist critique to Deren's films; see Rabinovitz, *Points of Resistance*, 27: "The Project, however, has continued to reproduce auteurism's basic assumption that an artist's life (and particularly early life) is the best source of evidence for understanding the themes and meaning of her *oeuvre*. The result is that so far the redress of women filmmakers' neglect has been to counter silence with an overwhelming amount of information on one woman filmmaker."

29. Jones, *Tracing the Subject*, 35.

30. Mary Anne Doane, *Femmes Fatales: Feminism, Film Theory, Psychoanalysis* (New York and London: Routledge, 1991), 17–32, at p. 26. This essay is a revised version of an earlier essay by Doane, "Film and the Masquerade: Theorising the Female Spectator," *Screen* 23 (1982).

31. Ibid., 33–43. This essay is a revised version of one that first appeared in *Discourse* 11 (1988–89).

32. Jones, *Tracing the Subject*, 45.

33. Silverman, *Acoustic Mirror*, 209, further states compelling reasons for this lack of interpretation of experimental films by women: "To the degree that feminist theory and criticism of the late seventies and the eighties have concerned themselves centrally with authorship, they have shifted attention away from the classic text to experimental cinema, and specifically to experimental cinema made by women. The author often emerges within the context of these discussions as a largely untheorized category, placed definitively 'outside' the text, and assumed to be the punctual source of its sounds and images. A certain nostalgia for an unproblematic agency permeates much of this writing to which I refer." Doane, "Masquerade Reconsidered," 42–43, calls for a reconsideration of the problems concerned with feminist aesthetics and the concept of subjectivity in film. In this light, Patrice Petro's assessment in *Camera Obscura* 22 (1990): 8–26, is interesting if not totally persuasive. She believes that the project of feminism in film history has prevented it from being accepted as "historical," because it relegates feminist work to gender criticism and speculative theory. She follows Silverman by locating gender criticism in the concept of the *auteur*, particularly in regard to female Hollywood directors. She locates speculative theory in the discourse on female spectatorship, regarding it again as mainly directed at the depiction of women in Hollywood film. She does not deal with the important criticism of avant-

garde and experimental women directors, in spite of Silverman's earlier book. Rabinovitz, *Points of Resistance*, 68, argues that Deren herself foreclosed a feminist interpretation of her films: "Deren did not champion her own films as woman's discourse, she curbed the possibilities of interpretations linking her pleasures in the irrational to woman's language by surrounding the films with intellectual discourse emphasizing the rational order of the films." As the *Legend* illustrates, Deren surrounded her films with all kinds of discourse: psychologizing, rationalizing, historicizing. What really happened is that historiographers on the avant-garde chose to emphasize Deren's "rationality," with the result that Deren's work was criticized by Rabinovitz and others (and against the evidence of *Anagram*) as being masculinized discourse. I would argue that this discourse is not that of Deren but that of her interpreters.

34. Benveniste quoted in Silverman, *Acoustic Mirror*, 200.

35. Maya Deren, *An Anagram of Ideas on Art, Form and Film* (New York: Alicat Book Shop Press, 1946), 5.

36. Deren, preface to *Anagram*.

37. Silverman, *Acoustic Mirror*, 187–202.

38. On the significance of the Futurist Manifesto for the documentary avant-garde of Joris Ivens, see Bill Nichols, "Documentary and the Turn from Modernism," in *Joris Ivens and the Documentary Context*, ed. Kess Bakker (Amsterdam: Amsterdam University Press), 142–59.

39. Deren, preface to *Anagram*.

40. Deren, *Anagram*, 9.

41. Mikkel Borch-Jacobsen, *The Freudian Subject*, trans. by Catherine Porter (Stanford: Stanford University Press, 1988), 3.

42. Deren, "Cinema as an Independent Art Form," in *Legend*, vol.1, pt. 2, 345.

43. Deren, "Cinema as an Independent Art Form," in *Legend*, 348.

44. Alexander Hammid, "New Fields-New Techniques," *Screenwriter* 1 (1946): 22. This small treatise by Hammid on film theory deserves more attention than I can provide in the context of this essay. His work on the differences between documentary and fiction film and their relationship to Hollywood movies is an important document in postwar film history and links the theory of the American avant-garde directly with a European documentary tradition.

45. See Soussloff, *Absolute Artist*, for the extended historical argument referred to here.

46. Pierre Bourdieu, "L'illusion Biographique," *Actes de la Recherche en Sciences Sociales* 63 (June 1986): 70–71.

47. *Legend*, vol.1, pt. 1, x.

48. *Legend*, vol.1, pt. 1, 167, 498n13. There is some discrepancy in the accounts published here in the dates when the Derenkowskys changed their names. Eleanora would have been somewhere between five and seven when it happened.

49. The first and best exploration of this kind of anecdote can be found in Ernst Kris and Otto Kurz, *Legend, Myth, and Magic in the Image of the Artist: An Historical Experiment*, trans. E. H. Gombrich (New Haven and London: Yale University Press, 1979).

50. *Legend*, vol.1, pt. 2, 74 and 636n68.

51. *Legend*, vol.1, pt. 2, 74–75.

52. For a good survey of the artist portrayed in other genres of painting see Michael Levey, *The Painter Depicted: Painters as a Subject in Painting* (London: Thames and Hudson, 1981).

53. *Legend*, vol.1, pt. 2, 35.

54. Hammid's extensive use of close-ups and "portrait" photography in this film is justified by John Steinbeck in the preface to the book that publishes extensive stills from the film; see John Steinbeck, Rosa Harvan Kline, and Alexander Hackensmid [*sic*], *The Forgotten Village* (New York: Viking, 1941), 5: "A great many documentary films have used the generalized method, that is, the showing of a condition or an event as it affects a group of people. The audience can then have a personalized reaction from imagining one member of that group. I have felt that this is the more difficult observation from the audience's viewpoint. It means very little to know that a million Chinese are starving unless you know one Chinese who is starving. In *The Forgotten Village* we reversed the usual process. Our story centered on one family in one small village. We wished our audience to know this family very well, and incidentally to like it, as we did. Then, from association with this little personalized group, the larger conclusion concerning the racial group could be drawn with something like participation."

55. For the strengths and pitfalls of these strategies, see Judith Butler, "Collected and Fractured: Responses to *Identities*," in *Identities*, ed. Kwame Anthony Appiah and Henry Louis Gates (Chicago and London: University of Chicago Press, 1995), 439–47.

15

"THE MOURNER'S BENCH" from
"SOUTHERN LANDSCAPE"

16

Mark Franko

Aesthetic Agencies in Flux

Talley Beatty, Maya Deren, and the
Modern Dance Tradition in *Study in Choreography for Camera*

There has been no work to my knowledge that links Maya Deren to the American modern dance tradition. Perhaps this is because Deren's own presence in her films is so elusive in this respect: she appears as a dancer, but as a dancer not dancing. This manner of self-presentation matched Deren's often-cited filmic strategy of "creating dance out of non-dancing elements."[1] Nevertheless, we know of her professional ties to Katherine Dunham, from whose company Deren recruited performers for films, notably Rita Christiani and Talley Beatty.[2] In this essay, I begin to assess Deren's location in the dance modernism of the 1940s, not only as concerns her immediate artistic milieu or cinematic craft but also with regard to the representation of agency—that of women and men, black and white, but also of dance, choreography, and film.

I maintain a double focus: 1) on the relation of camera and editing to choreography (or their merger) and 2) on the relation of the black male dancer to the historical modern dance personae of the thirties and forties (or their friction). I shall develop this double focus particularly through Deren's short film *Study in Choreography for Camera* (1945; hereafter *Study*) in relation to two other dances: Martha Graham's 1930 *Lamentation* (in

Figure 15. *Study in Choreography for Camera* (1945). Talley Beatty in motion. Courtesy of Anthology Film Archives. Figure 16. Talley Beatty in publicity photograph for *The Mourner's Bench* in *Southern Landscape* (1947). Courtesy of San Francisco Performing Arts Library and Museum.

the 1941 film study by Dwight Godwin) and Talley Beatty's 1947 *Mourner's Bench*, a solo from his larger ballet *Southern Landscape*, a work he choreographed for his own company.[3] Graham's solo, *Lamentation*, in addition to providing a modern dance filmed for more than documentary purposes in the 1940s, also helped establish some influential criteria for dance modernism that Beatty later implicitly critiqued in his solo *Mourner's Bench*.[4] Working through this dance's critical intervention, it will be seen that canonical American modern dance of the thirties and forties promulgated modernist convictions about the relation of the dancing body to space and time—a relation whose dominant rhetoric also contained racial dimensions—and that the formalism of Deren's *Study* invokes the differences that existed in modern dance of the 1940s between the female white (and black) dancer and the black (and white) male dancer. In avant-garde cinematic practice Deren attempts in some sense to come to terms with these differences.

By complicating the narrative of modernism in modern dance, I wish to nuance Lauren Rabinowitz's statement that Deren, in *Study*, "literally freed the gesture and rhythms from their geographic backdrops and real-time constraints in an attempt to make dance the direct representation of universal expression."[5] The idea that modern dance purveyed "universal expression" was subscribed to by many choreographers. Deren rewrites this conceit for avant-garde cinema as the "utterly imaginative concept" resulting from the merger of dance and cinema.[6] Dance, when enhanced by film technology, allows for a ritual statement unmoored from the burden of traditional knowledge. In the 1940s, Deren opened an interface among modernist movement, film technology, and ethnography.[7]

But what could it mean politically for the film apparatus to further this modernist project by "literally" freeing the body from its static stage setting and real time? Is the freedom from "real time" also a liberation from historical time? An important aspect of the freedom Deren associated with the cinematic manipulation of time and space was the causation of a "semi-psychological reality" on the screen.[8] Never fully grounded in the psychological subject per se as a representation, the specter of the psychological could nonetheless emerge from "a filmically visual integrity, which could create a dramatic necessity of itself."[9] The ingredients of a formalist drama and a "semi-psychological reality" important to the functioning of Deren's "ritual," which is founded on narratives of transformation, were visually configured by Deren through the female physiognomy (frequently her own) in the film frame. How did her ritual project work when the object of "visual integrity" in the film frame was no longer the face and body of a woman but of a black male? And given the social engagement implied in Beatty's later choreography for *Southern Landscape*, was it really feasible for Beatty to be "freed" in this way?

I

In many ways, *Lamentation* sets forth the aesthetic program of North American dance modernism. Graham's much noted percussive movement style is in evidence, replete with her decomposition of expressive gestural elements and their repetitive reassembly into a depersonalized statement. Graham presents a "transcendentalizing version of subjectivity" in which the white female modern dancer is presented as a universal subject.[10] All Graham's moves are performed from a sitting position on a bench. There is a modernist reduction to essentials: nonlocomotive movement and the bench as property, a thirties trope for the reduced and essential object.[11] The theme of lament or mourning is enacted from a universalized perspective where mourning reduces to the geometrical figuration of its gestures, highlighted and ambiguated by the stretch fabric that abstracts the particularity of limbs and anatomy. Graham's lament is emotionally departicularized: we don't know who or what is being mourned. Her expression is impassive in that the face is not a privileged locus of expression. This bundle of strategies has been called "absolute dance" and constitutes an attempt to render dance autonomous from other performing arts by asserting its uniquely indigenous, in fact, essential properties.

The observations I can make from a filmic perspective either confirm the choreography's modernist commitments or (perhaps unwittingly) work against them. Graham's percussive discontinuity is accentuated by the seeming indifference of an immobile camera eye. Her movement leads her in and out of a static frame, and there is a focus on what might be thought of as random detail. This focus equalizes the relative value of her body with respect to surrounding space, a strategy tending to favor impersonality. The close-up of Graham's face as she mimes the drying of tears (however distanced and hieratic this gesture actually was in live performance) relocates the dance's interpretation in particularities of facial expression and therefore in psychologism, which I believe runs counter to the dance's intent.

Let us retain, however, this notion of absolute dance as a position of aesthetic modernism favoring impersonality, the abstraction of movement rather than its particularism, and a universalized subjectivity. One of the goals of absolute dance was self-reflexivity, a way in which the dance could take itself for subject matter regardless of its theme and the performer's body as its essential message or the basis for its thematic accumulations. A certain conceptual similarity issues from Deren's thought on ritualization in her films:

> The ritualized form treats the human being not as the source
> of the dramatic action, but as a somewhat depersonalized element
> in a dramatic whole. The intent of such depersonalization is not
> the destruction of the individual; on the contrary, it enlarges him
> beyond the personal dimension and frees him from the specializa-
> tions and confines of personality.[12]

Deren probably considered all the performers in her films, but certainly the principal ones, as depersonalized. She explains depersonalization, however, not in terms of autonomy or as an absolute but in terms of ritual. I will return to her use of this term.

These aesthetic strategies were, of course, for both Graham and Deren, collated with notions of the primitive. Graham's modernist discourse connected the primitive to race and nationality. In 1926, she said: "We must first determine what is for us the Primitive—that expression of its [America's] psyche only possible to a supremely cultured and integrated people."[13] Graham also used the term "integrated" to characterize American Indian culture, whereas she linked African American dancing to "a rhythm of disintegration":

> Our two forms of indigenous dance, the Negro and the Indian, are as dramatically contrasted rhythmically as the land in which they root. The Negro dance is a dance toward freedom, a dance to forgetfulness, often Dionysiac in its abandon and the raw splendor of its rhythm—it is a rhythm of disintegration. The Indian dance, however, is not for freedom, or forgetfulness, or escape, but for awareness of life, complete relationship with that world in which he finds himself; it is a dance for power, a rhythm of integration.[14]

Thus, although the white female dancer is a primitive figure of integration inasmuch as she models herself on the virile Indian to project her feminine subjectivity as a universal and, ultimately, national trait, the black dancer might be thought of within this rhetoric as the antimodernist in that his presence was difficult for white audiences to accept as a "universal," and the role of his maleness in the projection of national identity was also problematic. Thomas DeFrantz has identified the semiotic heritage of the black male body since slave culture as one of potent/impotent. It is, as DeFrantz explains, a body expected to evidence the potential of immense labor power but also social passivity and docility.[15] Some variant of this semiotic baggage is in conflict with the athletic white male body projecting national identity. Examples of this could be drawn from Leni Riefenstahl's male figures in her 1936 film *Olympia* and from Graham's staging of Erick Hawkins in her 1938 *American Document*.[16] In this sense, Deren's recourse to the "utterly imaginative concept" of combining cinema and dance places her work outside prevailing images of the "modern" male dancing body in the late thirties and early forties.

This brief and schematic analysis raises the specter of the black male modern dancer's ideological baggage in North American dance modernism. His presence on the modern dance concert scene was, it should be noted, contemporaneous with Graham's earliest innovations of the twenties and thirties. Talley Beatty's male predecessors were Asadata Dafora and Hemsley Winfield. Dafora introduced a West African aesthetic to the New York concert stage in 1934 with his ballet *Kykunkor*. Winfield took a modernist position in works such as *Life and Death* and *Negro* (1931). *Life and Death* apprehends its theme as a universal conflict between a black male chorus (Death) and a single black man (Life) who is ultimately overwhelmed by the group. Life, it would seem, is individualized, and death is the mass that engulfs him. This trope is in line with Graham's *Heretic* (1929) in which a single woman is engulfed and crushed by a female group. The white female soloist and the white female group were dominant in American modern dance, with the exception of Hemsley Winfield's black male group in *Life and Death* and Ted Shawn's all-(white)-male dance company. It is interesting to compare Graham and Winfield for this reason. Winfield's presentation of the solo male figure can be more problematic than Graham's with respect to the universalizing procedures of aesthetic modernism. In Winfield's *Negro*, for example, the black male dancer does not stand alone as a transcendental subject. On the contrary, his presence is riddled by ambivalence and irony. A brief choreographer's description, which is all that remains of this dance, describes the work in these terms:

> A Negro comes out very nonchalant. Music that accompanies
> his walk is a very slow blues. The music is low and played as a slow
> opera. Music changes and becomes barbaric and more negroid. The
> figure fights against this music, but finally succumbs. The figure
> moves, becomes heathenish and uncouth, and he becomes negro.[17]

Although this description is minimal, it suggests with some irony the conceived difficulty for the black male soloist to negotiate an image of transcendentalized subjectivity and self-reflexiveness in concert dance.

At the same time, it also suggests that black modernism engaged in what Henry Louis Gates Jr. has called "Signify'n," or a set of formal revisions like tropes, turning on "repetition of formal structures and their differences."[18]

II

Like Graham, Beatty choreographed himself in *Mourner's Bench* as a solitary body lamenting, and he thus reiterated Graham's choice of spare stage setting: bench and dancer. Yet he introduced differences as well. Rather than confining himself to the sitting position, Beatty stood on the bench, balanced across it, ran around it, and rolled away from it. I would like to say that Beatty transferred his emotion onto the bench rather than performing a transcendentalized subject objectifying loss. He did not seek to objectify mourning through his formal emplacement on the bench as much as he sought to depict the complications the bench represented for the mourning process. The subtext, as Beatty explained in his brief introduction to the reconstruction on video, is the prohibition of public mourning in the slave era, and therefore his choreographic drama of mourning was situated in a hidden, nocturnal place rather than in full view and public space.[19] The bench evoked a place the black body was assigned for the purpose of mourning as a socially erased act. In a "Tropicana" program within which *Southern Landscape* was included, the death is said to be caused by the Ku Klux Klan.[20]

Social impediments block Beatty's mourning on several levels. His dance thus engages not an absolute theme but a complicated social reality colliding with an emotional necessity. As a corollary to its social complexity, the male dancer in *Mourner's Bench* does not explore a psychological space within which time can be transfigured into eternity and the mourning body sublated into an absolute theme. Along with historical issues of race evoked by *Mourner's Bench*, the fact that the dancer is male furnishes a further impediment to interiorization. It thus becomes clear that Graham's famous "inner landscape" primarily enables a feminine introspection. There is no such equivalent "inwardness" for the male dancer, black or white. Yet—and this is where the dilemma of the black male modern dancer arises—there is also no acceptable position of pure exteriority for the white male modern dancer to inhabit.

Graham's presence is monumental, Beatty's is mobile; Graham's is ahistorical, Beatty's historical.[21] The socially clandestine status of mourning in Beatty's work is perhaps what accounts, somewhat paradoxically, for his greater choreographic mobility than Graham's in *Lamentation*, his attempts to explore all the physical possibilities provided by the bench, all of which are unsatisfactory, since they issue from a prohibition. Something like this prohibition applies to male dancers, black and white, as performers of modern dance.

Maya Deren's *Study in Choreography for Camera* provides a glimpse of 1940s modern dance, indeed a very historical glimpse of Talley Beatty in his dancing prime. This very short film also focuses so unrelentingly on dance that it introduces the notion of choreography as a cinematic operation. Although in her other films nondancing elements became dancelike (with the exception of the Christiani/Westbrook duet in *Ritual in Transfigured Time*), here, indubitably, is a dancer dancing. Beatty's choreography is not "for" the camera in the sense that it addresses the camera or adapts itself to the camera's potentials but rather "of" the camera, in that much of his dance is synthetically derived by editing and by a fluid construction of space that itself vies with the dancer for dancerly qualities. In *Study*, it is very unclear who or what is choreographing and who or what is dancing. This fuzziness is a direct result of Deren's thinking on the dialectic between photography and editing: "[F]ilm-making consists of two distinct but inter-related processes: *photography*—by which actuality is recorded and revealed (by the refined optics of the lens, the slow-motion analysis of movement, etc.) in its own terms; and *editing*, by which those elements of actuality proper may be re-related on an imaginative level to create a new reality."[22]

Figure 17. *Study in Choreography for Camera* (1945). Deren edited Talley Beatty's leaps to bridge spatial gaps. Space is thus a construct of movement for which the basic materials are the body and the camera. Spatial topography ultimately derives from the editing process. This location photograph was intended to be used in a poster for the film. Courtesy of Catrina Neiman.

III

This ambiguation of agency with respect to the black male dancer could be viewed as a useful alternative to absolute dance and the universal, if also psychological, female subject it purveys. That is, Beatty's presence prevents the experimental aspect of the film from espousing any universalizing pretensions whereas, by the same token, the lack of differentiation between his agency and the film's agency enables him to circulate freely within it, abnegating the necessity to adopt any position toward the "primitive" that dance—and particularly black male dance—had to cope with in the thirties and forties. As Deren herself wrote: "*A Study in Choreography for Camera* was an effort to remove the dancer from the static space of the theatre stage to one which was as mobile and volatile as he himself."[23] This statement acknowledges Beatty's role in the "utterly imaginative concept" of this film dance. His own volatility becomes the model for what the film attempts to manipulate and get beyond. In this sense, the habitual ritualized depersonalization is incomplete in *Study*, and the locus of movement's agency becomes its focal point.

Beatty's movements explore the spaces proposed by the film so that we experience those same spaces visually, perhaps more than we experience his dancing itself. Beatty is both present and absent, a product of the film's manipulation of time and space as well as the vehicle wherein the film itself attains movement. This is what Deren identifies as film dance: "a dance so related to camera and cutting that it cannot be 'performed' as a unit anywhere but in this particular film."[24] Given the formal preoccupations of film dance as Deren articulates them, *Study* does appear to be aligned with the modernist notion of an absolute. The film dance cannot be enacted; there is no first time because it is never performed, but rather it is constructed on the editing table. Yet, despite this way in which the film stands outside real time, it is also the result of a hybridization—that of dance with film, and of modern dance with a black male body. At this point, it might be useful to reflect again on agency, to ask, What operates on what?

Deren conceptualizes choreography as a dialectical operation: "Choreography," she writes, "consists not only of designing the dancers' individual movements but also of designing the patterns which he and his movements, as a unit, make in relation to a spatial area."[25] For Deren, the limitations of dance arise from the limitations of architecturally defined space germane to live performance. The mobility of the camera and the manipulations of editing disrupt such limitations and transfigure them. Through the agency of camera and editor, "a whole new set of relationships between dancer and space could be developed."[26]

Some of these premises are worked out in *Ritual in Transfigured Time*, a film in which black dancer Rita Christiani plays Deren's alter ego. Also notable in this 1945 film is the presence of a white male modern dancer, Frank Westbrook. At the beginning of the film, Christiani wanders through an alienating party scene inhabited by white men and women engaged in a stylized and superficial social choreography constructed with the help of slow motion, stop motion, and careful editing of crowd movements. The transition from this indoor scene to the outdoors reveals Christiani involved with the energetic and sinister Westbrook, who prolongs the imposing web of "social" movements that haunts Christiani and from which she must escape. Westbrook's appearance is marked as "male modern dancer" and is assertively aggressive. Christiani and Westbrook literally dance together, but she and Deren, who is also intercut here, escape his sphere of control by running into the sea and submerging themselves. In these final shots of the female body descending, the film switches to negative. Images of Deren and Christini merge through quick intercutting as black and white reverse their valence under water in a transfiguration of woman as self-sufficient (but also perhaps suicidal) psychic subject: black veils become white cocoon, black skin turns white, white skin turns black, water becomes air, the body sinks but also floats. *Ritual in Transfigured Time*, made in the same year as *Study*, is perhaps the Deren film in which dance, film, and ritual most explicitly merge. The white male dancer epitomizes taut, muscular, and airborne solidity, whereas Christiani and Deren are fluid subjects of the spiritual, the unconscious, and perhaps the tragic. Most important, Deren makes the *female* dancer the subject of transformation, or to use Deren's favorite term, transfiguration. The male is at best a catalyst, at worst, an obstacle.

As a dancing subject moving through interiors and exteriors in *Study,* Beatty enjoys the same fluid potential as Christiani and Deren. Yet the continuity he provides to every magical switch, the undialectical editing principle he seems to embody, qualifies his role as a protagonist of transfiguration. Beatty's dance in *Study* renders spatial disjunction possible in that he dances through the disruption of montage. His dance thus appropriates to itself the potentials of montaged space rather than experiencing those conjunctures in transformational stages of "semi-psychological reality." I think, in particular, of the moment when the switch from the forest to the apartment is literally bridged by his foot, which carries him from one frame to the other. The movement is thoroughly mundane, and extremely undialectical. The polar opposite example might be the final leap he makes from the Egyptian Hall of the Metropolitan Museum to the Palisades cliffs, a leap that is extended and constructed by editing and that ends in an impossible landing, which is the most kinesthetically magnetic moment of the film: his hovering over the water in the deep second position plié. Yet even here what is manipulated is the dance itself rather than a ritual process.

The film suggests an elasticity to space and the time spent moving through it, which is in actuality very condensed. In retrospect, the film seems much longer than its mere four minutes, which indicates to me a concern with time. Whereas in modern dance one might think of space as an analytic tool or aesthetic dimension for choreography, *Study*

Figure 18. *A Study in Choreography for Camera* (1945). Courtesy of Anthology Film Archive.

Figure 19. *A Study in Choreography for Camera* (1945). Talley Beatty's final landing at the end of the film. Beatty's "leap" takes him from the Egyptian Hall of the Metropolitan Museum of Art to the Palisades cliffs. The impossibility of the leap, achieved through editing, adds to its dramatic impact. Courtesy of the Museum of Modern Art/Film Stills Archive.

18

19

reconceptualizes the trope of choreography as a *temporal* analysis accomplished by spatial means. Space is thus felt to be a construct of movement for which the materials are the body and camera but whose ultimate effect derives from the editing process.

The dancer's movements, his choreographic patterns, and the spatial area in which they occur are all the products of cinema. But the real product of this construction is time, and particularly time remembered: "TIME TIME TIME—not SPACE."[27] Thus if choreography is no longer identifiable as an authorial phenomenon appropriating a particular use of space, neither is space "naturalized" as an unlimited and "wild" choreography. Rather, space becomes a social/visual construct. "A person," wrote Deren, "is first one place and then another without traveling between."[28]

Along with the fairly formal aspect of *Study* goes an easy association of exterior and interior with nature and culture. Deren's "culture" interiors are a very specific, bohemian bedroom of the Morton Street apartment and the Egyptian Hall of the Metropolitan Museum. Beatty ventures through these interiors (rising from a bench to spin and spiral through the apartment, leaping and running in the museum hall), but he takes a rooted stance in nature (the final locus of the Palisades cliffs). In the opening forest panning shot, Beatty's movement is also grounded. The black male body inhabits nature and culture only by virtue of a cinematic illusion, giving the impression of lingering in these places or being on the periphery of place(s). Unlike the bench in Graham's and Beatty's solo dances, Beatty cannot be reduced to an object or magnified to that of a (depersonalized) "individual." Perhaps this is why he dances. His dancing induces us to reconstruct the film's condensed sequences as a meditation on time, and thus in that very apprehension of them, to mourn them as past. History returns to the "utterly imaginative concept" of conjoining dance and cinema in a way that cannot be explained away by a voyage into the unconscious of a dramatic subject. The female body is the locus of this exploration that transfigures representation from a "natural" (spatial) to a "psychic" (temporal) phenomenon. Woman in modern dance is the humanist and autonomous subject, not man. In modern dance and in *Study*, man spatializes time, rendering it historical, whereas woman temporalizes space, rendering it universal.[29]

In her films, Deren manipulates two discourses of dance modernism whose recognizable icons are the white or black female and the white male. The white male dancer drives the female body through space, inducing the ritual of her transformation. In *Ritual*, Christiani becomes a psychological subject, although her blackness is also a constant reminder of Deren's transfiguration in that everything in the film pointed toward an aestheticization of transfiguration of the autonomous subject: from black to white in the performers' skin colors, switches from positive to negative film images, and the theme of widow to bride, which also contained a temporal reversal. These transfigurations relate intimately both to the issue of depersonalization and to the transformations proper to ritual, of which the female subject is normally the dramatic site.

> [T]he pattern, created by the film instrument, transcends the
> intentions and the movements of individual performers, and for
> this reason I have called it *Ritual*. I base myself upon the fact that,
> anthropologically speaking, a ritual is a form which depersonalizes
> by use of masks, voluminous garments, group movements, etc.[30]

Deren goes on to explain that ritual serves to accomplish a "critical metamorphosis." Thus, as Deren links the techniques adapted by film from choreography both to the aesthetic concerns of depersonalization *and* to the ritual imperative, she points toward the female dancing body as the entity meant to occupy the frame of these operations. But Talley Beatty's gender defuses his ritual potential. *Study* only depersonalizes Beatty in the technical sense: his body participates in a filmic reality, one in which his relation to space is largely complementary and his role in the construction of time largely invisible. Yet, as a black male dancer, he cannot become a "ritualized" subject founding a "semi-psychological reality" as can Deren or Christiani. Nor does he represent the social motor of pure externality and history, as does Frank Westbrook. The issue of Talley Beatty's agency in *Study* thus remains unresolved.

Deren herself suggests a way out of this impasse in a 1945 letter she wrote to Beatty about his financial remuneration for his role in the film. Deren said: "I thought it important that this was one of the rare cases when a Negro was presented, not as and because he was a Negro, but purely and simply because he was an artist."[31] In this supplementary depersonalization outside the film Deren abstracts Beatty from typecasting but also seems to acknowledge the failure of *Study* to attain a ritual dimension. She also implies a ritual status change from "Negro" to "artist." It is as though Beatty's transfiguration occurs outside the film's manipulations of time and space.

Having entered the Morton Street apartment, Beatty rises from a bench. It was shortly after the filming of *Study*, in 1947, that Beatty formed his own company and choreographed *Mourner's Bench*, a work in which the uncertainties of agency are also unresolved but have the advantage of a historical rather than ritual grounding in the imagination.

Notes

1. Maya Deren, "Ritual in Transfigured Time," in *Film Culture* 39 (winter 1965): 5.

2. Katherine Dunham, America's first "dancing scholar," was a dancer and anthropologist who studied under Melville Herskovitz at the University of Chicago and did fieldwork in Haiti from 1935 to 1936. By the 1940s she had established herself as a modern dance choreographer of international repute specializing in Caribbean source material for the creation of dance dramas such as *Rites de Passage*. She gained wide popular exposure through her work on the films *Cabin in the Sky* and *Stormy Weather*. Maya Deren became Dunham's secretary and editorial assistant, traveling with the road company of *Cabin*. Dunham's research on Haiti in the thirties thus prefigured, and surely influenced, Deren's subsequent Haitian project.

3. Talley Beatty came from Chicago to New York with Katherine Dunham's company to appear in the YMHA's "Negro Dance Evening" in 1937. He received his classical training in Chicago working with Ruth Page. He also appeared in *Black Face*, which was choreographed by Lew Christiansen for Lincoln Kirstein's Ballet Society. He began his own choreographic career in 1947. *Southern Landscape* was his first piece,

inspired by Howard Fast's *Freedom Road.* In 1949 he founded his own company, Trop-icana, which toured internationally and used his choreography until 1955. Beatty died in 1995 at age 76.

4. For a fuller discussion of Graham's modernism, see Mark Franko, *Dancing Modernism/Performing Politics* (Bloomington: Indiana University Press, 1995).

5. Lauren Rabinowitz, *Points of Resistance. Women, Power and Politics in the New York Avant-garde Cinema, 1943–71* (Urbana and Chicago: University of Illinois Press, 1991), p. 70. A similar point was made by Richard Lippold in a 1946 review. What dance and film do, according to Lippold, is free each other from undue preoccupa-tion "with the problems of their own craft." What cinema lacks is "the real physical agony," whereas what dance lacks is a spatiotemporal mobility that would free it from "the physical entity as the reification of human experience in visible form." Richard Lippold, "Dance and Film: A Review in the Form of a Reflection," in *Dance Observer* (May 1946): 58–60.

6. Maya Deren, *An Anagram of Ideas on Art, Form and Film* (New York: The Al-icat Book Shop Press, 1946), p. 15. The "utterly imaginative concept" is what distin-guishes the "modern primitive," in Deren's terms, from the primitive saddled with traditions.

7. See Jeannette DeBouzek, "Maya Deren: A Portrait of the Artist as Ethnogra-pher," in *Women and Performance: A Journal of Feminist Theory* 5, no. 2, #10 (1992): 7–28.

8. Preface, in *Anagram.*

9. Ibid.

10. This phrase is borrowed from Andrew Ross, *The Failure of Modernism: Symp-toms of American Poetry* (New York: Columbia University Press, 1986).

11. See William Carlos Williams, "Five Dollar Guy—A Story," in *New Masses* (May 1926). The narrator begins with the project "to put down, to find and to put down some small, primary thing" and discovers in the process a bench, "a long slat-back yellow bench" (p. 19). A similar kind of bench appears in Vertov's *Three Songs for Lenin* (1934). Filmed lovingly throughout the opening sequence, this bench was immortalized by a photo of Lenin sitting on it in the park outside the room where he died. Thus, in Vertov the bench also becomes an object of the utmost simplicity, an object at which to mourn, and an object of reduction to essentials—here, the absent body of Lenin.

12. Ibid., p. 20.

13. Martha Graham, "Seeking an American Art of Dance," in *Revolt in the Arts: A Survey of the Creation, Distribution, and Appreciation of Art in America,* ed. Oliver M. Saylor (New York: Brentano, 1930), p. 253.

14. Merle Armitage, ed., *Martha Graham* (New York: Dance Horizons, 1966), p. 99. This statement by Graham was made in 1932, and the Armitage anthology in which it was republished appeared in 1937. Amy Koritz relates this racial performance topol-ogy to ideas on rhythm culled by Graham from Mary Austin's *The American Rhythm*

(New York: Harcourt, Brace & Co., 1923) in "Re/Moving Boundaries: From Dance History to Cultural Studies," in *Moving Words: Re-writing Dance*, ed. Gay Morris (London: Routledge, 1996), pp. 88–106. For further discussion of Austin's influence on Graham, see my "Nation, Class, and Ethnicities in Modern Dance of the 1930s," in *Theatre Journal* 49 (1997): 475–91. Although Graham characterizes racial movement qualities in this passage, her model for nationality is assimilationist. In the same 1932 remarks, she adds: "The dancers of America may be Jewish and Spanish and Russian and Oriental, as well as Indian and Negro. Their dancing will contain a heritage from all other nations, but it will be transfigured by the rhythm, and dominated by the psyche of this new land. Instead of one school of technique ever becoming known as the American dance, a certain quality of movement [which is what Graham means by 'rhythm'] will be recognized as American" (ibid., p. 100).

15. Thomas de Frantz, "Simmering Passivity: The Black Male Body in Concert Dance," *Moving Words: Re-writing Dance*, ed. Gay Morris (London: Routledge, 1996), pp. 107–20.

16. The role of the male body in the artistic projection of national identities as fashioned by female directors/choreographers in the 1940s is a subject that demands further analysis in another context.

17. Hemsley Winfield, "Negro," in Joe Nash Collection, Schomburg Center for Research in Black Culture, New York Public Library, Manuscripts, Archives and Rare Books Division.

18. Henry Louis Gates, Jr., *The Signifying Monkey. A Theory of African-American Literary Criticism* (New York: Oxford University Press, 1988), p. 52.

19. Beatty's remarks to this effect are recorded on the video of the New Dance Group Gala Retrospective produced by the American Dance Guild, New York (1993).

20. Part 1 of *Southern Landscape* is "The Defeat in the Fields." "While working in their fields, the people are terrorized by the newly formed Ku Klux Klan. The men go off to fight and are defeated." This section is followed by the "Mourner's Bench." The ballet contains three more sections: "My Hair was Wet with the Midnight Dew" ("under emotional stress the survivors wandered at night through their ravaged fields"), "Ring Shout" ("the defeated seek release through the ring-shout, a survival of an African dance), and finally "Settin' Up" ("The dead are mourned."). Talley Beatty program file, San Francisco Performing Arts Library and Museum.

21. For further analysis of these differences, see my *Dance as Labor: Performing Work* (Stanford: Stanford University Press, forthcoming).

22. "Film in Progress. Thematic Statement," in *Film Culture* 39 (Winter 1965): 11.

23. *The Legend of Maya Deren*, vol. 1, pt. 2, 458.

24. "Film in Progress. Thematic Statement," in *Film Culture* 39 (Winter 1965): 4.

25. Ibid., p. 3.

26. Ibid.

27. Maya Deren and Gregory Bateson, "An Exchange of Letters," in *October* 14 (Fall 1980): 23.

28. "Film in Progress. Thematic Statement," in *Film Culture* 39 (Winter 1965): 3.

29. For a similar phenomenon in a contemporaneous dance of Graham, *Dark Meadow*, see my "History/Theory—Criticism/Practice," in *Corporealities: Dancing Knowledge, Culture and Power*, ed. Susan Foster (London: Routledge, 1995), pp. 25–52.

30. Maya Deren, "Ritual in Transfigured Time," p. 6.

31. VèVè A. Clark, Millicent Hodson, and Catrina Neiman, *The Legend of Maya Deren*, vol. 1, pt. 2 (New York City: Anthology Film Archives, 1988), p. 281.

Ute Holl

Moving the Dancers' Souls

Verses Reversed

Among the bohemian artists in New York's Greenwich Village in the 1940s who challenged traditional lifestyles and mores, two women stand out: Anaïs Nin and Maya Deren. Both turned their lives into artistic experiments. They were neighbors, friends, and collaborators; later they were each other's critics, and, finally, they were enemies. Their relationship has been described as a matter of personal rivalry. A closer investigation shows that their argument originated in opposing theories about art, psychology, and the identity of the artist in a rapidly changing world. In light of their biographical and scientific background, Deren and Nin's dispute turns out to concern an issue that would dominate postwar discourse on aesthetics: the impact of technology on perception and, consequently, on art.

While Nin's thoughts have been widely read and received in a feminist literary community, Deren's theory on media and subjectivity still awaits discovery. In the 1940s their respective theories were clearly avant-garde, but both women were famous mainly for their artwork. As true Greenwich Village artists, they staged their theory in everyday poetry and artist's diaries. Maya Deren started the discussion that turned into a feud on August 19, 1945, in a poem for Nin:

For Anaïs Before the Glass

The mirror, like a cannibal, consumed,
carnivorous, blood-silvered, all the life fed it.
You too have known this merciless transfusion
along the arm by which we each have held it.
In the illusion was pursued the vision
through the reflection to the revelation.
The miracle has come to pass.
Your pale face, Anaïs, before the glass
at last is not returned to you reversed.

This is no longer mirrors, but an open wound
through which we face each other framed in blood.[1]

Maya Deren, who in her films portrays herself as an absentminded dancer and dreamer, was in fact a master of technical film tricks. In her poetry she proves to be a master of literal tricks too. In her poem to Anaïs Nin she challenges techniques of self-reflection, self-perception, and identity by alluding to the myth of Narcissus and his lethal misrecognition of himself. Anaïs Nin had called her diaries mirrors. She had expected the process of writing down her experiences to turn into a revelation of herself. It is the miracle of this transformation that Deren refers to in her poem: "This miracle has come to pass."

Deren's verses are ambiguous. "Your pale face, Anaïs, before the glass at last is not returned to you reversed" can be read as a warning or a promise. As a warning it refers to the illusory belief that a simple process of writing can be a revelation of identity. The mirror will finally consume the life or presence of the writer instead of returning it. This seems to be an old romantic metaphor, but Deren investigates the real, not the metaphorical, functions of artistic technique. In "Cinema as an Art Form" she writes:

> When we agree that a work of art is, first of all, creative, we actually mean that it creates a reality and itself constitutes an experience.

The antithesis of such a creative work is the merely communicative expression whose purpose it is to register, through description, an existent reality or an experience.[2]

Mirrors, in this sense, are devices that can only register. Therefore, writing according to a mirror technique can never be creative. Along with this allusion to the vanity of Nin's work, Deren's offers another solution. The verses, if read with the emphasis on "not reversed," turn out to be a promise. The mirror can only reflect the reversed picture of the self, but there is, at last, a method to reflect it unreversed: the film image. Read thus, the battlefield that Maya Deren opens up between Nin and herself is between two media, literature and film. For Maya Deren, these media have completely different creativity values: "But whereas the typewriter can hardly be considered capable of creative action, the camera is, potentially, a highly creative instrument."[3]

Anaïs Nin defended narcissism as an artistic method. Maya Deren experimented with the formal techniques behind any form of self-recognition. For her the pleasures of narcissism merely result from ignorance about the technical conditions of self-recognition. For Narcissus, the trapper of Greek mythology, everything he saw in nature was prey to his deceptive tricks, but he did not realize that his own image resulted from that same trick and trap. He deceived himself about himself; he proved susceptible to his own techniques. He fell into his own trap and in love with his visually reversed self as other. In her poem, Maya Deren set an imaginary trap for Anaïs Nin, and the great author of seduction was herself seduced into playing a part in Maya Deren's *Ritual in Transfigured Time*.

Maya Deren felt very content about the finished film. Other collaborators, who contributed time, money, and themselves, like Anaïs Nin, did not. The quarrel of the two artists that followed the first viewing of the picture is well known. Nin noted in her diary: "I remembered this returning from Maya's, when we saw the finished film. (. . .) A close-up

of me, twice natural size, was shiny skinned and distorted by mag-
nification. Everyone found his flaw there. Maya said: 'It is always so.
Everyone is shocked when he first sees himself in film or hears his voice
for the first time. That is why I made you sign a release. You will get
over it.' "4

Maya Deren's poem appears to be an anticipation of this incident:
"This is no longer mirrors, but an open wound through which we face
each other framed in blood." Actually, Deren had reflected on an everyday experience: the gaze at one's own mirror image is filled with wishful
projections, while seeing oneself in a film is an experience stripped of all
imaginary powers, stripped of all narcissistic magic. The picture of the
"self" on film remains a plain representation of the physically real body
until a director uses all his craft and tricks to transform it into art. In this
case the "self" becomes "another." This process is, like any ritual, a violent transformation.

This narcissistic disillusionment through film, as Nin described it in
her diary, is a matter of *self*-perception, to be sure—others thought that
Anaïs looked very good on screen.5 Likewise, Deren's poem deals with
techniques of self-perception in art. Its conclusions are as ambiguous
as the verses themselves: while the mirror reflects a pleasing image, it
consumes the life of the artist who relies on its revelatory power. The
film image, on the contrary, does not please the "I," but it shows reality unreversed and can thus be used to create new and strange experiences of the self. Deren had implicitly raised the question of psychology in film and media. For her, representation and identity in art are a
matter of technical transformation. Anaïs Nin had well understood this,
and consequently her critique of the making of *Ritual* was aimed at the
camerawork:

> Maya, the gypsy, the Ukrainian gypsy, with the wild frizzy hair like
> a halo around her face. Sasha Hammid placed her face behind glass
> and in that softened image she appeared like a Botticelli. The cam-
> era can be a lover, or a hater, or a sadist, or a defamer, as the press
> cameramen well know. It lies. (. . .) Maya's actors happened to be

Figure 20. *Ritual in Transfigured Time* (1946). Anaïs Nin as an unnamed character in the film who observes the initial interaction between Christiani and Deren. Courtesy of Catrina Neiman.

beautiful. She uglified them. I had never seen as clearly as in Maya, the power to uglify in the eye behind the camera.[6]

Nin is referring to Hammid's famous "Botticelli shot" of Maya Deren in *Meshes of the Afternoon*. This film was Hammid's and Deren's honeymoon experiment, shot when they were just married. But even if Hammid definitely beautified her in the softening effects and double reflections of the windowpane, the filmic interest and the filmic techniques in *Meshes* go beyond the intention to create beauty. In the course of the film, the identity of a young woman is radically dissected, and in the end she is shown bleeding amid fragments of a shattered mirror. What is left is the open wound of identity: the impossibility of self-assurance.

In her poem, Deren had addressed Anaïs "Before the Glass." This could be read in a spatial sense: the real Anaïs in front of a mirror, not the beautified artwork behind a glass, windowpane, or lens. Or, since the

Figure 21. *Ritual in Transfigured Time* (1946). Maya Deren with her back to the camera, Rita Christiani facing Deren, and Anaïs Nin in the background. The film does not provide cast credits. Deren's concerns lie less with self-expressive acting and individual credit than with the impact of character, characters, movement, and editing as a totality. Courtesy of Catrina Neiman.

poem was written along with the script for *Ritual in Transfigured Time*, the address could be read in a temporal sense: Anaïs before the glass would not be the same after her transformation by the camera. From Maya Deren's writings on film, Anaïs Nin could have known that for Deren films were never a depiction of reality, neither beautified nor uglified, but the creation of a new experience.

Anaïs Nin's strong reactions during the viewing of the film and her continuing angry remarks about its shooting could suggest that the pictures had triggered in Anaïs Nin a memory of another story of which Deren was not aware. In seeing the camera as "a lover, a hater, a sadist or a defamer," Nin recalls the primal scene of abuse by her father, as she has reconstructed it again and again in her diaries and texts. This primal scene is recorded as a photograph that her father took of the naked little Anaïs.[7] The photograph was all the evidence she had. The unrecallable and inexpressible facts attached to this picture she then rewrote into her many stories of seduction. Gradually her literary work developed into a subtext of the origins of classical psychoanalysis in Freud's (later withdrawn) theory of seduced children. In her criticism of camera technique she names the classic masquerades of psychoanalytic transference through which she will seduce a series of psychoanalysts, of whom Otto Rank was the best known.

Pictures of her "self" were the lever with which Anaïs Nin would throw the father-imagos out of their authoritarian seats in psychoanalysis. In her literature she emancipated the speech of the "talking cure"—as one of Freud's patients had called his therapy—from the father's verdicts.

Tracing Trance

In Maya Deren's biography, in contrast, the camera was an extremely positive and productive link to her father's science. Salomon Deren had been a psychiatrist for children in Syracuse, New York, after the family fled the civil war in the Soviet Union in 1922. In his early career in St. Petersburg he was part of the Russian experimental school for a new objective psychology.

In the years before the Russian revolution Salomon Derenkowsky had been educated at the Psychoneurological Institute of Vladimir Bekhterev. In 1916, Dziga Vertov had studied and conducted a series of self-experiments at that same institute. Bekhterev revolutionized traditional introspective psychology in Russia and used different devices to prove the objectivity of mental activity. One of them was the camera. Bekhterev had studied with the founders of modern neurophysiology and psychology: Charcot in Paris, Wundt and Flechsig in Leipzig. He had brought the new and then experimental science of artificial nervous excitations back to Russia, where shamanistic methods were still part of everyday healing. Bekhterev's work on trance, hypnosis, possession, and the induction of certain nervous states as scientific psychology was a novelty to Russia. Shamanism had been considered magic and charlatanism, and now Bekhterev reimported the art as avant-garde science. His scientific investigation of the nervous processes in trance and their application in medical therapy was always regarded suspiciously by the changing regimes. Derenkovsky worked in a department that treated alcoholics with hypnosis and group therapy, a method that from today's neurological point of view turns out to have been a progressive experiment in health care.[8]

Maya Deren followed the traces of her father's scientific work, although she approached it from an altogether different angle. Deren's studies of possession evolved through her passionate interest in dance. Around 1940, while working with the dancer and anthropologist Katherine Dunham, Maya Deren studied Caribbean culture and religion. In an article on trance dancing published in 1942, she credits her father for "criticisms, suggestions and helpful reading." Comparing the phenomena of hysteria and possession in religious dancing, Deren immediately confronts the origins of her own Western culture, with its fusion of belief, knowledge, and power in medical science, with the totally different approach in Haitian communities. In examining possession, suggestibility, and affectivity of the nerves, she returns to the roots of European medical discourse and thus to the favorite fields of Charcot—and consequently of Bekhterev and Freud.

Deren's first observation is that in studying hysteria she is dealing with social phenomena or, rather, social techniques, not individual pathology: "One of the similarities is that hysteria, as possession, also occurs only within a social context, when there are one or more witnesses to the scene."[9]

Second, she observes that in European medicine the nervous id is transformed into a diseased ego by an epistemological operation: through individualization, a fact that is only perceived if viewed from a vantage point outside a given culture. The possessed person in Western cultures is considered sick, because the disease is not traced back to the social context that caused it. The same phenomena, which are reasons to hospitalize individuals, especially women in modern Europe, enjoy great prestige in shamanistic cultures or cultures with an emphasis on collectivity. "If one compares hysteria with possession in terms of the individual, the similarities become so striking as to tempt one to combine the two phenomena into a single category. Exciting causes for both include psychic conflicts and insults and resultant nervous instability. Both are marked by the retraction of cerebral control and the emancipation of a complete sub-conscious system of ideas."[10]

In Western medicine, possession was studied by determining the meaning of the various symptoms, as Charcot and Freud had done. This individualization of social phenomena marked the foundation of psychoanalysis in Freud's and Breuer's first studies on hysteria. Deren, however, traces possession back to its social roots in different societies and their collective rituals. In her article of 1942, she is interested in the physiological processes and the technical influences that induce states of possession or trance. Comparing the phenomena of hysteria, hypnotism, and possession, Deren examines the trance techniques and the effects they have on perception and consciousness:

[J]ust as various mechanical devices such as crystals and light are employed in hypnotism, so, I believe, drum rhythms are extremely important in inducing possession.

As we know, rhythm consists in the regularity of the interval between sounds. Once this interval has been established, our sense-perceptions are geared to an expectation of its recurrence. (. . .) Even more important, sustained rhythmic regularity and the fact that the source of it is outside the individual rather than within, means that consciousness is unnecessary, as it were, in the maintenance of this concentration.[11]

This approach corresponds to the method taught in St. Peterburg's Psychoneurological Institute: instead of analyzing personal symptoms as psychoanalysis would, Bekhterev and his students investigated all kinds of mental activity by experimenting with neurological factors that induced certain states of mind.

It is interesting to note that in this early essay on dancing, Deren has formulated a basic hypothesis on social techniques and mental activity that she maintains in her film theory. She will remain concerned with the physiological functioning of perception rather than with subconscious meaning. She will theorize film form in terms of form and perceptual effects rather than of psychoanalytic symptoms. The rhythm of twenty-four frames per second, the rhythm of light and darkness in the pictures, the rhythm of varying and repeating speeds in her films affect perception much more than the symbolic value of the pictures. The "intervals" of light, speed, and spaces create a sense of perception that is "geared to an expectation," as she described sense perception in a ritual trance.

It should be mentioned—although it cannot be elaborated in this context—that Vertov's theory of the interval derives from the same psychoneurological school: in his manifestos, the subject of perception is technology, the camera-"I" of the Kinoki. The truth of film perception, as Godard would later keep repeating, is not a general truth, but the truth of film technique that uses twenty-four frames per second to produce an illusion of movement in human minds. It is the mind that is moved.

Far away from St. Petersburg or Paris, Maya Deren would modify her father's studies in her own experimental way. She remained concerned with the cinematic factors in mental activity, and she would compose her films from ideas of technology, technique, and form.

In her first film, *Meshes of the Afternoon*, every subjective sensation of the protagonist corresponds to an objective film trick. The trick can be as simple as dimming the lens to simulate the protagonist's state of mind when falling asleep or swaying the camera in the staircase to induce dizziness. Other tricks are more intricate, as when two accelerated pans are joined by montage, and thus two different speeds of movement or two different rooms are linked to form new time and space experiences. The

most obvious trick in *Meshes of the Afternoon* is, of course, the multiplication of the protagonist by masking the lens and triple-exposing the film.
This was the classical film trick that inspired Otto Rank's essay on *The
Student of Prague* and the doppelgänger. In *Meshes of the Afternoon*, the
"uncanny," as Rank called it in Freud's terminology, is cinematically produced. Already in her first experimental film, Deren ensured that it could
no longer be decided whether the uncanny is an effect *of* the individual
or an effect *on* the individual. Cinema is a collective ritual. It is a matter
of technical transformation, not of individual neurosis.

Meshes of the Afternoon is, according to Deren's intention, "concerned
with the inner realities of an individual and the way in which the sub-
conscious will develop, interpret and elaborate an apparently simple and
casual occurrence into a critical emotional experience."[12] In Deren's description of the film, the various techniques of the subconscious are already transformed into cinematic techniques: "Using cinematic techniques
to achieve dislocations of inanimate objects, unexpected simultaneities,
etcetera, this film establishes a reality which although based somewhat
on dramatic logic, can exist only on film."[13]

Deren planned her film work in ritualistic terms: a method of stimulating emotion and perception through a collective technique or, in other
words, a method of inducing a special psychic activity in the minds of a
group of people. This seems an unfamiliar approach, but one of the first
film theorists followed exactly the same logic: Hugo Münsterberg, who
was in fact a famous colleague of Bekhterev—and Salomon Derenkowsky,
for that matter. Trained as an experimental psychologist, in 1916 Münsterberg had applied his science of perceptual techniques to the new
medium of film to show that cinema worked exactly like his experimental devices in the psychology laboratories at Harvard: the cinematic apparatus can induce mental processes. Thus, a close-up in cinema is the
objective equivalent of a subjective feeling of attention; a flashback is, sub-
jectively, involuntary memory; and superimposition is association. Emotions can be transferred to the minds of the public by shooting and edit-

ing the frames in a way that produces new experiences of time and space. Film—or the photoplay as Münsterberg called it—is a translation of visual stimuli into the neural logic of the mind. "The photoplay tells us the human story by overcoming the forms of the outer world, namely, space, time, and causality, and by adjusting the events to the forms of the inner world, namely, attention, memory, imagination, and emotion."[14]

Nearly thirty years after Münsterberg declared the unconscious in psychology and cinema to be no more than an ensemble of mental operations, Maya Deren pursued this path in her filmic experiments. "My first concern was to emancipate the camera from theatrical traditions in general and especially in terms of spatial treatment," Deren wrote in 1945.[15] She used devices of the camera and editing techniques for a "controlled manipulation" of time and space so that "the intentions and the movements of the individual performers"[16] would be transcended and transfigured.

Deren's criticism of psychoanalysis, or rather of its popularized form in most surrealist art production, is well known. Around the time when she wrote the poem for Anaïs Nin, she noted in the early outlines for *Ritual in Transfigured Time* that "there is a larger visual, or rather psychological habit: the search for the romantic personality as the prime value, whether in literature or painting; and this tendency, aided and abetted by popularized notions of psychoanalysis, has found its final expression in sur-realism."[17]

Much of Deren's criticism may be due to her resentment of European art invading, under the leadership of Breton, avant-garde positions in the New York art scene of the forties. The surrealist credo of the unconscious or its archetypes—C. G. Jung had lectured in Yale during 1937—as the origin of all art production had influenced American art criticism. What was true for the fine arts was true for experimental film. Maya Deren personally faced this dilemma when Iris Barry, as the head of the Museum of Moderns Art's film department, rejected a screening of her films with the explanation that Deren was only repeating the experiments of the French avant-garde of the twenties. But apart from efforts to secure screening venues, Deren's criticism of the surrealistic notion of the unconscious gives a clue to her argument with Anaïs Nin.

From the time Nin had met Artaud in Paris, she considered her writings to be surrealistic, although there are no traces of montage or collage techniques typical of surrealist art forms in her texts; the only surrealistic technique she actually applied is that of free-flowing associations that are supposedly uncensored by any conscious agency. Nin believed that the immediate expression of the unconscious self in art was the strongest drive of her productivity.

Deren instead argues that it is an illusion to believe in a consistent, self-contained ego within. To find the conditions and determinations of the self, one has to understand the social techniques that produce it, that gear it to its functions. The sources that affect the mind, the techniques that construct identity, are to be found outside the individual.

Making Experiences

Maya Deren's polemic against surrealism seems strange, considering her admiration for Jean Cocteau's *Sang d'Un Poète*, which she saw in New York after having made *Meshes*. In fact, her own methods bear a strong resemblance to surrealistic procedures: the isolation and the strange rearrangement of certain objects, her techniques of fragmenting and then reassembling time and space, subjects and objects. Deren's cinematic tricks that associate, condense, and displace the visual material actually correspond to what Freud described as the processes of dream work and to what the surrealists called expressions of the subconscious. The difference between her art form and that of the surrealists is that Deren never thought that these techniques derived from a hidden, unconscious secret self or soul. She insisted that they were the result of consciously applied effort by the artist through his or her art instruments.

My repeated insistence upon the distinctive function of form in
art—my insistence, that <u>the distinction of art is that it is neither</u>

simply an expression, of pain, for example, nor an impression of pain but is itself a form which creates pain (or whatever its emotional intent)—might seem to point to a classicism.[18]

In this sense, Cocteau's film was a true classic. Experimental film historian Amos Vogel pointed out about Cocteau's work what Deren had underlined for any real art: "Often mistaken for a surrealist work, this is a carefully constructed, entirely conscious artifact mingling symbol and metaphor to project anguish, apotheosis and conception of the struggling artist."[19]

Using film technique Deren set out to produce a reality of which the surrealists could only dream. By analyzing matter, time, and space, as the sciences do, in their historical implications, she considered art to be an experiment with reality itself: "The reality from which man draws his knowledge and the elements of his manipulation has been amplified not only by the development of analytical instruments; it has, increasingly, become itself a reality created by the manipulation of the instruments."[20]

Vertov's Kinoki manifestos echo in these passages from Deren's *Anagram* essay. As a filmmaker she relied on her instruments to discover reality, because the camera is a time-space instrument, as are "the radio in communication, the airplane and the rocketship in transportation, and the theory of relativity in physics."[21] Therefore, the task of cinema or any other art form is not to translate hidden messages of the unconscious soul into art but to experiment with the effects contemporary technical devices have on nerves, minds, or souls. The aim of film art is to engender movement in other minds, to move other souls. And others will be moved.

Today, the airplane and the radio have created, in fact, a relativistic reality of time and space. They have introduced into our immediate reality a dimension which functions not as an added spatial location but which, being both temporal and spatial, relates to all other dimensions with which we are familiar. There is not an object which does not require relocation in terms of this new frame of reference, and not least among these is the individual.[22]

In her first experiments Deren had demonstrated that in film the so-called individual can be divided, like the woman in *Meshes*, or multiplied, like the men in *At Land*. Maya Deren worked with dancers so that she could experiment with the manipulation of time and space. Movements that are formalized and rhythmical can be fragmented by tricks of the camera, prolonged in slow motion, and condensed in time-lapse; they can be reversed, inversed, or edited against the laws of gravity and spatial logic.

In *Ritual in Transfigured Time* the dance montage from the early films is transferred to everyday situations. Deren worked with a metronome to have divisible movements shot from different camera angles, and later she reassembled them according to temporal intervals, against common spatial logic, imposing her own filmic rhythms on the movements of the dancers. Through this technique a party is transformed to create the feeling of an uncanny and aggressive ritual. A dance appears on screen that has never been danced, that has instead been created by camera and editing work. Emotions are artificially, almost mathematically, produced by technical devices. They are engendered beyond the intentions of the actors.

It is even conceivable that Deren not only planned to use slow motion and freeze-frames, as she finally did in the finished film, but that her instructions "reverse" and "converse" in the shooting list originally also referred to printing instructions. Other films, *At Land*, for example, actually do work with reversed material.

By using a metronome, the basic instrument of all experimental psychologists from Charcot to Wundt, she could fragment the dance movements and reassemble them in the editing process. This process, of course, meant that the actors had to submit their feelings to the technical side of filming. Anaïs Nin was frustrated during shooting and offered her help—as a writer:

> It was then I noticed the theme of the party I had written about:
> that nothing happened because there was no connection of thought
> or feeling between the people acting, and so no tensions, no exchange
> of dramatic or comic moments. It was empty. I wanted to tell Maya:
> use my words to describe what is happening! But of course film-
> makers have a contempt for words.[23]

But filmmakers can work with the empty spaces between words—or people. After technical processing, the event turns into an impression that does not owe anything to the personal feelings of the persons involved but results from a cinematic transformation. Therefore, it is not just the invention of a filmmaker, but an experiment on social systems: in *Ritual in Transfigured Time* a party conversation occurs through the manipulation of time. Suddenly emotions and relationships appear, as well as movement patterns that had not been conceivable before the transformation.

Although the cinematic operations are simple technical permutations, the dance that the cinematic trick creates on the screen possesses emotional value: it appears to be uncanny—though still full of grace. The movements of the cinematically transfigured actors produce an effect that Heinrich von Kleist once described in his essay on the puppet theater: the strange line that the puppet's center of gravity follows and that creates the impression of grace in the spectator. In Kleist's text it is called the "path of the dancers' souls." But neither the intentions of the puppeteer nor the mechanics of the puppets' limbs nor the interpretation of the spectator could have produced it. The secret of Kleist's text is that the origin of the movement can be traced to the elliptical path of the reader's desire to understand the text. It is produced by an ensemble of techniques, and it leaves us with the Nietzschean question: What makes us dance, if we are, in fact, being danced?

In the puppet theater, Kleist observes the strange logarithmic relations between techniques and the emotions they produce. Maya Deren experiments with the cinematic tricks that transfigure mechanical, photochemical, and editing techniques into emotions. This transition is more than the expression or the impression of subjective emotions; it is, as Deren demanded in her *Anagram*, "*itself a form which creates*" emotion. This objectively engendered emotion—as opposed to subjective feeling—was the reason for Anaïs Nin's disappointed reaction at the screening: her idea of an artist was to be the source, not the instrument, of emotion.

Deren made her films not according to the logic of a literal character but according to cinematic laws of space, time, and movement. She called this method ritualistic: "Above all, the ritualistic form treats the human being not as the source of the dramatic action, but as a somewhat depersonalized element in a dramatic whole. The intent of such a depersonalization is not the destruction of the individual; on the contrary, it enlarges him beyond the personal dimension and frees him from the specializations and confines of personality. He becomes part of a dynamic whole which, like all such creative relationships, in turn, endows its parts with a measure of its larger meaning."[24]

Deren understands depersonalization not in the psychoanalytical sense of the term as decomposition or decay of the personality but, on the contrary, as growth and enlargement. This understanding is due to the fact that for her the individual is subjected to the historical development of social techniques. With the help of science and technical inventions, art must explore and simulate the conditions that produce historical subjects and their possible emancipation: "In its method—a conscious manipulation designed to create effect, in contrast to the spontaneous compulsions of expression—and in its results—the new, man-made reality, in contrast to the revelation or recapitulation of one which exists—the ritualistic form is much more the art equivalent of modern science than the naturalism which claims to be so based."[25]

In this sense her understanding of "ritualistic" is not a (pseudo-)primitive one but refers to the media aspect of art: art forms, as she will further elaborate in *Anagram*, are historical techniques of transmission that produce reality. The technical reality of man produces the emotional reality as a secondary effect. Conscious use of technical art instruments can relocate the individuals in the relativistic universe of the twentieth century. Yet the relocation itself may not be consciously experienced, because these techniques affect the nerves, the cortex, and the unconscious performance rather than conscious perception. As a shaman—and this is a comparison Deren herself never made but that can be derived from her work on Haitian Voudoun—the filmmaker, like any craftsman, applies his technique consciously, but its effects may lead into an abnormal state of the nerves, into a state of trance, that cannot be consciously perceived. It is in this state that the transformation of the self takes place.

With her understanding of the unconscious in this technical sense, Maya Deren also enlarges the usual anthropological notion of the term "ritual." Rituals are collective events in which common laws of time and space are repealed for certain groups in order to create extraordinary experiences. Rituals do not simply end in ecstasy that dissolves the person as social being; rather, during the seemingly anarchic process of the ritual, the participants are transformed into their new social status according to certain rules. While the participants' bodies dance and tremble in a state of unconsciousness, the same techniques that have thus affected their nervous systems will implant new cultural significations and social identities. This is as true for archaic drums and crystals as it is for the flicker of cinematic projection. And whether it is gods or media that are responsible for these procedures, their laws can be known.

It is no coincidence that Deren as well as Kleist chose dance forms when they experimented with the effects of media. In dancing, the functioning of social techniques is a common experience: representation and self-representation, social orders and individual expression are no longer distinguishable. In dance the body experiences what the subject experiences in language: to be located, displaced, and relocated according to social significations. It was Jacques Lacan's pleasure to hold up a mirror to psychoanalysis that has formulated a notion of media as, simultaneously, producer and transformer of identities. By giving an example from the psychoanalytical experience he projects the imaginary self-formation of the child in what he described as the mirror stage onto the formation of identity in general: "We only have to understand the mirror stage as an identification, in the full sense that analysis gives to the term: namely, the transformation that takes place in the subject when he assumes an image."[26]

It is exactly in this double sense of the word "assumption" that Maya Deren would have wanted Anaïs Nin to understand her way of making pictures: constructing *and* transforming subjects. The mirror stage, according to Lacan, is not an individual self-reflection but a socializing situation; in fact, it is *the* socializing oedipal situation when the child transcends the dyadic contented self-sufficiency it shared with the mother. According to Lacan this is an experience through images. Through the mirror the child perceives itself as something that it is not yet physically: a whole self-containing body. In the imaginary engendered by the mirror image, the child enlarges itself beyond its physical possibilities, yet at the same time it is really transfigured into a social being, located in the presence of the Other. Deren's description of the ritualistic form contains all these elements.

The poem to Anaïs Nin is an amplification of the idea that art cannot be a revelation of the self, but that art is a means to engender transitions of the self, the dangerous crises every social being has to go through several times in life. These *rites de passage* always leave traces of the wounds they open.

Through this notion of the ritualistic form Deren's theory on art and film form turns into a theory on media as techniques of social transition. Unlike Nin, who is primarily curious about herself, Deren is interested in the culture of self-transformation. She experiments with the technological engendering of emotional states, and she celebrates the cinematic form as a means to understand modern social and political relationships.

Daughters of Invention

Being a technician of emotions is no innocent project, however, and in the forties this was certainly a science of dictatorships. Maya Deren worked at a time when totalitarian propaganda machines had occupied psychotechniques as their scientific means and used film as their most efficient medium. Still, Deren defended cinema as the art form that permits a total experience of contemporary reality: "If cinema is to take its place beside the others as a full-fledged art form, it must cease merely to record realities that owe nothing of their actual existence to the film instrument. Instead, it must create a total experience so much out of the very nature of the instrument as to be inseparable from its means."[27]

This, of course, is dangerous ground: to demand total experience out of the instrument, that is, out of the effects, not the contents of film, seems to offend all notions of reason and political enlightenment. To understand Deren's film theory, her argument has to be followed back to its roots in anthropology and psychoneurology and her insight that film always affects the nervous system of people before messages are conveyed. The perception of movement in film is based on unconscious mental activity. If this activity were conscious, there would be twenty-four frames of still pictures per second—the technical truth, as Vertov and Godard pointed out. Deren's decision—based on the fact that film depends on physiological activity beyond perception—was to study these processes and apply them to the construction of her films. She then drew attention to the new form of experiences achieved. Experimental filmmaking could only be critical toward mainstream film production if it *consciously* used filmic means to manipulate *unconscious* processes of the mind. This seeming contradiction is the reason for confusion and feuds over Deren's theory.

Nowhere in her writings does Deren actually reflect on the contemporary political consequences of this media aspect of film, except perhaps for a few remarks on wartime filming in *Anagram*. It is in her film work that Deren pursues her radical quest for those films that would generate new and appropriate forms of experience.

Examples of slow-motion or time-lapse filming that invoke unconscious subtexts have already been cited. Another example of Deren's efforts to use and at the same time analyze filmic means is a sequence in *Meshes of the Afternoon* in which the (temporal and spatial) labyrinth of desire that threatens the protagonist takes form by technical means.

Toward the end of the film the fear of the desiring self is reflected in a truly visual form: in a face, which is a mirror that does not reflect anything at all. While the surrealists would paint and photograph bulls and fauns as symbols of their unconscious desires, Deren shows visually how unconscious psychic terrors are produced by means that aim at the blind spots of perception. The danger that is so threatening to the integrity of the individual is not an unconscious sexual drive from within that deceives consciousness. Rather, the danger that threatens the identity of a person is the fact that the subject can never know its own desire but can only reflect it through the psychic position of another social being or through artificial devices beyond himself. Those positions and devices, in their old, archaic or modern, electronic forms, have their own law and order and will inflect the desire of the subject accordingly. But the real danger in this external manipulation of desire comes if the reflection of the self is denied. This is the case with the woman who has a mirror for a face in *Meshes*. She denies self-reflection to the younger heroine. The distortion of self-reflection in society can mean pain, but the denial of self-reflection means social and also physical death.

Deren's films investigate archaic and modern ritualistic forms. They were dangerous yet promising adventures, because, as she described it in her poetic invitation to Anaïs Nin, they created life and reality. Anaïs Nin's writing process could only try to compensate for suffering in reality, without changing its technical preconditions. Maya Deren wanted to invent new forms and means to extend the visual horizon of perceivable selves.

It has been observed that cinema's history concerning the politics of bodies and identities starts with Charcot's series of photographs at the Salpêtrière. These pictures and their significance mark the beginning of

institutional control over the unconscious and involuntary movements
of the body. Charcot developed a system to submit the "wilderness of
paralysis, convulsions and spasms" to a numerical and literal order.[28] Wild
states of possession were tamed into psychological dictionaries. In cinema, those states appear to escape into the wilderness of their physical
reality again. Maya Deren, writing as a film technician, knows that the
old story continues as social technique: in classical cinema, transgressions
of what is presumed to be normalcy are always linked to fear, often to
the fear of the savage other. Hollywood is at its best when it directs wild
passions and systemizes them into good and evil, healthy or sick: in this
case it returns film form to its historical origin. In the article dedicated
to her psychiatrist father, Deren wrote: "It is revealing that the best use
of cinematic form (camera, editing, etc.) appears in those commercial
films which seek to describe an abnormal state of mind and its abnormal
perception of reality."[29]

In the abnormal state of mind, commercial cinema is screening its own
essential technique: to manipulate perception unconsciously to create the
illusion of movement. But commercial cinema, from *The Cabinet of Dr.
Caligari* to zombie B movies, had to deny the positive, enlarging elements
of trance in order to deny the fragility of identity and perception that
constitutes the basis of Western societies. Deren's aim in filmmaking was
to liberate the cinematic techniques of trance, hypnosis, and possession
from classical narration. To do so, she did not simply change the value
of signification: on the contrary, she considered symbolic or metaphorical signs in her films altogether meaningless. It was not the symbolic value
of the knife that was important in the story of *Meshes* but, for example,
the editing techniques that exposed the different visual and emotional
functions of a knife. Deren set out to challenge the complete cinematic
system of signification.

In her writings on film Deren did not go back to Charcot and the early
days of neuropathology, but, following the medical traces of body politics, she picked up the studies when they became important to film history. In her first essay on possession she replaced Western medicine's

pathological verdict on trance with a positive understanding of trance as prestigious social transformation. All the figures in Deren's films are animated cinematically through slow-motion or artificially joined spaces to dance across normal time and space experience. These figures are reassembled in the minds of the spectators as a response to film technique. Cinema itself turns into a ritualistic place where people are not only moved through trance but transfigured by it.

Maya Deren's film theory can be read against the background of her anthropological studies. At the interface of film and anthropology, a theory of media emerges that analyzes the relationships among techniques, bodies, minds, identities, and political power in the frame of the twentieth century. But while Marshall McLuhan, twenty years later, called media the "extensions of man," Deren is well aware of the fact that the crucial transmission runs in the reverse direction: the minds of men and women are affected by the social impact of technical inventions. Or, radically speaking, the souls of people are moved by communication systems—unconsciously in the technical sense.

As Deren had written in *Anagram*, film, like any other art form, is not an expression of man "but a form which creates" emotions and creates experiences "out of the very nature of the instrument." Therefore, Deren's radical aspiration was to liberate cinema from the domain of the entertainment industry or governmental propaganda. She knew what she was writing about, because Alexander Hammid was working for the Office of War Information during World War II, where most of the creative inventions on 16mm film were made. To subvert the dominant media strategies, she needed to study the functioning of the art instrument, not the symbolic meaning of pictures.

At this point the controversy between Maya Deren, pursuing the tradition of psychoneurology, and Anaïs Nin, writing in the tradition of psychoanalysis, returns on an elementary level. Nin became one of Deren's fiercest critics. She had doubts about Deren's intentions to work with the media side of film: "Her obsession was to employ symbolic acts but to deny that they had symbolic significance."[30]

For Deren, critics like Anaïs Nin are part of an old anachronistic literary culture that cannot judge reality as produced by film's instruments:

> Another habit is the current tendency to psycho-analyse anything which deals with an imaginative reality. The special conditions of film production, where it is the camera which perceives and records, according to its capacity, introduces a non-psychological censor. The spontaneous associational logics of the artist cannot be retained intact by an instrument which eliminates certain elements by virtue of its refined optics, its ability to remember details, which the subconscious might not have considered significant.[31]

Psychoanalysis versus psychoneurology—the two daughters continue an old feud, but they subvert the rules of science. Anaïs Nin had been a patient and scholar of Otto Rank, the author of a fundamental text on narcissism.[32] Rank was also famous for psychoanalyzing films, for example, the classical doppelgänger story *The Student of Prague*.[33] In applying Freud's theory of narcissism, Rank discovered the double to be no more than the representation of the repressed and disavowed parts of a personality. After succumbing to Nin's seduction, he left Vienna and his family to live in New York as the American doppelgänger of his European self. Nin's techniques of transformations were as practical as they were literal: she immediately confronted her theoretical father with his own theory and assumed the analyst's chair herself.[34]

Deren proceeds in the opposite direction. For her, repression or disavowal is not a matter of personal neurosis but of social conventions and communication systems. The unconscious part of our self-perception is ignorance about the making of our image. Therefore, her films show transitions and techniques of transition at the same time. The final sequence of *Ritual in Transfigured Time* is an example of how Deren would experiment with the narcissistic trap of self-perception. It is a disillusionment of self-assured identity, but it is also a disillusionment of the nature of female identities: these are mere products of culture and therefore subject to change.

Toward the end of *Ritual* we see the transformation of widow into bride, two classical symbolic significations of women's bodies that every culture introduces with special rites and rituals. Deren shows this change not as the story of a single figure but as movements of a depersonalized ensemble. The movements of the film show that a transition is not a matter of personal reflection but of a collective distortion and dislocation of individuals in time and space (see figures 34, 35, and 36, p. 255).

Deren's means in *Ritual* are radically cinematic. The picture of the final transition is a matter of photochemistry: the film negative presents the figure of the widow, played alternately by the dancer Rita Christiani and by Maya Deren herself, immersed in water, whose surface had been Narcissus's lethal deceit. Underwater the widow, in negative, turns into a bride. In terms of film, the reversed picture of the widow is the bride. But even the bride is not a final picture. Her white gown works like an afterimage of all the other states of women's bodies we have seen, and our perception, "geared into expectation" by the silent black-and-white rhythm of the film, floats back through the different stages of female metamorphosis. As we sit in the cinema we experience a trancelike state induced by projected light and skillfully transported motionless pictures. While our minds are unconsciously moved to perceive bodies in movement, we can consciously understand that the dance of identification we see is a social ritual in which we ourselves participate.

Notes

1. Maya Deren, "For Anaïs Before the Glass," in *The Legend of Maya Deren: A Documentary Biography and Collected Works*, vol. 1, pt. 2, *Chambers (1942–47)* by VèVè A. Clark, Millicent Hodson, and Catrina Neiman (New York: Anthology Film Archives Film Culture, 1988), p. 537

2. Maya Deren, "Cinema as an Art Form," in *The Legend*, vol. 1, pt. 2, p. 313

3. Deren, "Cinema as an Art Form," p. 317.

4. Anaïs Nin, *The Diary of Anaïs Nin, Summer 1946*, vol. 4 (New York: Harvest Books, 1973), pp. 156–57.

5. Cf. James Merrill interview, *The Legend*, vol. 1, pt. 2, p. 539.

6. Nin, *The Diary of Anaïs Nin, 1955–1966*, vol. 6. (New York: Harvest Books, 1975), pp. 351–53.

7. Cf. Noel Riley Fitch, *Anaïs: The Erotic Life of Anaïs Nin* (Boston and New York: Back Bay Books), 1993.

8. Cf. George L. Ponomareff, M.D., "Commentary on the Bekhterev Psychoneurological Institute," *Current Psychiatric Therapies*, no. 23 (1986): 281–85.

9. Eleanora Deren, "Possessed Dancing in Haiti," quoted according to the typescript in the Maya Deren Collection, Mugar Library, Boston University, p. 5.

10. Deren, "Possessed Dancing," p. 8.

11. Deren, "Possessed Dancing," p. 10.

12. Maya Deren, "Magic Is New," *Mademoiselle*, January 1946. Reprinted in *The Legend*, vol. 1, pt. 2, p. 309.

13. Deren, "Magic Is New," p. 309.

14. Hugo Münsterberg, *The Film—a Psychological Study: The Silent Photoplay in 1916*, with a new foreword by Richard Griffith (New York: Dover, 1970), p. 74.

15. Maya Deren, "Choreography for the Camera," *Dance* (October 1945); reprinted in *Film Culture*, no. 39 (winter 1965): 3.

16. Deren, "Choreography for the Camera," 3.

17. Maya Deren, "Notes on Ritual and Ordeal," 1945, *Film Culture*, no. 39 (winter 1965): 10.

18. Maya Deren, *An Anagram of Ideas on Art, Form and Film*, in *The Legend*, vol. 1, pt. 2, p. 17. Underline in original.

19. Amos Vogel, *Film as a Subversive Art* (New York: Random House, 1974), p. 81.

20. Deren, *Anagram*, p. 17. Underline in original.

21. Deren, "Cinema as an Art Form," in *The Legend*, vol. 1, pt. 2, p. 319.

22. Deren, "Cinema as an Art Form," p. 319.

23. Nin, *The Diary*, vol. 4, p. 135.

24. Deren, *Anagram*, p. 20.

25. Deren, *Anagram*, p. 20.

26. Jacques Lacan, *Écrits: A Selection*, translated by Alan Sheridan (London: Tavistock, 1977), p. 2.

27. Maya Deren, "Cinematography: The Creative Use of Reality," *Daedalus* (winter 1960): 171.

28. Cf. Sigmund Freud, "Charcot," in *Gesammelte Werke*, vol. 1 (London: Imago Publishing, 1952), p. 22. My translation.

29. Deren, "Cinema as an Art Form," p. 315.

30. Nin, *The Diary*, vol. 6, p. 35.

31. Deren, *Anagram*, p. 43.

32. Otto Rank, "Ein Beitrag zum Narzißmus," in *Jahrbuch für psychoanalytische und psychopathologische Forschungen*, vol. 3, 1911.

33. Otto Rank, *Der Doppelgänger. Eine psychoanalytische Studie* (Leipzig: Internationaler Psychoanalytischer Verlag, 1925), pp. 57–59

34. Fitch, *Anaïs*, p. 180 ff.

22

23

Jane Brakhage Wodening

Maya Deren

Isadora Duncan was a beautiful and wild dancer who had danced in her own way and become known everywhere for her strange form of dancing. She was also a Communist and made strikes and confusion among the people. Everywhere she went, she was adored and her way of dancing became the new way of dancing and it was called Modern Dance. She always wore a very long scarf around her neck and one day the other end of it wrapped around the wheel of her car and killed her. Maya Deren heard the stories of Isadora Duncan and wanted to be like that.

Maya Deren's father had come over from Russia and he was studious and an anthropologist and he had wanted a boy. Her mother was brash and dumpy. Maya was brash too but she was slim and graceful and full of fire. She was a born dancer and she had rages that were fierce and wild and she was so small and dainty that no one could disobey her.

When she was very young, Maya went to Oregon where she found many lumberjacks who were all big powerful men with bulging muscles and she roused them and organized them and led them in a wildcat strike and thus she was a Communist leader.

But Maya Deren wanted to dance too so she went to Los Angeles and there she met Sasha Hammid and they made a film together. That was

Figure 22. *Meshes of the Afternoon* (1943). Courtesy of Anthology Film Archives.
Figure 23. Maya Deren (1942). Photographed by Alexander Hammid. Courtesy of the Czech Center of Photography.

during the War. After the War, she traveled across the land showing her film and talking about it and about Art. And she and Sasha were no longer together but Sasha had another woman and they all lived in New York City in two separate places and she and Sasha and his new woman made a film about a cat having kittens. Then she used Parker Tyler who was a poet and a critic and Anaïs Nin who wrote diaries that told everything and John Cage the composer in a film and she made other films too and after that she went to Haiti.

In Haiti, she was fulfilled. She learned about voodoo, a religion of shamanic power, and this religion was based on dance. And when she danced in Haiti, she was possessed of the voodoo gods and she had power over men. And so she became a priestess and her red hair stuck out all over her head like sparks and she wore her hair that way the rest of her life.

Maya Deren came back to New York City and became a priestess there and she had jars with gnarled roots in them preserved in rum and other jars with strange spices or colored powders for voodoo rituals. And she wrote a book about voodoo and it was acclaimed a good anthropological book but before it was even begun, her father was already dead so she couldn't prove to him that she was as good as if she had been a boy.

Teiji Ito ran away from home when he was not yet grown and he was eating garbage and sleeping in movie theaters between the rows of chairs and one day Maya Deren went back into the movie theater because she had left her gloves and there between the rows of chairs she saw Teiji Ito lying asleep and she took him home with her and he was her man for the rest of her life and he became a composer and made musical instruments.

Maya kept cats and named them after voodoo gods and many of these cats hated each other. Ghede and Erzulie had the run of the house but the others had to be locked up in rooms and behind fences.

When Maya showed her films in New York City, her mother would always come to the shows, and before the show Maya and her mother would scream at each other in front of the theater. Sometimes Willard Maas would hold meetings of the filmmakers and then Maya would scream at everyone and they would scream back too and Willard Maas would defend her because she was a woman and so small although she didn't need him to defend her.

There was a doctor in New York City who gave everyone the same thing, it was a brown liquid and they would inject it into their rumps and then they would feel good. And he was called Doctor Feelgood and many artists went to him, even President Kennedy went to him, or so I've heard, and they all got the brown medicine to inject into their rumps. Tennessee Williams who wrote great plays used Doctor Feelgood's medicine all the time and he felt he couldn't bear to live without it. One time, Tennessee went all the way to the Middle East, and when he arrived he found that he had forgotten to bring Doctor Feelgood's mixture so he came right back. Maya Deren, although she was always very poor, always paid the very high price that Doctor Feelgood asked and sometimes she would inject the medicine into her rump in the presence of men and they would always be very pleased to see her leg all the way up to her rump.

Geoffrey Holder the dancer was going to marry his leading lady. Geoffrey was Haitian and he believed in voodoo but he was also hungry to be a star in the eye of the public so he didn't insist on voodoo. He was to have a big Wedding and it was to be News.

He asked Maya to be in charge of the voodoo rituals and decorations at the Reception. She was very excited about it, hoping that now she would have glory. Maya was always looking with a raging hunger for her big chance. She went to the big house where the Reception was to be. She should have known it was going to be bad by the tiny room she was given. She started getting angry when they wouldn't give her money to buy the things that were needed, shoved her into the background whenever she pushed herself forward. By the wedding day, she was screaming at them now and again. She had asked Stan Brakhage to come and bring the film-maker Larry Jordan too and they could both help her by photographing on film. Stan helped her with the floating candles in the goldfish pond and when they were all alight and afloat, he photographed them. And in her mind, in that small gesture, he was the only one who helped her.

And so, when all the people were gathered at the Reception, Maya Deren became possessed by the voodoo god Papa Loco. She went into the kitchen and she started to roar and she picked up the refrigerator that weighed several hundred pounds and she threw it across the kitchen. The women who had been preparing the food came running out with their hands waving and their eyes rolling and Geoffrey Holder and some other people went into the kitchen and took Maya and carried her upstairs to her room. Members of the Wedding who understood voodoo stayed with her there, got her into bed where she sat roaring and demanding things to be brought to her. And the way she roared was she would roll her head from side to side and roar with each breath. She asked for rum to be brought and set aflame and she asked for Stan to be brought. They brought another Stan, Stanley Haggart, but she didn't want him, she wanted Stan Brakhage, so Stanley Haggart went down again and got Stan Brakhage and sent him up to her room.

Stan Brakhage had had an experience with Papa Loco before this and it had been in this wise. He was making a film in Colorado in the mountains and he had only the mornings to work on it. As it happened, that summer in the Colorado mountains, it got cloudy every day in the mornings and Stan couldn't make this film in the rain and the clouds. After many days of this, he complained of his problem to his friend, the painter-sculptor Angelo di Benedetto, who had been to Haiti too and to Africa where they have voodoo also and Angelo said, "Why didn't you tell me sooner?"

Angelo got out some of his father's homemade wine, and with the wine he drew a circle on the table and, mumbling in a language Stan couldn't hear or understand, he spoke with Papa Loco who was the god of the weather and of ritual and of art. And from that day on, the sun shone every morning in the Colorado mountains and Stan could finish his film.

Stan went up to Maya's room and she was sitting up in her bed and rolling her head and roaring. The other people there, Haitians, were caring for her and they were not afraid because they knew it was Papa Loco. And the rum was burning with blue flames in a bowl beside the bed and

Maya put her hands into the bowl of blue flames and flung them all over Stan Brakhage and blessed him in the name of Papa Loco. It was Stan's only suit and he feared to lose it and he tried to brush the blue flames off but the Haitians told him the flames wouldn't hurt the suit and they didn't. Later, Maya tried twice to curse Stan; once, when he was two hours late to a gathering everyone was to come to and fold and stamp papers to advertise a show and the other time, when he made a film of the birth of his first child because, she said, he had revealed too much of the mysteries of women. But Papa Loco shielded Stan, and Maya's curses didn't take effect.

From the Afterword in *from the Book of Legends*

Once I was introduced to Maya Deren. It was at a party and she was little and bursting with fiery grace and I was big and young and pregnant. And we moved toward each other to shake hands but as our hands approached each other, something told each of us not to touch the other. There was some electricity in the air between us and we neither one wanted to shake hands. We both stepped forward and reached out and as our hands almost touched, we both pulled them back and stepped back. And we both said, "How do you do?" and after that we kept as far apart as we could.

Note

This essay originally appeared in *from The Book of Legends* (New York: Granary Books, 1989; reprint, London: Invisible Books, 1993).

24

· · 1C
· · ·
· · ·

Lucy Fischer

"The Eye for Magic"

Maya and Méliès

[M]ore than anything else, cinema consists of the eye for magic—*that which perceives and reveals the* marvelous *in whatsoever it looks upon.* **—Maya Deren**

[I]t is the trick, *used in the most intelligent manner, that allows the supernatural, the imaginary, even the impossible to be rendered visually and produces truly artistic tableaux.* **—Georges Méliès**

It is common for the critical literature on Maya Deren to place her work within the broader framework of cinema history. P. Adams Sitney, for example, in his seminal text *Visionary Cinema*, positions her films squarely within the European experimental tradition—relating them to the work of Jean Cocteau, Salvador Dalí, and Luis Buñuel.[1] In a similar, though oppositional, gesture, Annette Kuhn finds parallels between Deren's films and the commercial domain—specifically, between *Meshes of the Afternoon* (1943) and Hollywood gothic melodrama.[2] What have been slighted in this genealogy, however, are Deren's connections to the primitive cinema—a link that avant-garde filmmakers have frequently cultivated in their work. Ken Jacobs's *Tom, Tom the Piper's Son* (1969) is a literal reworking of a 1905 movie. Andy Warhol's protracted, single-view

Figure 24. Maya Deren in Los Angeles (1942). Photographed by Alexander Hammid. Courtesy of the Czech Center of Photography.

"stares" at sights like the Empire State Building are, on one level, ironic citations of turn-of-the-century "actualities."

One of the few critics to link Deren to early cinema is Michael O'Pray, who states that: "With the exception of perhaps the . . . 'primitive' films of the Lumières, Maya Deren's *A Study in Choreography for Camera* was probably the simplest film . . . to be made at the time, 1945."[3] Yet it is the work of another pioneer filmmaker that bears fullest comparison to that of Deren—Georges Méliès, the master of the "trick-film" genre.

That Deren's films and writings would be informed by a sense of magic should come as no surprise to us. Born Eleanora, she changed her name to Maya, in honor of the Hindu goddess of sorcery.[4] Beyond that, Deren's poetry and theoretical musings on art and cinema were laden with references to prestidigitation. In a verse entitled "He," she chants: "Lips to my magic flute, I call you."[5] In another, she intones.

LISTEN

THE MAGIC SIGN AND THE SECRET WORD

THE SONG OF A CHILD AND THE CRY OF A BIRD

ARE ALL THE HEART BEATING[6]

Finally, in a work entitled "Genesis," she writes:

Let us reserve this hour for magic.
Beginning with nothing, let it be swiftly perfect
      with impossibility . . .
Let the impossible be real.
Let the incredible be true.[7]

In her theoretical essays, Deren also draws on metaphors of illusion to describe the process of creation. In an article published in *Mademoiselle* (significantly entitled "Magic Is New"), she writes: "I had always been impatient with what I felt was a criminal neglect [in the cinema] of [its] potent magic power."[8]

Beyond such theorizing, Deren projected an occult aura to those who had personal contact with her. Her husband Teiji Ito remarked that "upon walking into her apartment for the first time, he felt its magic immediately bring his life into focus."[9] Similarly, Anne Clark (who acted in *Witch's Cradle* [1943]) claimed that one "could always feel [Deren's] ideas about magic and ceremony" in her presence.[10] But it was not only Deren's private world that exuded a sense of magic but her cinematic universe as well. Parker Tyler, for example, finds Deren's movies noteworthy for their "magic ability to make even the most imaginative concept seem real."[11]

Though Deren's intellectual and artistic interest in magic makes parallels to the cinema of Georges Méliès inevitable, the differences between the two filmmakers are as compelling as are the similarities. Although, as the epigraph makes clear, for Méliès, magic is fundamentally a "trick," for Deren it constitutes access to the "marvelous."

Star Film and the Star System

Maya Deren was an expert at manipulating images. **–Maria Pramaggiore**[12]

Maria Pramaggiore has shown that Deren, as the "leading lady" of her own experimental texts, "participated in a process of persona construction during the 1940s that looks surprisingly similar to the construction of mainstream film stars in that era."[13] Clearly, Deren's "cult" status was augmented by her gorgeous, exotic demeanor as well as by her grace in movement. (Ephraim Katz, for example, calls Deren a "dark beauty" in his encyclopedia entry on her.)[14] Casting herself in such works as *Meshes of the Afternoon, At Land* (1944), and *Ritual in Transfigured Time* (1946), she became an icon of the experimental film community. But her celebrity role went beyond that of an ersatz movie star. It is significant that she gave herself no screen credit as actress. Rather, her renown was tied to the personal appearances she made in prominent art cinema venues as a lecturer accompanying her films. This tradition (of independent artists discussing their work) is one that continues today. Thus, as an early master of media self-promotion, she was as interested in "manipulating" her public image as in glorifying the one that filled the screen.

Georges Méliès, too, was highly identified with his work and production company, Star Film. Having begun his career in vaudeville with live magic shows, Méliès moved into cinema in response to the growing popularity of the medium. Like a stage magician, he continued to be featured in his own routines, "headlining" such films as *Extraordinary Illusions* (1903), *The Enchanted Sedan Chair* (1905), and *The Untamable Whiskers* (1904). Hence, his visage (when not disguised) became recognizable on screen.

In addition to populating their films, both Deren and Méliès had a habit of multiplying their own celluloid effigies. In *The One-Man Band* (1900), Méliès appears sitting on a chair and "replicates himself into six musicians . . . and a centered orchestra conductor."[15] In *The Man With the Rubber Head* (1902), a doubled image of Méliès's skull is poised on a scientist's laboratory table.[16]

Likewise, in numerous Deren films, versions of herself miraculously propagate. In *Meshes of the Afternoon*, one Deren figure seems constantly (through shot/countershot editing) to be staring at another. In one famous image (based on a multiple exposure), three Derens sit together at a dining room table. Similarly, at the end of *At Land*, while one Deren runs along the beach, two others pause to observe her flight. Hence, both Deren and Méliès fit into the tradition of actor/directors who simultaneously command and control their celluloid appearances. The third member of this triumvirate is Orson Welles, who gave voice to his love of prestidigitation late in his career in his essay-film *F for Fake* (1975).

It would seem that those cineastes who seize on the metaphor of magic to explain the creative process are often those who demand total control of the medium—"triple threats," as it were. Significantly, in her writings, Deren makes her authoritarian stance quite apparent. As she notes: "The artist is a magician who, by his perception of the powers and laws of the non-apparent, exercises them upon the apparent. . . . The master-magician commands: he makes manifest the other dimensions to those who have no power to make them manifest."[17] Here, magic, perhaps, meets megalomania.

The Inn Where No Man Rests

Where is the door? I don't remember
climbing stairs; nor whether at the
corner I turn right or left . . .
Someone has changed the houses on
the street.
                                    —Maya Deren[18]

Clearly, from a retrospective stance, the verse above seems preparatory of *Meshes of the Afternoon*—a film that chronicles a person's nightmarish disorientation within a house. As the film opens, a woman (played by Deren) enters a cottage after struggling with her key. Once in the residence, mysterious things proceed to happen. Beyond the woman discovering various incarnations of herself, objects inexplicably change form. At one point a key turns into a knife; later, the knife turns back into a key. At other moments, things suddenly disappear. After reaching down to the pavement to pick up a flower, Deren's arm vanishes. After she spies a black-hooded figure on a path, the phantom fades from view. Finally, each time Deren reenters a space she has previously traversed, something is inscrutably altered. A phone that is off the hook is suddenly on; a phonograph that is playing stops.

While we can look to Deren's poem for a precedent for *Meshes*, we can also investigate a subgenre of Méliès's films.[19] In such works as *The Black Imp* (1905), *The Apparition* (1903), and *The Inn Where No Man Rests* (1903), Méliès stages an ongoing narrative concerning a hapless traveler who must spend the night in a hotel room that is strangely haunted (like the bungalow in *Meshes*). In *The Inn Where No Man Rests*, a candle floats through the room, clothes come to life, and boots walk on their own—acts that rival the anomalies taking place in *Meshes*. As in Deren's work, a bed figures prominently in Méliès's *The Inn* (as it does in *The Black Imp*, where it bursts into flames). In *Meshes* the bed is also the site of much disturbance. As Deren reclines on it, a man (codirector and husband Alexander Hammid) hovers over her prostrate body. A flower she is holding turns into a knife; she throws it at his face—which is suddenly transformed into a photographic surface that seems to tear. As the titles of Méliès's *The Apparition* and *The Black Imp* indicate, these films also involve the appearance of a ghostly spirit who menaces the traveler—not unlike the black-hooded figure with a mirrored face (also played by Hammid) that stalks Deren in *Meshes*.

While on the surface these Méliès and Deren films bear comparison (based on the quizzical events that confront their luckless protagonists), on a deeper level, the works are quite opposed. While Méliès's films convey a sense of antic absurdity (like the confusion one experiences in an amusement-park "fun house"), *Meshes* communicates a sense of hallucinatory terror (like the distorted world of *The Cabinet of Dr. Caligari* [1919] or the Magic Mirror Maze in *The Lady from Shanghai* [1948]). If Deren borrows tropes from the primitive era, she clearly shifts their emotional valence.

A Trip to the Moon

People in the twentieth century are increasingly occupied with magic, mystical experience, transcendental urges . . . the belief in extraterrestrial intelligence . . . so that, in this sense, fantasy, the supernatural, the magical documentary, call it what you will, is closer to the sense of the times than naturalism. **–Stanley Kubrick**[20]

One of the most acclaimed and recognized images in all film history is that of the face of a grimacing, anthropomorphic moon with a rocket ship stuck in its eye. This picture is, of course, taken from *A Trip to the Moon* (1902), one of many Méliès's works to imagine space exploration.

Also noteworthy here is Méliès's *The Eclipse* (1907), a tale of scientists assembled at a conference who peer through telescopes to witness extraordinary astronomic events. Richard Abel calls the film a "dream of celestial bodies" that "hovers over the sleeping scientists."[21] The first part of *The Eclipse*, with its story of "The Courtship of the Sun and Moon," as rendered by grotesque humanoid/planetary faces, echoes his *Trip to the Moon*. Its second part, "The Wandering Stars," introduces a new motif. Filling the night sky is a series of tableaux in which "stars," "constellations," and "planets" circulate (among them Gemini, Uranus, Urania, and Noctambulo). A traveling star (labeled Venus) opens up to reveal a woman inside. Comets (with women riding on them) soar through the sky. Finally, galactic maidens drift through the firmament as part of a meteor shower. Clearly, here Méliès is less interested in scripting an adventure narrative than he is in mounting a picturesque occasion to display his pretty soubrettes. Hence, a sense of the wonder of *womanhood* informs the film more than an impression of interplanetary awe.

It is not difficult to see in this Méliès film a naive ancestor of Deren's *The Very Eye of Night* (1952–1959)—an abstract work that uses dancers (choreographed by Anthony Tudor) to represent the constellations in a bright, twinkling sky. Using negative imagery (which renders the dancers ethereally white), Deren places them against a black faux-sky background. Through camera movement, superimposition, and optical processing, she achieves the illusion of figures floating through the heavens.

While for Méliès "trips to the moon" were a genre of science fiction (with camera stunts employed to add a sense of futuristic display), for Deren the sky was a site of rapture. *The Very Eye of Night* begins with a title sequence featuring a drawing of an eye—reminding us that Deren associated magic with vision (both literal and metaphoric). But clearly, for her, the image of the cosmos also had mystic resonances. As Deren wrote: "I am interested . . . in discovering the laws of the unknown forces which compulse the universe."[22]

While Deren's interest in extraterrestrial enigmas seems a long way from her love of dance, the two realms intimately intertwine in *The Very*

Eye of Night. For just as outer space presents a field in which earthly laws are violated and superseded, so the domain of film dance liberates the body through the magic of cinematography and editing.

The Human Fly

I can say without bragging . . . that it was I myself who successively discovered all the so-called "mysterious" processes of the cinematograph. **–Georges Méliès**[23]

Among the most famous production numbers of the American musical is the routine from *Royal Wedding* (1951) in which Fred Astaire walks on the walls and ceiling. This illusion is, in fact, produced by a "special effect" that dates back to the days of Méliès. In *The Human Fly* (1902), a Russian dancer executes handstands and somersaults up the wall and across the ceiling of an Oriental stage set.[24] Clearly, such sequences were rendered without actors having magical powers. Rather, by creating sets whose mise-en-scène positioned a fake "wall" or "ceiling" on the actual floor (and then matting shots together), performers apparently defied the constraints of normal space.

While no Deren film presents an episode precisely like that of *The Human Fly*, there are moments in *Meshes* in which characters are made to challenge the laws of gravity through certain camera and postproduction techniques. Central here are the interior stairs of the bungalow in which the film unfolds. As Deren ascends for the first time, the angling of the frame makes her appear to be clinging to the ceiling, as though her equilibrium were being tested. Another time, as she mounts the staircase, she looks as though she is being tossed from side to side—an effect achieved by angling the camera in precise opposition to the direction in which she "falls." (Here we recall the line in Deren's poem "I Cannot Place the Face" in which she cries: "I am afraid the walls will gradually move in.")[25] A more complex variation on the theme occurs later in *Meshes* around the site of a window. Early on, Deren enters an upstairs bedroom, arriving through a window, as though she were blown in, with mesh curtains clinging to her body. In a later scene, what seems to be a reverse printing of the same shot creates the effect of her being sucked out of the portal backward. Spatiotemporal laws are also "overcome" in *Meditation on Violence* (1948), where (through freeze-frame technique) a man's jump is arrested in midair. Similarly, in *Ritual in Transfigured Time*, a dancer's movement is halted in medias res.

While the two latter examples share something of the heady, virtuoso spirit of *The Human Fly* (where a cinematic trick is gleefully flaunted), Deren's *trucage* often conveys a sense of the uncanny—of the unsettling (versus emancipating) effects of bending the bounds of regular time and space.

An Impossible Voyage

To show something as everyone sees it is to have accomplished nothing. *—V. I. Pudovkin*[26]

Georges Méliès once stated that trick effects allow "the impossible to be rendered visually" in film.[27] Clearly, one of the incredible feats that the cinema can achieve is to configure a fully synthetic space. Significantly, in Méliès's film *An Impossible Voyage* (1904), the scientists who assemble to plan a groundbreaking trip are members of the Institute of *Incoherent* Geography. While in that movie the novelty of travel involves the scientists' use of every known means of locomotion (automobile, dirigible, submarine, and so forth), in other Méliès films, amazement is tied to their arrival at an exotic (and unfilmable) locale (the moon, the North Pole, the bottom of the sea).

In the work of Deren, the "impossible voyage" implies something else—the magical shift (though a matched cut on action) from one realm to another. Such a feat transpires quite dramatically in *Meshes* when Deren ominously begins to stride across the room with a knife in her hand. Suddenly, she is standing in tall grass and then, in a series of consecutive shots (based on matched cuts), her feet touch upon five discrete domains: water, earth, grass, pavement, and rug. While Méliès promised a world of "in-

coherent" geography in his films, the terrain negotiated by his characters remains rather logical, if fanciful. If explorers set off from the earth
in a rocket, they land in outer space; when they fall from the sky, they
end up in the sea. It is Deren who produces a universe of truly incoherent relations in *Meshes*, with her consecutive steps across five disjunct territories. Furthermore, Deren's landscape has symbolic significance, since
her foot touches down on the principal "turfs" of the human world.

In Deren's later work, "creative geography" becomes a more dominant theme. *At Land* begins with Deren washed up on shore from the
ocean (like one of Méliès's mythical sea queens from *The Kingdom of the
Fairies* [1903] or *The Mermaid* [1904]). As Margaret Warwick describes
the scene, "[a] Woman . . . issues forth from the sea, a mythological being from another world."[28] Deren pulls herself up on a piece of driftwood and begins to look around. Strangely, however, the next shot (ostensibly from her point of view) implies that she is gazing at a smoke-filled
room in which a party is taking place. We next see her crouching under
a table. However, when we cut to a close-up of her feet, they are perched
on driftwood. Finally, she begins to crawl across the table, but the scene
is intercut with matched images that depict her plowing through dense
foliage (which suggests another locale).

In other works, Deren's impossible journeys are linked to movement.
In *A Study in Choreography for Camera* (1945), Talley Beatty (filmed in
slow motion) lifts his leg in one room and (through a cut in action), deposits it in another. Further, reminiscent of moments from the diving
sequence in Leni Riefenstahl's *Olympia* (1938), Deren edits together
several moments of his leap—stretching and extending his balletic trajectory. A similar strategy is employed in *Meditation on Violence*, which
depicts a Chinese martial-arts routine. At one moment the athlete jumps
up within a room, and in another shot, he lands outside.

Beyond representing tricks of montage, these sequences have allegorical overtones. For Deren's mythic/ritualistic perspective on the universe leads her to question the finite categories that we usually accept:
the distinction between nature and culture (the ocean/the cocktail party)

and the difference between inside and out (the beach/the reception hall). Finally, the distended jump of her dancer constitutes a "leap of faith," by which the camera reveals to us a temporality that we, generally, ignore.

A Spiritualist Photographer

The world is full of strangers bearing faces I cannot place. —*Maya Deren*[29]

Both Deren and Méliès were "spiritualist" photographers in the sense that they were fascinated by metamorphoses of identity facilitated by the intervention of cinema. In fact, the early trick films were called "transformation" views—a term that stressed the fluid, evolving nature of the magical world they presented. In *A Spiritualist Photographer* (1903), Méliès transmutes a female model into a life-sized poster (much as the face of Hammid in *Meshes* becomes a flat photographic surface). In *The Cook in Trouble* (1904), a chef chases goblins through his kitchen as they repeatedly change form: from old man to king, to imp, to woman.

While Méliès achieves these effects through classic "stop motion," Deren, in *Ritual*, accomplishes such identity transformations through editing. In one shot, dancer Rita Christiani begins to execute a turn, which is "completed" by Deren in another. Thus, the two women are "merged" through a perfectly matched cut. While in *Extraordinary Illusions*, Méliès transforms a mannequin into a living female through a "substitution trick," in *Ritual*, Deren shifts from a mannequin-likeness of herself (in one shot) to her living being (in another).

Aside from utilizing an opposing technique, Méliès's transformations are produced in a different tone. The changes of persona that confront the "cook in trouble" are humorous ones that keep him guessing just whom he will next see. In *A Spiritualist Photographer*, it is a self-reflexive joke (live person turned into image) that fuels the illusory trope. In all cases, Méliès wants his transformations to be sensational: his preferred term for the cinematic effect was *fantastic view*.[30]

In Deren's films, it is a sense of mystery that informs such flux, be it the eccentric dream logic of *Meshes* or the mythic alchemy of *Ritual*. Furthermore, when her figures fluidly transmute into other beings (in a manner opposed to Méliès's shocking substitution cuts), what is communicated is a sense of characters existing without boundary or individuality—a stance consonant with a mythic worldview. As Deren once wrote:

> [T]he ritualistic form treats the human being not as the source
> of the dramatic action, but as a somewhat depersonalized element
> in a dramatic whole. The intent of such a depersonalization is not
> the destruction of the individual; on the contrary, it enlarges him
> beyond the personal dimension and frees him from the specializa-
> tions and confines of personality.[31]

While in Méliès's world each individual "should" remain discrete (and hence a joke arises when he or she does not), in Deren's world the blending of personae is the norm.

The Magic Lantern

Myth is the facts of the mind made manifest in a fiction of matter. **–Maya Deren**[32]

Clearly, while both Deren and Méliès were consumed with the magical potential of cinema, their films employ "trickery" for very different ends.

Méliès was part of the commercial enterprise of his time. Having started on the musical-hall circuit, he moved into film—choosing it as an updated and more promising mass-entertainment outlet. The purpose of Méliès's cinema was largely recreational—to offer people a whimsical attraction as relief from the strains of everyday life. His goal was to "provide a veritable pleasure"—to fill the viewer with amazement at the astounding conceits the camera could generate.[33] Fittingly, Méliès's trick films were, primarily, *comedies.* When the magician produced ten ladies from an umbrella, made a phantom appear or disappear, or animated a series of decapitated heads, the audience was to find these acts not only fabulous but *funny.* It is no accident, then, that certain Méliès films (like *The Magic Lantern* [1903]) employed the figures of Harlequin and Pierrot—remnants of the ancient slapstick tradition of commedia dell'arte. In reviving these clowns for a new medium, Méliès surely "tipped his hand."

Clearly, Deren's goals were other. She set her work in opposition to the popular cinema (working as an enlightened "amateur"). Furthermore, she felt that "the more casually circus-like [film] is, the more it fills the role of an . . . accessible divertissement"—a function she denigrated.[34] Rather than merely constituting a means of amusement, magic, for her, had momentous implications.

First, it could transport people to a rare and alternate reality—one normally hidden from view. As she notes: "In the dimension of the real [the magician/artist] creates the manifestations of the apparently non-real which is always astonishing to those who do not admit of the existence of laws apart from the limits of their own intelligence."[35] Here Deren assumes an elitist stance: she is one of the initiated who can make spirits known to those who remain in the dark.

Second, magic could link people to ritual and myth—occult forms that also fascinated Deren. Margaret Warwick refers to a "mythological sense" in Deren's work.[36] P. Adams Sitney likens the three women in *Ritual in Transfigured Time* (played by Deren, Christiani, and Anaïs Nin) to the three Graces—personifications of beauty, charm, and elegance.[37] Deke Dussinberre (who speaks of the filmmaker's "recourse to myth") compares them to the legendary Fates or Furies.[38] Here Deren's attraction to ancient religion meets her invocation of "ancient" cinema—both discourses that serve as refreshing antidotes to modern life.

Both Sitney's mention of the Graces and Dussinberre's reference to the Fates have interesting implications from a feminist perspective as well. The Graces were female beings associated with the arts—similar to the Muses. Moreover, the Fates, who spun, measured, and cut the web of life (as Deren wrote, shot, and edited a film) were so powerful that they rivaled Zeus.

Ironically, the clearest indication of Deren's interest in myth and ritual came in her brief foray into documentary work. In 1946 she won a grant from the Guggenheim Foundation to make a film about Haitian Voudoun. She spent some eight months there, shooting and writing—returning again on numerous occasions.[39] Her book *Divine Horsemen: The Living Gods of Haiti* (with a foreword by scholar Joseph Campbell) was published in 1953. While Deren never completed her Haitian film (shot between 1947 and 1951), after her death, Cherel Ito compiled, organized, and edited the footage, then released a movie under the same title as the book.

According to Campbell, Deren was not limited by an "academic" interest in the subject. As he notes, she

> performed the feat of delineating the Haitian cult of Voudoun,
> not anthropologically—as a "relic of primeval ignorance and archaic
> speculation" . . . but as an experienced and comprehended initiation
> into the mysteries of man's harmony within himself and with the
> cosmic process.[40]

While for Méliès myth provided merely a set of recognizable characters and narratives to serve as colorful backdrop for his magical skits (as in *Jupiter's Thunderbolt* [1903]), for Deren, it furnished a means of conjuring a precious but elusive reality. Hence, the film version of *Divine Horseman* introduces us (through voice-over narration) to a series of Haitian gods and explains, quite respectfully, their diverse powers. Significantly (given Deren's status as a female filmmaker), one of the primary figures in the system is the goddess Ezili, who has "exclusive title to [the] capacity to conceive beyond reality." Hence, she is the "divinity of dream" and the "muse of beauty."

Clearly, Deren was also interested in altered states of human consciousness. Thus, she saw myth as "the facts of the mind made manifest." In creating a sense of ritual in her work, she was perhaps intrigued by inducing heightened mental states in her viewer, just as the rites of Voudoun did in its practitioners. Thus, by analogy, she is a "Divine Filmmaker" (like the "Divine Horseman" who "mounts" and "rides" the Voudoun celebrant during his trance).

From this perspective, the illusory world of *Meshes* seems not only one of nightmarish delusion but of spiritual possession whereby the protagonist confronts (in the mirror-faced specter) an apparition of Death (just as Ingmar Bergman, another magic enthusiast, later had his protagonist confront a ghoulish chess master in *The Seventh Seal* [1956]). Interestingly, given *Meshes*'s relentless focus on domestic space, Deren once noted that "to enter a new myth is . . . to enter, in one's mind, *the room which is both tomb and womb.*"[41] No better description exists of the Hollywood bungalow in which *Meshes* transpires—a space both quotidian and extraordinary. Hence, for Deren, film trickery allows access to a realm normally hidden from the spectator. Her magic was proposed not for the filmgoer's diversion but to help the viewer "meditate upon the common human experience which is the origin of the human effort to comprehend the human condition."[42]

Furthermore, while Deren was interested in cinematic special effects (like slow motion, negative printing, and reverse motion) and employed them in several works—unlike Méliès, she saw these devices as potentially destructive of the human creative role. As she remarks: "In such cases, the camera *itself* has been conceived of as the artist"—a fact that subverts the personal touch.[43]

Deren's sense of cinematic wonder was also tied to a bolder notion of editing than that of Méliès —whose stop-motion and substitution tricks were accomplished by *masked* cuts. As Deren comments: "In film, the image can and should be only the beginning."[44] Montage must, then, be employed to fashion "the sequential relationship which gives . . . new meanings to the images."[45] Editing, however, must be rendered without subverting the documentary weight of the image, "without distorting [its] aspect, diminishing [its] reality and authority."[46] Hence, for Deren, cinema is a medium based on the combination of "discovery and . . . invention."[47] This balance of "fact" and "fiction" also informs her sense of the mystical. Thus, what intrigues her is the "manifestation of the unknown

in the known."[48] For Deren, the magician must convince the uninitiated
of the existence of an alternate universe through the concrete details of
conventional reality rather than through fanciful themes. Here she describes the magician's role in a manner reminiscent of a sequence in *At
Land* in which she crawls across the table:

> Only the magician who presents me with a banquet table convinces
> me when I am hungry; I must touch the plate and eat the grape. He
> who merely speaks of the feasts he has had in private, I take for a
> blackguard, a liar.[49]

As ritual and magic issue from the real world, so too must the photographic image.

For Melies, the magic of cinema is based on making discontinuous
shots appear continuous; for Deren, the mysteries of film often take place
across a visible, if paradoxical, cut (like the one that connects a dancer
lifting his leg in one space and lowering it in another). As she notes:

> [S]uppose that the fact that a camera can stop, wait indefinitely, and
> then start again, was used, not as a substitute for the intermissions
> during which the stage scenery is shifted, but as a technique for the
> metamorphosis . . . in spatial dimension?[50]

Clearly, here she confronts Méliès's quintessential strategy and declares
it lacking.

Given Deren's interest in Voudoun, we might also think of the cinematic cut as a kind of formal "crossroads"—a figure central to Haitian
ritual discourse. In Voudoun, the crossroad represents an intersection of
two worlds—precisely the same power Deren harnessed through the
filmic cut.

Beyond transformation, Deren saw profound implications in the
process of animation—both in relation to its broad cinematic application (making still images move) and in its status as a specific technique.
Significantly, in *At Land*, as some women play chess on the beach, the
game pieces begin to move on their own. For Deren, animation has a

potent mystical resonance: "If [something] can move, it lives. This most primitive, this most instinctive of all gestures: to make it move to make it live. So I had always been doing with my camera . . . nudging an ever-increasing area of the world, making it move, animating it, making it live."[51]

Thus, Deren's "magic" is not in the service of Mélièsian distraction but of illumination—working to reveal the spatiotemporal "secrets" of the world. As she asserts: "Whatever the instrument, the artist [has] sought to re-create the abstract, invisible forces and relationships of the cosmos, in the intimate, immediate forms of his art." Hence, for Deren the cinema is an instrument of "profound importance."[52]

The difference between magic as revelation and magic as entertainment is made clear in the film version of *Divine Horsemen*. The first half of the work focuses on Voudoun rites and rituals as practiced in a quotidian context by Haitian villagers. The film ends, however, with a huge costumed parade (much like Mardi Gras) in Port-au-Prince. As we watch a host of dancers and musicians perform, the narrator informs us that they are talented professionals whose routines are not produced by the spell of "possession." Clearly, Deren's film and dance work seeks to walk the line between the poles—drawing on mysticism and aesthetics, inspiration and craft, in the creation of her art.

Afterword: Double Exposure

When I undertook cinema . . . it was not like discovering a new medium so much as coming home into a world whose vocabulary, syntax, grammar, was my mother tongue; *which I understood, and thought in, but, like a mute, had never spoken.* **–Maya Deren**[53]

This essay has put into stereoscopic view the work of Deren and Méliès. On one level, this perspective has sought to disclose a crucial link between modernist and primitive filmmakers, one neglected elsewhere in the history of cinema. Thus, when Deren admits to experiencing a certain "déjà vu" in picking up the camera, it is, perhaps, the legacy of those like Georges Méliès that makes her feel that she is "coming home" to the medium, already able to speak its "mother tongue."

Though this essay has drawn numerous parallels between the two artists, it has also aspired to highlight distinctions. While the work of Méliès tries joyfully to fool us into believing in the validity of a world that we know to be false, Deren's oeuvre seeks earnestly to convince us that an alternate universe is "true." Hence, for Deren, Méliès's beloved camera "tricks" are not mere technological stunts but sacred devices for linking the "real" to the "unreal." Significantly, in describing, rather mystically, the conjunction of the known and unknown (which she felt we experienced, in cinema, as an uncanny "recognition"), Deren drew on a metaphor straight out of Méliès's toolbox of special effects. She notes: "As we watch a film, the continuous act of recognition in which we are involved is like a strip of memory unrolling beneath the images of the film itself, to form the invisible underlayer of an explicit *double exposure.*"[54]

Notes

Thanks to Jessica Nassau for bibliographic help and to Bill Nichols for editorial suggestions.

Epigraphs: Maya Deren, quoted in VèVè A. Clark, Millicent Hodson, and Catrina Neiman, *The Legend of Maya Deren: A Documentary Biography and Collected Works,* vol. 1, pt. 1, *Signatures* (New York: Anthology Film Archives and Film Culture, 1984), 310 (my italics). Georges Méliès, "Cinematographic Views," in Richard Abel, ed. *French Film Theory and Criticism: History/Anthology, 1907–1939,* vol. 1 (Princeton: Princeton University Press, 1988), p. 45, my italics.

1. P. Adams Sitney, *Visionary Film: The American Avant-Garde* (New York: Oxford University Press, 1974).

2. Annette Kuhn, *"Meshes of the Afternoon," Monthly Film Bulletin* 55 (June 1988): 186.

3. Michael O'Pray, "A Study in Choreography for Camera," *Monthly Film Bulletin* 55 (July 1988): 218.

4. Clark et al., *Legend,* pt. 1, p. 1.

5. Deren, quoted in Clark et al., *Legend,* pt. 1, p. 70.

6. Deren, quoted in Clark et al., *Legend,* pt. 2, p. 72.

7. Deren, quoted in Clark et al., *Legend,* pt. 1, p. 370.

8. Deren, quoted in Clark et al., *Legend*, pt. 2, *Chambers*, p. 308.

9. Teiji Ito, quoted in Clark et al., *Legend*, pt. 2, p. 132.

10. Anne Clark, quoted in Clark et al., *Legend*, pt. 2, p. 132.

11. Parker Tyler, quoted in Clark et al., *Legend*, pt. 2, p. 308.

12. Maria Pramaggiore, "Performance and Persona in the U.S. Avant-Garde: The Case of Maya Deren," *Cinema Journal* 36, no. 2 (Winter 1997): 17.

13. Pramaggiore, "Performance and Persona," 17.

14. Ephraim Katz, *The Film Encyclopedia*, 3d. ed. (New York: Harper Collins, 1998), p. 360.

15. Abel, *Cine Goes to Town*, p. 63.

16. Abel, *Cine Goes to Town*, p. 63

17. Deren, quoted in Clark et al., *Legend*, pt. 2, pp. 142–43.

18. Maya Deren, "I Cannot Place the Face," quoted in Clark et al., *Legend*, pt. 2, p. 369.

19. Though Méliès is the best-known filmmaker within the trick film genre, others made similar movies (for example, *Dream of a Rarebit Fiend* [1906] by Edwin Porter).

20. Stanley Kubrick, quoted in Vivian Shochack, *Screening Space: The American Science Fiction Film* (New York: Ungar, 1991). p. 57.

21. Abel, *Cine Goes to Town*, p. 72.

22. Deren, quoted in Clark et al., *Legend*, pt. 2, p. 142.

23. Méliès, "Cinematographic Views," p. 44.

24. Abel, *Cine Goes to Town*, p. 62.

25. Deren quoted in Clark et al., *Legend*, pt. 1, p. 369.

26. V. I. Pudovkin, quoted in Richard Dyer MacCann, *Film: A Montage of Theories* (New York: Dutton, 1966), p. 31.

27. Méliès, "Cinematographic Views," p. 38.

28. Margaret Warwick, "*At Land*," *Monthly Film Bulletin* 55 (June 1988): 185.

29. Maya Deren, "I Cannot Place the Face," quoted in Clark et al., *Legend*, pt. 2, p. 369.

30. Méliès, "Cinematographic Views," p. 38.

31. Maya Deren, *An Anagram of Ideas on Art, Form and Film* (New York: Alicat Book Shop Press, 1946). Reprinted in George Amberg, ed. *The Art of Cinema: Selected Essays* (New York: Arno Press and the *New York Times*, 1972), and in this volume, *Anagram* p. 20.

32. Deren, *Anagram*, p. 21.

33. Méliès, "Cinematographic Views," p. 45.

34. Maya Deren, *Anagram*, p. 44.

35. Deren, quoted in Clark et al., *Legend*, pt. 2, pp. 142–43.

36. Warwick, "*At Land*," p. 186.

37. Sitney, *Visionary Film*, p. 32.

38. Deke Dussinberre, "*Ritual in Transfigured Time*," *Monthly Film Bulletin* 55 (July 1988), p. 217.

39. Maya Deren, *Divine Horsemen: The Living Gods of Haiti* (London and New York: Thames and Hudson, 1953), p. 5.

40. Joseph Campbell, quoted in Deren, *Divine Horsemen*, p. xi.

41. Deren, *Divine Horsemen*, p. 24 (my italics).

42. Deren, *Divine Horsemen*, p. 24.

43. Maya Deren, "Cinematography: The Creative Use of Reality," in Gerald Mast, Marshall Cohen, and Leo Braudy, eds., *Film Theory and Criticism: Introductory Readings*, 4th ed. (New York and Oxford: Oxford University Press, 1992), p. 66 (my italics).

44. Deren, "Cinematography," p. 67.

45. Deren, "Cinematography," p. 67.

46. Deren, "Cinematography," p. 67.

47. Deren, *Anagram*, p. 46.

48. Deren, quoted in Clark et al., *Legend*, pt. 2, p. 142.

49. Deren, quoted in Clark et al., *Legend*, pt. 2, p. 142.

50. Deren, *Anagram*, p. 50.

51. Deren, quoted in Prammagiore, "Performance and Persona," p. 27.

52. Deren, *Anagram*, p. 52.

53. Maya Deren, quoted in Pam Cook, "Chambers and Corridors—Maya Deren," *Monthly Film Bulletin* 55, no. 654 (July 1988): 220 (italics mine).

54. Deren, "Cinematography," p. 63.

25

Moira Sullivan

Maya Deren's Ethnographic
Representation of Ritual and Myth in Haiti

In 1946, Maya Deren received the first Guggenheim Fellowship for creative work in motion pictures. Her application for renewal included a proposal for a "cross-cultural fugue" of Haitian and Balinese ritual and Western children's games linked through montage. Soon after her arrival in
Haiti the following year, she made a significant detour from her original
conception in order to authenticate the rituals she observed and studied.
The result was a skillful synergy of art and ethnography that significantly
altered her filmmaking. The purpose of this essay is to bring aspects of
this work that remain unexplored in film scholarship to light.[1] The intersection of the Haitian project and her filmmaking practice will be examined in a discussion of two major projects: 20,000 feet of 16mm film
she shot during a Haitian Voudoun ceremony and her exposé on the
mythical roots of Voudoun, *Divine Horsemen: The Living Gods of Haiti*
(1953).[2] It is the thesis of this essay that the footage deserves recognition
as ethnographic documentation and belongs in appropriate archives for
historical research. Furthermore, the principles of Haitian Voudoun described in *Divine Horsemen* expanded Deren's vision as a filmmaker and
opened new dimensions for creative work in ethnography.

One year before her first trip to Haiti, Deren wrote *An Anagram of
Ideas on Art, Form and Film* (1946) in which she analyzed the disruption
of consciousness caused by the division of magic, science, religion, and

Figure 25. Maya Deren in Haiti (no date). Courtesy of Tavia Ito.

207

philosophy in the seventeenth century and its effect on art. According to anthropologist Bronislaw Malinowski, the discussion of the relationship between magic or religion, the "sacred," and science, the "profane," was at the apex of modern anthropology.[3] Deren argued that the process of creation for the artist/magician and the scientist was similar: making the *invisible* visible. She discovered this was also true of the priest/priestess of Haitian Voudoun. Embracing this rich, metaphysical vision, Deren worked to combine the elements of ritual, myth, and dance in film and written representation.

The framework essential for a discussion of Deren's interdisciplinary work in art and ethnography is her use of a *conceptual* anagram. This anagram can be visualized as a series of ice floes on an open sea. The traveler can move from one floe to another and keep the journey in motion, but standing on any piece too long will result in isolation. The key exists in linking the pieces to the whole. "The whole is so related to every part," she wrote of the anagram, "that whether one reads horizontally, vertically, diagonally or even in reverse, the logic of the whole is not disrupted but remains intact."[4] Deren cautioned that "modern specialization" discouraged holistic approaches (one might add especially by a woman) that encroached on the provinces of knowledge.

The Use of Ritual in Deren's Films

Deren's early interest in the use of ritual and myth in poetry became a guiding force in her creative work. The French symbolist school and T. S. Eliot were particular key influences. The symbolist effort to *spiritualize* language and Eliot's *mystical method*, which transformed the architecture of modern poetry, influenced both the nature and form of her films. Sir James Frazer's *The Golden Bough*, about the return to basic rituals as a source of creativity, was indispensable to Eliot. "The Waste Land," his notable (and "symbolist," according to Deren) poem, was based on primitive rituals and myths.

Because they embodied the element of a *depersonalized* individual within the dramatic whole, Deren later came to call the form of her films *ritualistic*. She vigorously endeavored to develop a new syntax or vocabulary of filmic images, arguing that the filmmaking of her time was dominated by the narrative, with characters as causal agents, and by the documentary, with its convention of *recording* reality. Instead, she promoted the poetic or *vertical* film characterized by a "downward plunge" of imagery as an alternative to *horizontal* or linear development.[5]

Deren's later concerns centered on "rituals involving minimalization of personal identity."[6] This focus is reflected in films made after her first visit to Haiti. In *Meditation on Violence* (1948), the forward and reverse shots of a Shao-lin boxing ritual represent the principle of eternity. *The Very Eye of Night* (1952, released in 1958), an "astronomical ballet" of the Gemini twins and the Satellites, also conveys the repetition and duration of form characteristic of ritual.

Commencing with *A Study for Choreography for Camera* (1945), all Deren's films use ritualized dance as a primary tool of communication. Dance was an ongoing interest from the early 1940s, when she served as secretary to choreographer Katherine Dunham (see figure 26). Through this association she met several dancers from the West Indies such as Talley Beatty, who was cocreator of *A Study for Choreography for Camera*, and Rita Christiani, who was a protagonist in *Ritual in Transfigured Time* (1945–1946). Lyricist John LaTouche also helped to finance *The Very Eye of Night*.

Dunham conducted field studies in the West Indies in the 1930s and even filmed in 16mm under the supervision of Melville Herskovits at the University of Chicago. Deren's access to this material led her to publish a series of articles about religious possession in dancing.[7] Her initial focus in this early work was on the "personality of the possessed," but later she carefully notes in *Divine Horsemen* how the conception of the individual is obliterated during possession, that is, how it becomes a receptacle that serves as a vehicle for the *loa* (gods). This shift is already evident in *Ritual in Transfigured Time*, in which the individual becomes part of a larger collective consciousness. In a "tribal dance" of social encounter,

Figure 26. Katherine Dunham dance class, New York City (ca. 1953). Photograph by Maya Deren. From the Deren Collection, Boston University, Mugar Library, Special Collections.

a man loses sight of a woman he has just met. When he later finds her, she escapes by plunging into the sea, becoming both "widow" and "bride." Her underwater movement appears in negative images, making these two "selves" conjoined by a reversal of black to white. This sequence symbolized a new dimension in Deren's films.

After *Ritual in Transfigured Time*, Deren expanded her work in negative images. As such, her films of the early 1950s profoundly illustrate the impact of the mythology of Voudoun. In *The Very Eye of Night*, dancers float in planes within black space. Released from horizontal and vertical orbits and gravitational fields, the movement of the dancers and camera becomes "fourth dimensional."[8] For a film workshop that Deren supervised for the Toronto Film Society in Canada in 1951, *Ensemble for Somnambulists*, there are no planes at all, just a void of blackness. "I would like them to become aware of pulse . . . a perspective which begins to live because a figure descends into its depth," she explained of this film.[9] Each "sleep walker" is twinned, journeying to the heavens, the abyss, and inward to the self, a notion that finds correspondence in the ending of *Ritual in Transfigured Time*. "Plunging into the depths" had a particular connotation within Haitian Voudoun; it is reflected in the iconography of these films. The positioning of figures in blackness symbolizes the "abyss," the permanent home of the *loa*, or Haitian gods, located at the bottom of the sea. "If the earth is a sphere," Deren rhetorically states in *Divine Horsemen*, "then the abyss below the earth is also its heavens."[10] Through a series of ordeals, characters in her earlier films move on familiar ground such as dinner parties or beaches. Beginning with *Ritual in Transfigured Time*, the terrain begins to disappear, and figures float in the "abyss." Blackness (negative film) was used by Deren as a metaphor for the process in which the individual tries to find his or her divinity, a principle within Voudoun. *Ensemble for Somnambulists* illustrates how the "blackness of night erases the horizontal plane of the earth's surface," where sleepwalkers begin their journey.[11]

Deren claimed that the artist crosses the threshold separating him from the void, "where he creates a plane of earth where his foot has been."[12]

Her later films especially represent this distinction. References in film scholarship to the *trance* motif in her work scratch the surface of a larger truth that emerged during Deren's study of Voudoun.[13] The "somnambulists" or "sleep walkers" of her films had a mythical anchor that went beyond surface appearances. As in Voudoun, theirs was a journey to the *crossroads* or point of access to the world of cosmic memory. At this junction, a vertical plane "plunges" into the "world of the invisible," while a horizontal plane remains fixed in the mortal, "visible world."[14] For Deren, diving into the abyss was a way of symbolizing the processes involved in creativity.

The Haitian Footage

In addition to twenty thousand feet of film, Deren's extensive documentation of Voudoun ceremony in Haiti included one thousand stills (see figure 27) and fifty hours of audio recordings. What is notable in the footage is that retakes are extremely rare. On the back of her Bolex she taped the commands *Speed Stop Focus Finder Motor.* These prompts allowed her to safeguard shots that could never be redone. Other techniques she perfected that served her well in Haiti were *shoot to cut*, which reduced the necessity of editing, and *plan by eye*—the reliance on a visual shorthand of the profilmic event.[15]

According to Deren, the precedents for filming Voudoun rituals in Haiti were rare in the late 1940s and early 1950s, since in those instances when it was permitted, ceremonies were interrupted by comments or gestures that destroyed their solemnity. Because animal sacrifices were forbidden, photography was also discouraged. Although it was unusual for an outsider to be permitted into ceremonies, Deren received permission from the *houngan* (priest) Isnard of a *hounfor* (temple) outside Port-au-Prince. She described the major portion of the initial 5,400-foot footage shot in 1947 as part of an eight-day *ceremony caille*—a benediction to the specific *loa*, or god of the *hounfor*. Because the basic form of the ceremonies was similar, Deren was able to capture aspects from different perspectives,

Figure 27. Ethnographic documentation of a Haitian Voudoun "king" and other *serviteurs* from a *Ra-ra* Festival, Haiti (ca. 1954). Photograph by Maya Deren. From the Deren Collection, Department of Special Collections, Boston University.

including cornmeal drawings of deity, or *vevers*, chicken and goat sacrifices offered to the four directions, and other ceremonial preparations. There are numerous possessions in a variety of forms in which the individual is dressed either in the accoutrements of deity or in ordinary attire. In addition, drumming, singing, and forms of prayer are filmed. Deren admitted her difficulties in structuring this material, a process that sheds light on the problems of editing ritual enactments in ethnographic filmmaking.

> In the second batch of my material [1949], I concentrated on various dance and ritual movements, many of which were photographed in slow motion, with the action of the body clearly delineated . . . whenever I tried to "stop" a moment, to isolate

it from its context, it projected an impression which was not at
all what the Haitians meant. In fact it often did not even look like
dance—at least dance in the sense in which we think of it. And it
became clear to me that certain fundamentals governing ritual had
to be established before any specific statements about Haitian dance
could be made to make sense . . . dance is only part of the ritual and
its form is governed by the larger pattern, rather than being contained in itself. This larger "logic" is known, rather than constantly
"visible," and for this reason the dance may seem itself formless and
anarchic.[16]

Deren wrote of her difficulties in editing her material: "sitting over the
viewer, the splicer,—so many nights—pushing together shots which would
not marry," calling "the creative act fundamentally unreasonable and irrational."[17] It is for this reason that although the Haitian footage remained
largely unedited, it should be seen as *complete* in accordance with the aims
Deren insisted were crucial to an understanding of Voudoun.

Before visiting Haiti, she made negotiations with several production
companies who wanted documentaries, projects that for various reasons
were canceled. Borrowing editing facilities whenever possible, Deren
tried to find commercial and educational forms for her material without
success, a tremendous frustration in her filmmaking career. In a second
application for renewal of the Guggenheim Fellowship, she submitted
four categories from the footage for consideration, pointing out that the
Library of Congress was interested in rerecording portions of her audio
recordings to broadcast on WNYC radio in New York.[18] Deren argued
that her footage was an important contribution to both filmmaking and
ethnography.

This material has actually two separate values. Until I sat down and
carefully went through it to make an outline catalog of the 5,400
feet, I had failed to realize that quite independent of its aesthetic
value in relation to my film, it had enormous historical and anthropological value as well. It seems that my ability to establish unusually

sympathetic relations with the Haitian country people resulted in the recording of ritual material which had not previously been put on motion-picture film.[19]

Failing to receive renewed funding, Deren tried to elicit interest from anthropological sources at universities. Despite support from Margaret Mead, Gregory Bateson, and Melville Herskovits, the footage was rejected because she had no standing in the field. Deren disagreed with the criteria excluding her work: "In effect, sensitivity to form provides the artist with a vast area of clues and data that might elude the professional anthropologist whose training emphasizes . . . 'scientific detachment.'"[20] This observation reflects her radical methodology in ethnographic fieldwork. Several references are made in *Divine Horsemen* to the ineffective methods of other studies, including those of Herskovits. As Deren noted, "normal sensitivity and responsiveness to formal nuance and subtlety" made the scientific anthropologist "dependent upon the vagaries of informants' memory, intelligence and articulations."[21] She argued that even in Western culture verbal discourse proves unreliable; it would not suffice in Haiti "in a language which is largely imagistic and in reference to a religion which is completely couched in ritualist action."[22] Criticizing the dualism of anthropology, she stated that African cultures are "predicated on the notion that truth can be apprehended only when every cell of brain and body—the totality of a human being—is engaged in that pursuit."[23]

The Use of Choreocinema in the Haitian Footage

Central to a discussion of the Haitian footage is Deren's photography of ritual dance. In the avant-garde film of the 1940s and 1950s, her choreography of dance in film was groundbreaking. *New York Times* dance critic John Martin called it *choreocinema*, and it inspired artists such as Gene Kelly, who consulted her about her work.[24] Compared to dance films that were literally and spatially confined, Deren's techniques were revolutionary. Arthur Knight explained her impact in a special issue of a dance journal dedicated to "cine-dance."

> What Maya Deren did, and very consciously in *Ritual in Trans-figured Time, Meshes of the Afternoon,* and particularly *Choreography for Camera* was, in her own words, to "emancipate the camera from the theatrical tradition in general, and especially in terms of spatial treatment, began to think of giving the dancer the world as a stage." Because the camera can go out into that world—indeed, is perhaps a bit more at home when not confined to a stage—she photographed much of her material in the open air, assembling the fragments into a coherent and frequently compelling entity by the logic of the movements within the frame.[25]

Deren's success in choreocinema lay in the photography and editing of motion: "the filmmaker can leave dancers out altogether and yet follow the principles of dancing—which is the arrangement of movement. . . . My choreographies for camera are not dances recorded by the camera; they are dances choreographed for and performed by the camera and by human beings together."[26] Such a perception was based on Deren's belief that the task of the filmmaker was similar to that of a choreographer.

> The dance choreographer works within an essentially stable environment. Once the stage has been set, he is concerned with the arrangement of human figures on it, with their movements within that set location. The film-maker, however, arranges whatever he has in his frame—including the space, the trees, the animate and even the inanimate objects.[27]

In Haiti, she noted that Western culture had no "moral or principled dance" in reverence to deity. Secular dance, which imparted a particular "ethos" to the dancer, she argued, contrasted sharply from the *principled* dance she observed, "whose very *raison d'être* is the intent to affect the participant, the means by which the physical act creates a psychic state."[28]

The profound theorem of the Haitian footage is the arrangement of *principled* dance movement (see figure 28). The purpose was not simply to "record" rituals but to capture the mobile body involved in dancing, gesture, drumming, and other ceremonial motion and to blend this into a cohesive whole through panning and change of focal lengths. This unique perspective makes the footage of interest both to film scholars and to those in the field of ethnographic filmmaking. Deren's *planned-by-eye* footage allowed for movement of the human body or objects into the path of the camera. Incorporated into the overall motion, the individual is "depersonalized" and embraced by the collective, which is made evident by the almost exclusive use of medium or long shots. Typically, long shots provide the ceremonial framework followed by medium shots of the *serviteur* or devotees.

Deren argued that in Voudoun it was impossible to separate dance from its cosmology. Ritual forms, she explained, distinguish themselves from "secular movements" by "ulterior references" in which even a movement as simple as offering *libations*, the pouring of liquids on sacred ground, was done to please the gods. The rituals thus served the *loa* in an act of complete ceremony, with none of the increasing sense of physical exertion that characterized Western dance performances. An obvious intention of the footage was to provide a system of documentation that integrated mythical symbols through mobility. Deren realized that film was an incomplete state for the representation of *principled* states, and, she insisted, at best the ethnographic filmmaker could present a faithful representation of the ceremonies.

"Art" and Ethnographic Filmmaking

To situate the Haitian footage within the context of ethnographic filmmaking in the 1950s, it is essential to discuss the work of Gregory Bateson and Margaret Mead, whom Deren consulted before going to Haiti.[29] Mead and Bateson had achieved recognition for their arrangement into two impressive monographs of 25,000 photographs that Bateson shot in

Figure 28. Film still from Maya Deren's Haitian footage. The *Yanvalou dos bas* movement is executed by two apprentice priests in a Voudoun ritual (1947). Photograph by Maya Deren. From the Deren Collection, Department of Special Collections, Boston University.

the 1930s documenting Balinese behavior.[30] Ethnographic filmmaker David MacDougall argues that "representing the Balinese" ethos was more a case of arrangement in accordance with the gaze of the two anthropologists than of "objective" recording in the field.[31] Historically, the 22,000 feet of film Bateson shot in 1936 of Balinese behavior and ritual were considered less important than his still photography. Out of the footage, six films were later assembled and released in 1951 under the sole supervision of Mead. Bateson regarded the Balinese footage separately from their subsequent written findings; because Mead's intrusive voice-over was central to the final film versions, they should be separated from Bateson's original footage.

Claiming that accessibility was the principal purpose of photographic documents in ethnography, Mead thought film enhanced the disseminations of her fieldwork and sought to have it accepted within the field. Film was thereby introduced to American ethnography with the Balinese project in the mid-1930s, although the field did not begin to flourish until the 1950s.[32] Already in 1947 Maya Deren was meticulously studying Bateson's original footage, recognizing its value to both filmmaking and ethnography. Moreover, the footage gave her invaluable clues to how she should proceed with her film project in Haiti. In this respect, her work served as an advance in the ethnographic documentation of rituals: she learned from the limitations of Bateson's original footage, but she also avoided the didacticism of Mead's finished films.

The technical restrictions of the 1930s required a stationary tripod camera. Shots abruptly end without providing adequate context, notably in footage assembled for *Trance and Dance in Bali*, which was of particular interest to Deren. None of the choreography of the camera valued by Deren was possible. In light of her later filmmaking in Haiti, this is the strongest argument that can be waged against Bateson's footage. Of his cinematography, he remarked, "We had cameras on tripods just grinding."[33] Mead opposed the creative use of the film camera and defended the Balinese material, claiming that "it was important to hold the camera long enough to get a sequence of behavior."[34] She added that no one since Bateson had been as successful at taking stills and film at the same time and with the same focal length. Although restricted to long takes, he later admitted that a long sequence of behavior, in his vocabulary, lasted only twenty seconds.

It seems clear that Mead's attitude about artists working in ethnography in part stems from firsthand knowledge of Deren's work. She argued that her own approach allowed for subsequent study in which even without a thesis, one could review background details of a filmed sequence and apply findings from field studies. Afterward, Mead endorsed Deren's filmed footage but not her book, *Divine Horsemen*, citing its methodology as problematic. In truth, she was not only at odds with Deren but also with Bateson on this account: she insisted on a positivist approach to anthropology in both written and photographic records, a position she maintained throughout her career. This view was reinforced in a paper she presented in 1975 at the International Conference in Visual Anthropology, five years before her death.

> We do not demand that a field ethnologist write with the style of a novelist or a poet, although we do indeed accord disproportionate attention to those who do. It is equally inappropriate to demand that filmed behavior have the earmarks of a work of art. We can be grateful when it does, and we can cherish those rare combinations of artistic ability and scientific fidelity that have given us great ethnographic films. But I believe that we have absolutely no right to waste our breath and our resources demanding them.[35]

Several problems can be noted in Mead's assembled films. Because they were intended to be supplementary to written ethnography, conclusions that were reached after field studies were not represented. Mead's use of Bateson's footage was conceived as a preliminary step to the final analysis, yet after editing, the imagery seems inconsistent with the claims of her voice-over. Because alteration of film speed is considered problematic in ethnographic filmmaking, the faster film speed used by Bateson was claimed to distort the Balinese way of life.[36] The anthropologists confirmed that the camera was not especially noticeable to the Balinese because of their indifference to the Western notion of the stage; however, contradictions are evident in sequences in which people seemed to be looking for direction from the filmmakers.

In comparison, Deren's Haitian footage is an oppositional discourse. *Divine Horsemen* was a project conceived separately from the film, making no claim that it should serve as a supplement or guide to the footage. The [*hounfor* (temple) Deren visited esteemed her filmmaking] as a form of service to the *loa* and considered it an intrinsic part of the rituals. She and her film camera were considered a "natural part of the behavioral space," a virtually unprecedented relationship for camera and event.[37] Parts of Voudoun ceremony in the Haitian footage were specifically shot in slow motion and defended as an essential source of illumination for the delineation of the mobile body in principled states. Moreover, in response to the altering of film speed, Deren insisted that the ontological nature of film based on optical illusion could never render total authenticity to movement, a position she maintained as a former student of Kurt Koffka, one of the three founders of Gestalt psychology, which advanced the phi phenomenon as an explanation of apparent motion.

The strip of film consists of a series of exposures or snapshots taken at very short intervals so that they record closely successive stages of the movement. But no matter how short the interval between exposures, each exposure is fixed and does not itself contain the movement. To recreate the original movement, we must actually restore the time element to the film: when we project these fixed frames in succession, the eye bridges over from still to still, and we have the optical illusion of movement.[38]

A decision made later to add only ceremonial music to the appropriate sequences of footage was an effort to match image with location sound. A 1977 compilation documentary made by Teiji and Cherel Ito, which they made to finish Deren's work, opens up the footage to the contradictions of image and text that Deren tried to avoid. Ironically, her unaltered footage is relatively unknown, whereas the Itos's work has received wider public access.[39]

The only example of how Deren would have edited her material (which does not, however, include the sound she would have used) can be found in a short film entitled *CBS Odyssey*, which consists of material that she assembled for a two-minute television clip. In the introductory sequence, female *voyageurs* make their way to the market followed by sections of the *ceremonie caille* with ritual dancing, concluded by a ceremony to the *loa* of the sea, "Agwé." In notes to CBS, she cautioned technicians to save even the smallest pieces of her work print, intended for "my own use for the editing of my own film on Haiti."[40]

Divine Horsemen: A Study of Haitian Myth and Ritual

Despite exhausting efforts to have the Haitian footage recognized, the first public forum for Deren's field studies on Haitian Voudoun was a monograph. Joseph Campbell approached her to record her field observations for inclusion in his *Myth and Man* series. She agreed to the project, recognizing that her background as a filmmaker and artist allowed her to "illuminate areas of Voudoun mythology with which the standard anthropological procedure had not concerned itself."[41] *Divine Horsemen* consisted of seven chapters: the origin of Haitian myth, the transplantation of the religion to the "New World," the characteristics of deity, the priests and devotees, the rites, the role of drumming and dancing, and a chapter on Deren's own possession, which will be discussed later.

Sequences of the footage are identifiable in the monograph, such as, for example, "the small groups of *voyageurs*, making their way market/ward from the distant mountains."[42] With tactile precision, Deren describes the language used by these women: "the onomatopoetic rhythms and cadenced phrasing of Creole, which, being an unwritten language, lives primarily as a sound to be understood rather than a symbol of meaning."[43]

Divine Horsemen provides an important background to the ritual enactment of myth in Voudoun. As Deren points out in her introduction: "myth is the voyage of exploration in this metaphysical space."[44] Campbell's cross-cultural studies and Jungian conceptions served as foundations for this approach. References are also made to the kabbalistic elements of Voudoun. An essay by Odette Mennesson Rigaud is included in an appendix on sacred marriages between divinity and devotee in Voudoun ritual.

In his introduction to *The Anger of Achilles*, Robert Graves cites how the *mythology* of androgyny discussed in *Divine Horsemen* was inspirational to his study of Greek myth, noting how West African religions embraced bisexuality differently from how the Greeks did.[45] In the Haitian footage, sequences show both cross-dressing and cross-gender possession, such as a woman in a man's suit dancing with Lady Ghéde, the male *loa* of death. In editorial discussions with Campbell, Deren said "the term 'massissi' refers to homosexual *houngan*s, who are distinguished by the words *madodo* . . . the male role in such a relationship, and *madoda* for the female role."[46] Deren provided some mythical background to these designations within African belief systems; however, it was omitted from the monograph by Campbell, who considered the "general" material sufficiently difficult without it. Because anthropologists have historically been criticized for failing to provide data and background on gay and lesbian culture, Deren's research is important despite Campbell's neglect.[47]

Deren's treatment of the mythical properties of Haitian Voudoun was an example of what Gregory Bateson called the "artistic approach" to ethnography. In an early study on the Iamatul Indians in New Guinea, Bateson claimed that a culture could be studied by scientific or artistic techniques. Specific to the artistic approach was an ability to unconsciously grasp meaning through iconic or nonverbal communication.[48] He furthermore claimed that analytic and cognitive studies of culture were incomplete without an "emotional tone or ethos," something that Deren's study more than adequately provided.[49]

In the portion of chapter 6 entitled "The Collective as Creative Artist," Deren describes something that is evident from her footage: there are no individual artists in Haitian Voudoun; the designation of "genius" applied to the collective as a whole.[50] This fact was especially

Figure 29. Sea ceremony for Agwé (untitled, no date). Photographed by Maya Deren. Courtesy of Tavia Ito.

notable in ceremonies involving ritual dance. In another section of chapter 6, "Dance the Meditation of the Body," she describes the collective interaction of the dancer and drummer in which the beats of the drum create a certain tension in the dancer. The repetitive, meditative movements could be interrupted by a break in the drumbeat, creating long, exaggerated movements that often precede the arrival of the *loa*. Deren's film *Meditation on Violence*, made after her first visit to Haiti, reveals how the study of Voudoun ritual dancing affected her cinematography. In this film, music and cinematography illustrate the ritual momentum of Chinese boxing. The slow, meditative movements of what is called "interior boxing," the Wu Tang, are accompanied by the music of a solo flute. Haitian drums accompany the Shaolin and Sword Shao-lin, in which the movements become more aggressive. The actual "break" from the Wu Tang to the Shaolin is demonstrated with rapid cuts and jumps from long to close-up shots, which are reversed, full circle, to the meditative Wu Tang.

Anthropologists Melville Herskovits and Harold Courlander acknowledged the importance of *Divine Horsemen*, and in contemporary studies it is often cited as an authoritative voice, most recently in conjunction with the exhibition *Sacred Arts of Vodou* at the Musuem of Natural History and U.C.L.A.'s Fowler Museum. Here Deren's methodology is especially praised because "Vodou has resisted all orthodoxies, never mistaking surface representations for inner realities."[51]

After its publication, Deren saw the value of providing information about Haitian Voudoun on radio and television.[52] She forwarded an original thesis stating that rituals were capable of demonstrating abstract principles for educational purposes and were a "primitive" version of audiovisual instructional aids conveying scientific principles and theories. When given the opportunity, she actively promoted ritual as a form of communication in Western culture. Spots on television and radio also provided Deren with opportunities to discuss her film footage and her book *Divine Horsemen* and to air her wire recordings on ritual and secular music. Furthermore, they served as a platform to address the religion of Voudoun: its pantheon and "syncretism" of Catholic and African icons, and its transplantation and development in Haiti.[53]

Experience, Deren insisted, was essential to the investigation of myth. Her participatory observation of the rituals of Haitian Voudoun was well documented in *Divine Horsemen*. In editorial discussions, she insisted that a strong foundation be built to facilitate an understanding of one of the highest forms of *connaissance*, or knowledge, within Voudoun known as *possession*. The final chapter, called "The White Darkness," was a narrative of Deren's own experience with possession, which she cautioned should not be seen as an individual experience. "It is one of the most absolute statements of impersonality I know," she expressed to Campbell.[54] Contemporary readings confirm that the decision to include the account was problematic. In *Haiti, History, and the Gods*, Joan Dayan called it an "idealizing, impressionistic and gothic passage":

> I want, for a moment, to turn to Maya Deren's description of possession in "The White Darkness" in *Divine Horsemen*. "Never have I seen the face of such anguish, ordeal and blind terror as at the moment when the loa comes." Deren ends the chapter and the book by describing her own possession by Ezili, a dazzling journey under the waters. Hers is a glorious surrender, a loss that she can only remember in images of the rolling sea, fog, light, "a white darkness, its whiteness a glory and its darkness, a terror."[55]

An alternative reading comes from *Urban Voodoo* by Black and Hyatt, who suggest that Deren must have been embarrassed writing about her possession since she "hid" it in the appendix.[56] In conversations with Campbell, Deren stressed that one was afraid of possession but in terms foreign to a Western sense of fear. She argued that there was no personal feeling involved; the process was highly structured. The personality was, therefore, blocked out by the experience. This view is evident in the account in which she describes events before and after her possession. She reported that it was rare for a non-Haitian to become possessed, and that it was understood by priests and *serviteur* that she had attained the necessary levels of *connaissance* in order for it to happen. It is important to point out that Deren was not a priestess, as some accounts claim, but only an initiate of Haitian Voudoun.

Both *Divine Horsemen* and the footage are expositions of the dialectic of rites that developed in response to slavery in Haiti: the benevolent, or *Rada*, rites from West Africa and their New World counterpart developed out of rage, the so-called *Petro* rites. In an original thesis, Deren described the influence of the Indians of Spanish heritage in Haiti on the development of these rites and how this influence preserved the New World African culture. Although historians understood that a "ceremony" was an instigator to Haiti becoming the second free colony of African slaves in the Western hemisphere, Deren specifically identified it as a *Petro* rite.[57]

Deren distinguished between white and black magic, claiming that as Haiti experienced increasing political and internal difficulty, black magic appropriated parts of the religion as tools of control. She made it clear that black magic was not the same as Voudoun and that there were qualitative differences between the principles of the religion and the work of self-ordained magicians outside it. Because of the methodical and substantial way in which she worked to point out this discrepancy, there is no credible foundation to the myth that she would have put "voodoo curses" on her contemporaries simply because she became a *serviteur* of the religion.[58]

Conclusions

An "anagram" of Maya Deren's ethnographic work conveys ritual and myth allied with dance and film. These forms eventually helped her to represent the ethos of Haitian Voudoun and ultimately the organic nature of the universe. From the early use of poetry to the development of the poetic film, her representation of ritual significantly expanded with her Haitian project. With the exactness of an artist and scientist, she charted the elements of *connaissance* within Voudoun and plotted its mythical construction. Using a methodology that involved the sensorium as well as mechanical extensions of human perception, she provided a cartography of inner and outer domains of experience. Her work combines both speculative and tactile realms, evident in her footage, and the documentation of her participant observation of Haitian Voudoun.

Deren's encounter in Haiti forced her to reevaluate the dominant representational forms used in Western culture. She entered areas that were the turf of the orthodox ethnographer in search of the mythological characteristics of a religion. This perspective caused her to film in an authentic way, allowing her to capture the imagination of the rituals she observed.

The footage of this New World religion is an invaluable document deserving recognition within ethnographic film. Generally film scholarship sidesteps this and other contributions Deren made from her field studies in Haiti. Some claim that her filmmaking career withered once she ceased making films in the fashion of her work from 1943 to 1946. As Deren pointed out, striking out in a different direction was foreign to modern specialization.

The Haitian footage embraced unique techniques of choreocinema that evolved from Deren's early dance films. This perspective allowed her to film the fluid, spontaneous movements of ritual in Haiti. Deren argued that the time element was crucial to filming principled states within their ritualized contexts. The use of art in ethnography promoted by Gregory Bateson gave Deren the theoretical platform from which to use these choreocinematic principles. It can be argued that she, in fact, expanded the possibilities for ethnographic filmmaking through her own work. Her unique study of the origin of myth in Voudoun and its ritual enactment remains an important background for understanding her groundbreaking method of representation. Although she has received recognition for *Divine Horsemen*, her unedited Haitian footage still awaits the careful scrutiny of film scholars and ethnographers alike.

Notes

1. Additional unstudied aspects of Maya Deren's ethnographic work in Haiti include detailed annotations and wire and audio recordings of ritual and secular music (See *Voices of Haiti*, recorded by Maya Deren, Elektra Records, 1953). Deren was an early advocate of the importance of music to the study of ethnography, a fact that is reflected in this material. Notes and transcripts of public lectures, articles, extensive still photography, and records of television and radio appearances are all further evidence of an extensive system of documentation. Included was a proposal to start a 16mm avant-garde film industry and "Institute of Cinematography" in Haiti. These documents and others from this essay are from the Maya Deren Collection, Boston University Mugar Library, Special Collections, donated in 1972 by Marie Deren, Maya Deren's mother. Two inventories of the material were taken by Stephen Edgington in 1976 of catalogued material and by Moira Sullivan in 1993 of uncatalogued material.

2. Deren's spelling of Kreyòl terms appears in this essay. For an explanation of this usage, see Deren, *Divine Horsemen*, p. 18. For a recent assessment of the emergent orthography of Kreyòl, which is essentially a phonetic language, see also Cosentino, *Sacred Arts of Vodou*, p. xiv.

3. For a discussion of this relationship, which sheds light on the nature of Deren's research, see Malinowksi, *Magic, Science and Religion*, pp. 17–95.

4. Deren, preface to *Anagram*.

5. "Poetry and the Film: A Symposium. With Maya Deren, Arthur Miller, Dylan Thomas, Parker Tyler. Chairman, Willard Maas. Organized by Amos Vogel" (October 28, 1953), in *Film Culture Reader*, ed. P. Adams Sitney (New York: Praeger, 1970), p. 174.

6. Maya Deren, "Film in Progress, Thematic Statement," *Film Culture*, no. 39 (winter 1965): 11.

7. Deren, "Religious Possession in Dancing," pp. 480–96.

8. Maya Deren, "Original notes for 'Eye of Night' Scenario," *Film Culture*, no. 39 (winter 1965): 23.

9. Maya Deren, correspondence to Dorothy Burrit, Toronto Film Society. Maya Deren Collection, Boston University Mugar Library, Special Collections. Inventory by Moira Sullivan, box 7, 1951.

10. Deren, *Horsemen*, p. 260.

11. Deren, correspondence to Dorothy Burritt.

12. Maya Deren, "Letter to James Card," April 19, 1955, *Film Culture*, no. 39 (winter 1965): 30.

13. Deren's films were placed, after her death, in Parker Tyler and later P. Adams Sitney's "trance" film category, peopled by "somnambulists," "initiates of rituals," and "the possessed." See Sitney, *Visionary Film: The American Avant-Garde, 1943–1978*

(New York: Oxford University Press, 1974), p. 21. See also the television documentary "Ancient Mysteries: A History of Voodoo," *A&E Networks*, 1996. Here excerpts of "spirit possession" from the Haitian footage are juxtaposed with the staircase sequence of *Meshes of the Afternoon*.

14. Deren, *Horsemen*, p. 35.

15. Maya Deren, "Plan by Eye," Maya Deren Collection, Boston University Mugar Library, Special Collections. Inventory by Stephen Edgington, box 2 (n.d.). For "Shoot to Cut," see Maya Deren, "Creative Cutting," *Movie Makers*, part 1 (May 1947), in Clark, *Legend*, pt. 1, p. 616.

16. Maya Deren, research material, Maya Deren Collection, Boston University Mugar Library, Special Collections. Inventory by Stephen Edgington, box 4 (n.d.). The Haitian footage is housed at Anthology Film Archives, acquired through Grove Press in 1972. Parts 1–4 and 7 were shot in December 1947 and on a later trip in 1949, and parts 5–6 were shot in 1954. The footage of 1954 contains ceremonies, documentation of Voudoun altars, carnivals and festivals, and everyday Haitian life. For a detailed inventory of the footage at Anthology Film Archives, see Sullivan, pp. 309–10. See also World Wide Web page by Moira and Jay Sullivan, *The Maya Deren Forum.* "http://www.algonet.se/~mjsull/," 1997.

17. Deren, research material, Maya Deren Collection, Boston University Mugar Library, Special Collections. Inventory by Stephen Edgington, box 4 (n.d.).

18. The four categories were a general ceremonial film, two ceremonies to the Haitian *loa Ghedé*, god of the dead, and *Agwé*, god of the sea, and secular dances from the Mardi Gras and Ra-ra festivals in Port-au-Prince.

19. Maya Deren, "Notes to Film in Progress Bali," Maya Deren Collection, Boston University Mugar Library, Special Collections. Inventory by Stephen Edgington, box 4 (ca. 1954).

20. Deren, *Horsemen*, p. 11.

21. Deren, *Horsemen*, p. 11.

22. Deren, *Horsemen*, p. 11.

23. Deren, *Horsemen*, p. 12.

24. Maya Deren, grant proposal, Maya Deren Collection, Boston University Mugar Library, Special Collections. Inventory by Stephen Edgington, box 5 (n.d.).

25. Arthur Knight, "Cine-Dance," *Dance Perspectives* 30 (summer 1967): 6–7.

26. Deren, cited in Knight, "Cine-Dance," pp. 6–7.

27. Deren, cited in Knight, "Cine-Dance," p. 10.

28. Deren, *Horsemen*, pp. 240–41.

29. Bateson, Mead, and Deren met on several occasions in New York to discuss Deren's initial film proposal on ritual. Bateson privately contributed two thousand dollars to the 1947 Haitian trip, and the Institute for Cultural Study, where Bateson and Mead were affiliated, partially subsidized Deren's 1949 trip. Mead stored the orig-

inal Haitian footage at the American Museum of Natural History along with a duplicate that Deren had agreed to deposit with the institute.

30. Gregory Bateson, *Balinese Character: A Photographic Essay* (New York: Special Publication of the New York Academy of Sciences, 1942).

31. David MacDougall, "The Visual in Anthropology," in Marcus Banks and Howard Morphy, eds., *Rethinking Visual Anthropology* (New Haven: Yale University Press, 1997), p. 292.

32. Banks and Morphy, "Introduction," *Rethinking Visual Anthropology*, p. 13.

33. Excerpts from "For God's Sake, Margaret, Conversation with Gregory Bateson and Margaret Mead," *The CoEvolution Quarterly* 10/21 (June 1976), in "Margaret Mead and Gregory Bateson on the Use of the Camera in Anthropology," *Studies in the Anthropology of Visual Communication* 4, no. 2 (winter 1977): 78. *Trance and Dance in Bali* is archived at Anthology Film Archives, New York City. The original six films are housed at the Museum of Natural History in New York.

34. *Studies in the Anthropology of Visual Communication*, p. 79.

35. Margaret Mead, "Visible Anthropology in a Discipline of Words," in Paul Hockings, ed., *Principles of Visual Anthropology* (The Hague and Paris: Mouton Publishers, 1975), pp. 5–6.

36. Cf. Heider, *Ethnographic Film*, pp. 51–52.

37. Heider, *Ethnographic Film*, pp. 30–31. See also MacDougall in Banks and Morphy, *Rethinking Visual Anthropology*, pp. 291–92.

38. Maya Deren, "Logic of Voudoun," Maya Deren Collection, Boston University Mugar Library, Special Collections. Inventory by Stephen Edgington, box 1 (ca. 1954), p. 21. This was a draft of "Religion and Magic." *Tomorrow* 1, no. 2 (September 1954).

39. Although the original footage is Deren's, Teiji and Cherel Ito edited and added animation inserts in a documentary film called *Divine Horsemen* (1977). There is ceremonial music as well as voice-overs of excerpts from her monograph spoken by John Genke and Joan Pape. This documentary is an accessible introduction to the footage housed at Anthology Film Archives, although in the process of making the documentary, the original sequence was altered and no longer follows the order in which Deren filmed events.

40. *CBS Odyssey* is housed at Anthology Film Archives, New York. Maya Deren, "CBS Instructions," Maya Deren Collection, Boston University Mugar Library, Special Collections. Inventory by Stephen Edgington, box 5 (n.d.). It is unclear from archive material if or when this clip was aired.

41. Deren, *Horsemen*, p. 7.

42. Deren, *Horsemen*, p. 225.

43. Deren, *Horsemen*, p. 225.

44. Deren, *Horsemen*, p. 24.

45. Graves, *Anger of Achilles*, p. xxx.

46. According to African mythology, the differentiation of male and female came from the segmentation of a divine, androgynous, cosmic whole called the *Marassa* (*Horsemen*, p. 40). During possession a *serviteur* can embody either sex, which can be seen as a ritual reenactment of this myth. Donald Cosentino implies that this and other phenomena of trance possession are "a kind of voguing of unattainable divine and secular orders." (See Cosentino, *Sacred Arts of Vodou*, pp. 44–45.)

Perhaps out of devotion to the *loa*, there are homosexual lifestyles among *serviteur*. Deren defines *massissi* as a homosexual of either sex (*Horsemen*, p. 333), although the designation is commonly used for the *houngan*, who takes male apprentices as "wives." In *Divine Horsemen*, she cites a South Rhodesian creation myth about a man and his two wives who created the entire animal kingdom. One of the wives, *Massassi* (of which *massissi* appears to be a derivation) gave birth to the vegetable kingdom (*Horsemen*, p. 54). Prior to the publication of *Divine Horsemen*, Deren explained to Joseph Campbell that the vegetable reference might be an implication of the non-procreative aspects of homosexual relationships, but he suggested that she delete a discussion of this. (See "Notes on the Massissi," Maya Deren Collection, Boston University Mugar Library, Special Collections. Inventory by Stephen Edgington, box 3 [ca. 1952].) Leaving out this reference in her classification of Voudoun *loa*, Deren lists the "Dada" or "Dadal" as originating from Nago (Nigeria), serving as the early *loa* of farming, vegetables, and fertility, *Horsemen*, p. 82. Cf. Huxley's description of *massissi* in *Invisibles*, p. 203 and references in Courlander's *Haiti Singing*, pp. 10, 252.

47. Lewin and Leap, eds., *Out in the Field*, p. 23.

48. Bateson, *Naven*, p. 1.

49. Bateson, *Naven*, p. 2.

50. Deren, *Horsemen*, pp. 228–29.

51. Cosentino, ed., *Sacred Arts of Vodou*, p. xii.

52. Maya Deren, "Notes," Maya Deren Collection, Boston University Mugar Library, Special Collections. Inventory by Moira Sullivan, box 2 (ca. 1949–1961). Records by Deren list television appearances about Haitian Voudoun for CBC TV, Canadian Broadcasting System, Ottawa; P.M. East, March 20, 1961; CBS's *Vanity Fair*, October 10, 1950 (with footage on Haitian dance); a Mike Wallace interview for *Nightbeat* (without film); and "Interview with Mike Wallace," WBC, New York, May 30, 1957. Radio broadcasts include an hour-long program on Haitian music on January 19, 1949, for WNYC radio; NBC with Dave Garroway, June 5, 1953; and WBAI with Gideon Bachman in 1953.

A proposal for a film on Voudoun, "The Truth about Voudoun," was made for the 1950s television series *Omnibus* but never telecast. See Maya Deren, "Notes on Haiti for *Cadence* Liner." Maya Deren Collection, Boston University Mugar Library, Special Collections. Inventory by Stephen Edgington, box 4 (ca. 1954).

53. Desmangles, *Faces of the Gods*, pp. 7–8. Desmangles calls this relationship "sym-

biosis," citing the use of "syncretism" in the editions of work by Deren, Herskovits, and Métraux.

54. Maya Deren, outtakes of the original transcript of taped conversations between Maya Deren and Joseph Campbell by Anne Dubs, 1950. Maya Deren Collection, Boston University Mugar Library, Special Collections. Inventory by Stephen Edgington, box 1. Catrina Neiman has made an in-depth study and road map of these conversations in *The Legend of Maya Deren: Ritual (1947–1953)*, vol. 2, which Anthology Film Archives, New York, hopes to publish at a future date.

55. Dayan, *Haiti, History, and the Gods*, p. 110.

56. Hyatt, *Urban Voodoo*, p. 140.

57. Deren, *Horsemen*, pp. 61-71, 271–86.

58. Sitney, *Visionary Film*, p. 21.

Bibliography

Banks, Marcus, and Howard Morphy, eds. *Rethinking Visual Anthropology.* New Haven: Yale University Press, 1997.

Bateson, Gregory. *Balinese Character: A Photographic Essay.* New York: Special Publication of the New York Academy of Sciences, 1942.

———. "Exhibition Review, Art of the South Seas" (January 29–May 19, 1946), Museum of Modern Art, New York, *The Art Bulletin: A Quarterly Published By the College Art Association of America* 28, no. 2 (June 1946).

———. *Naven: A Survey of the Problems Suggested by a Composite Picture of a New Guinea Tribe Drawn from Three Points of View.* Stanford: Stanford University Press, 1936.

Clark, VèVè, Millicent Hodson, and Catrina Neiman. *The Legend of Maya Deren.* New York: Anthology Film Archives, vol. 1, pt. 1, 1984 ; vol. 1 , pt. 2, 1988.

Cosentino, Donald J., ed. *Sacred Arts of Vodou.* U.C.L.A. Fowler Museum of Cultural History, Regents of University of California, 1995.

Courlander, Harold. *Haiti Singing.* New York: Cooper Square Publishers, 1973.

Dayan, Joan. *Haiti, History, and the Gods.* Berkeley and Los Angeles: University of California Press, 1995.

Deren, Maya. *An Anagram of Ideas on Art, Form and Film.* New York: Alicat Book Shop Press, 1946.

———. "The Artist as God in Haiti." *Tiger's Eye* (December 1948).

———. "Creative Cutting." *Movie Makers* (May, June 1947).

———. *Divine Horsemen: The Living Gods of Haiti.* Man and Myth, ed. Joseph Campbell. London and New York: Thames and Hudson, 1953.

———. "Ethnic Dance." *Mademoiselle* (February 1951).

———. "Haitian Dance Sacred or Stage." *Haiti Sun* (February 6, 1955).

———. "The Influence of the French Symbolist School on the Anglo-American

Poetry." M.A. thesis, Smith College, 1939. Maya Deren Collection, Boston University Mugar Library Special Collections.

———. "The Poetic Film." *Canadian Film News* (January–February 1951).

———. "Reason or the Dyadic Relativity of the Seventeenth Century and Its Development Towards Modern Triadic Relativity in Science, Philosophy and Ethics." Graduate thesis, Smith College, 1939. Maya Deren Collection, Boston University Mugar Library Special Collections.

———. "Religion and Magic." *Tomorrow* 3, no. 1 (September 1954).

———. "Religious Possession in Dancing." *The Legend of Maya Deren*, pt. 1, pp. 480–96.

———. "Social and Ritual Dances of Haiti." *Dance* (June 1949).

Desmangles, Leslie G. *The Faces of the Gods: Vodou and Roman Catholicism in Haiti.* Chapel Hill and London: University of North Carolina Press, 1992.

Graves, Robert. *The Anger of Achilles.* Great Britain: Cassel & Co., 1959.

Hockings, Paul, ed. *Principles of Visual Anthropology.* The Hague and Paris: Mouton Publishers, 1975.

Huxley, Francis. *The Invisibles: Voodoo Gods in Haiti.* New York: McGraw Hill, 1966.

Hyatt, Christopher, and Jason S. Black. *Urban Voodoo: A Beginner's Guide to Afro-Caribbean Magic.* Tempe, Ariz.: New Falcon Publications, 1995.

Kerényi, Carl. *The God of the Greeks.* Man and Myth, ed. Joseph Campbell. London and New York: Thames and Hudson, 1951.

Knight, Arthur. "Cine-dance." *Dance Perspectives* 30 (summer 1967).

Lewin, Ellen, and William Leap, eds. *Out in the Field: Reflections of Lesbian and Gay Anthropologists.* Urbana and Chicago: University of Illinois Press, 1996.

MacDougall, David. "Prospects for the Ethnographic Film." *Film Quarterly* 23, no. 2 (winter 1969–70).

Malinowski, Bronislaw. *Magic, Science and Religion.* New York: Doubleday, 1954.

"Margaret Mead and Gregory Bateson on the Use of Camera in Anthropology." *Studies in the Anthropology of Visual Communication* 4, no. 2 (winter 1977).

Neiman, Catrina. "Art and Anthropology: The Crossroads." *October*, no. 14 (fall 1980).

Sitney P. Adams. *Visionary Cinema: The American Avant-Garde, 1943–1978.* New York: Oxford University Press, 1974.

———, ed. *Film Culture Reader.* New York: Praeger, 1970.

Sullivan, Moira. *An Anagram of the Ideas of Filmmaker Maya Deren.* Karlstad, Sweden: Karlstad University Press, 1997.

Traversi, Derek, ed. *T. S. Eliot: The Longer Poems.* New York and London: Harcourt Brace Jovanovich, 1976.

Tyler, Parker. *The Three Faces of the Film.* New York: Yoseloff, 1960.

Watts, Alan W. *Myth and Ritual in Christianity.* Man and Myth, ed. Joseph Campbell. Boston: Beacon Press, 1972.

Maria Pramaggiore

Seeing Double(s)

Reading Deren Bisexually

A well-known frame enlargement from *Meshes of the Afternoon* (1943), which Maya Deren used to adorn promotional materials for the film, depicts Deren standing at a window, caught in the act of looking through the glass. At that moment in the film, Deren is a spectator gazing through the window at "another" Maya Deren as the latter retraces certain ritualized physical actions the observing Maya has already performed. The simultaneous coexistence of these two Mayas forces viewers to re-think the traditional opposition between self and other, between same and different. Visually, the Derens are identical to and different from each other. Moreover, their repetitive actions, such as successive attempts to climb stairs, further question distinctions between like and unlike, be-tween original and copy. As four Derens (the dreamer and three "dou-bles") emerge sequentially during this short poetic film, only the most nuanced gesture or facial expression helps spectators to differentiate be-tween and among these multiple expressions of Deren's persona.

Not surprisingly in a film that uses repetition and matches on action to undermine distinctions between reality and dream, these many Mayas watch and are watched. The window in the scene I describe above serves as a metaphor for both the camera lens and the film screen—two sites where self might become other and identification might become indistinguishable from desire. The blurring of the glass in the shot en-

Figure 30. *Meshes of the Afternoon* (1943). Courtesy of Anthology Film Archive.

hances the camera's soft focus, making Deren's face more abstract, less individual. This visual effect speaks to the depersonalizing process of merging self and not-self, of encounters between and among spectator, camera, and actor in the transparent depths and surfaces of lens and screen.

A different kind of merging occurs in Anaïs Nin's often-quoted comment about this shot: Nin implicitly questions rigid boundaries between film and classical visual art. She wrote that Deren's husband and *Meshes* collaborator Alexander Hammid "caught a moment when Maya appeared at a glass window, and softened by the glass, she created a truly Botticelli effect."[1] By making reference to Botticelli's *Primavera*, Nin associates the film with the rhetoric of classical portraiture, although Deren's use of this particular shot more accurately resembled the promotional glamour photography of the Hollywood studio system. The painterly properties Nin identifies stem in part from the characteristics of reflection. Camera and window erase the markers of difference between the face and its reflection, merging image and transparent mirror image.

The erasure of difference and an examination of the limits of the individual persona, so palpable in the image of Deren's face at the window, are essential features of Deren's experimental approach to film. A refusal to obey the rules of subject and object informs her perspectives on the nature of cinematography (she called the film camera "independently active and infinitely passive"),[2] on the dynamics of movement (especially dance), and on film's unique capacity for capturing rhythm and ritual states and suspending chronological time. In an article entitled "Cinematography: the Creative Use of Reality," Deren laments the incursion of theatrical realism into film because it "deprives the motion-picture medium of its creative dimension."[3] She prefers to emphasize the "archetypal" potential of film images, including the mythic personas of figures such as Mary Pickford, Marlene Dietrich, Charlie Chaplin, and Marlon Brando. It is no accident that the passage in which she makes these observations is entitled "abstractions and archetypes." Deren's films deconstruct and aestheticize movement through her signature techniques of slow motion and graphically matched editing; making the visible world abstract is part of a process of mythifying the individual.

By multiplying her own image in *Meshes*, Deren engages with the mythic dynamics of identification and desire. Film theories of spectatorship, often relying on psychoanalysis, generally have conceived of identification as a narcissistic yearning for sameness (the spectator introjects an on-screen figure or projects him- or herself onto a character) and desire as an voyeuristic engagement with otherness (the spectator encounters a potentially threatening and eroticized other whose sexual and other differences must be mastered, contained, or assimilated).[4] In Deren's films, however, otherness is a function of the self—neither "internal" nor "external" to it but capable of producing effects both "within" the self and in the "objective" world the self inhabits. In *Meshes*, for example, Deren's doubles are imaginary, but they produce "real" effects. In this way, "otherness" is a mythic and abstract force beyond individual control—as is movement—yet is not located in the external environment alone.

Deren explores the contingency of self and other, of difference and similarity, through tropes of doubling, multiplication, and merging in three films concerned with self-representation. *Meshes, At Land* (1944), and *Ritual in Transfigured Time* (1946) explore the film medium's capacity to differentiate between *and* to blend same and different, with particular emphasis on bodies, movement, and space. These films treat the dialectics of individual identity as a limiting choreography that the film medium can defamiliarize and circumvent. Deren's films intervene in dichotomies, including individual and group, single and plural, active and passive, at rest and in motion. The films depict women whose inability to be categorized as either "same" (the same as other women or the same self from moment to moment) or "different" (different from others, from men, and from inanimate objects) is troubling and provocative. The woman protagonist's relation to her multiplied and fractured persona, expressive of both inner conflicts and social dynamics, remains unresolved at the conclusion of each film. Identity in these films remains a matrix of similarities and differences that is not amenable to an "either/ or" paradigm.

One way to interpret the fragmentation and multiplication of the protagonists, the resistance to limiting definitions of self and other, and the temporal circularity in these films is to read Deren's work from a bisexual perspective. Such a strategy is not simply a mechanistic template to be "applied" to any film; rather, I would argue that certain films call forth such a reading practice because they break down categories of opposition, producing fluid, nonexclusive spaces and times—the "in-between" and the "both/and." As they gesture toward abstraction, these three Deren films envision desire and identification as inclusive and overlapping processes, as fluid discovery rather than as certitude. Deren expressed a dialectical relation between self and other in the repetitive, open-ended structure of her films.

Deren's ritual-based films reject linear narrative trajectories; they also steadfastly refuse to embrace an erotics of either heterosexuality or homosexuality. The films focus on women whose behavior suggests discomfort with cultural imperatives surrounding gender and sexuality. The films' multiplication of similarity and difference produces social and sexual indeterminacies that, in addition to spatiotemporal fluidity, create a space for reading and seeing bisexually.[5] Before performing such a reading of these Deren films, I will first discuss the narrative and formal conditions of possibility for reading film bisexually.

Bisexuality and Film

Although gay and lesbian theories have been brought to bear on issues of film representation quite productively in the work of Andrea Weiss, Alexander Doty, Teresa de Lauretis, Chris Straayer, Judith Halberstam, and others, bisexual representation and spectatorship have been neglected, if not erased, in queer film theory.[6] Thus, even though textual queerness is acknowledged and sometimes privileged in recent critical discussions, the fact that specific formal, narrative, or extratextual elements of a film may repress or express possibilities for *bisexual* desire is rarely explored.

Merl Storr has usefully summarized competing concepts of bisexuality and points out that the coexistence of more than one definition of bisexuality remains a theoretical dilemma.[7] Bisexuality has been understood as a combination of two elements—although those elements have differed in various historical periods. The nineteenth-century sexologists considered bisexuals those people who were anatomically both male and female; Freud conceived of bisexuality as a psychological combination of femininity and masculinity. Since the gay liberation movement and queer theory have produced histories and theories of various sexualities, notions of bisexuality as a relation between heterosexuality and homosexuality have eclipsed earlier models. Social science approaches to bisexuality have adopted an additive paradigm, characterizing bisexuality as "dual attraction."[8] Under this rubric, elaborating bisexual desire is possible if the dynamics of heterosexuality and homosexuality are understood; rather than questioning what such a dualism might mean, the model consists of a straightforward combination of two terms. The blind spot in film theory may result from an implicit assumption that bisexuality conforms to an additive paradigm of sexuality: that the "bi" in bisexuality represents the sum of heterosexuality plus homosexuality and thus can be elaborated through these terms.

Some regard bisexuality as a border separating, or as a zone between, heterosexuality and homosexuality. Bisexuality may thus be considered a boundary or a mixture, an in-between or liminal space, a limit case or not a case at all but rather a subversion of any sexualities based on strictly gendered object choice. At the most basic level, bisexuality encompasses desires for more than one gender. Therefore, it is limiting to restrict theories of bisexual desire to those that posit bisexuality to be a combination of heterosexuality and homosexuality.

The approach I prefer takes as a point of reference the distinction between monosexualities (heterosexuality and homosexuality) and bisexualities to emphasize qualitative rather than quantitative differences among sexual identities, practices, and modes of apprehending the world. I define bisexual desire as nonsingular sexual desire that may be detached from gender oppositions: simply put, bisexual desire is non-mutually exclusive desire for same and different.[9] This intentionally abstract definition does not require that bisexual desire necessarily be associated with monogamy or nonmonogamy, with single or multiple partners (of any sex or gender), with any specific position regarding the relevance or irrelevance of gender, or with any particular stance on the relationship between gender and sexuality. It also resonates with earlier notions of bisexuality as located in the body or psyche—as a physical or psychological status of ambivalence and/or all-encompassing desire.

My argument that Deren's films invite a bisexual reading is not an argument that Maya Deren herself was bisexual, nor do I claim that any text, or any sexuality, is bisexual merely because it eroticizes boundaries or complicates identification and sexual desire. A bisexual film reading, I would argue, is encouraged by a text's specific representational practices, including: 1) the avoidance of a coupled resolution, whether heterosexual or homosexual; 2) the lack of a clear distinction between identification and desire among characters and, potentially, among characters and spectators; and 3) temporal and spatial regimes that undermine both progress and resolution, and therefore admit of the possibility of contingent identities, of subjects-in-process, particularly with respect to gender and sexual identity. Elsewhere I have argued that narrative structures assigning more weight to the conclusion—typical of Hollywood film rather than avant-garde or art cinema—may be less compatible with bisexual reading strategies.[10] Bisexual readings privilege the episodic quality of films that represent time as a field across which a number of sexual acts, desires, and identities might be expressed, not an inexorable march toward heterosexual maturity or the progress of discovery (and final certainty) represented by the homosexual coming-out narrative.

Deren's self-representation trilogy (*Meshes, At Land,* and *Ritual*) encourages a bisexual reading practice.[11] Her films depict conflicted women in liminal states who refuse to be defined in relation to men or women. At the conclusion of each film, the woman protagonist has escaped relationships, coupled or otherwise, with male and female others. Furthermore, the excessively watched, obsessively watching protagonists in the films repeatedly confound same and other, or, in the terminology of psychoanalytic film theory, the pleasures of ego idealization (narcissism) and libidinal investment (scopophilia). This confounding of identification and desire, I would argue, forms the basis for the pleasure of reading bisexually.[12]

Finally, the cyclical structures of these films—which draw heavily from Deren's study of Haitian Voudoun rituals and her growing interest in "the creative possibilities of Time"—disrupt chronology and elide closure, interrupting the dramatic teleology of crisis and resolution.[13] The films cannot guarantee any stable sexuality for their protagonists partly because their emphasis on ritual highlights liminality and transition instead of permanence, which has implications for the notion of a consistently gendered object choice.[14] In exploring difference and similarity, the films render moot the distinctions between self and other, male and female, object and subject, heterosexual and homosexual. What emerges from all three films is an aesthetic of self-elaboration rather than of taxonomy. Deren's interest in ritual possession and dance—two intensely physical states in which the self is suspended—underlies this film aesthetic. In that suspension, all social, representational, and physical categories are reevaluated. In what follows, I interpret each of Deren's three self-representation films in terms of the narrative and formal elements that encourage a bisexual reading.

Decoupling Sexuality and Deforming Narrative: *Meshes of the Afternoon*

Arguably, coupled resolution is the most important narrative trope restricting the possibilities for making alternative sexualities visible. Conventional coupled romance narratives, whether concerned with gay, lesbian, or heterosexual scenarios, make it difficult to recognize or to imagine bisexuality as anything but an obstacle to overcome or a confused developmental stage coming before "mature" monogamous monosexuality.[15]

Furthermore, triangulation can serve as an important device in the formation and subversion of the romantic couple as well as in narrative closure, particularly in film.[16] Romantic triangles offer opportunities for expressing overlapping identification and desire between and among three figures, elaborating rather than restricting similarities and differences the way a dyadic structure might. According to literary theorist René Girard, Western representations of love, romance, and sexuality rely on a triangulated structure of desire.[17] Eve Sedgwick, examining the implications of male homosociality in English literature, concludes that the bonds between male rivals are as strong as those between each of the men and the female love interest.[18] Writing specifically about bisexuality, Marjorie Garber observes that erotic desire depends on one's position within the triangle rather than on essential gender or sexual identities. She stresses the importance of examining "the connections among the 'other' partners that need articulating."[19]

What Garber suggests is that the rivalry and jealousy that characterize relations between two characters in a triangle who are competing for the third do not only involve identification (their shared desire for the third person). This construction is incomplete, because these relations may encompass rivalry, identification, *and* desire; the competition for the third figure might reflect or embody erotic desire between the competitors. Similarities and differences multiply within the triangle, offering the possibility that desire for same and other—what I am deeming critical to bisexuality—might be articulated. Bisexual desire does not arise within every romantic triangle; however, the triangle creates hospitable conditions for expressing non-mutually exclusive desire.

Because the (romantic) triangle offers the possibility for simultaneous desire and identification, triangulation may help to highlight the both/and quality of bisexual desire, including its apparent liminality as a zone "in-between" and yet connected with straight and gay sexualities. The third term produced within a triangulated context becomes a metaphor for and/or agent of structural instability in dyadic relations in general. Deren repeatedly uses triangulation in her trilogy to intervene in traditional modes of sexual- and self-definition.

In *Meshes of the Afternoon*, Deren invariably situates the protagonist (played by Deren herself) as a third term within triangular structures of looking and desire, often as both looking subject and observed object. The dreaming protagonist's desire for self and other is expressed in the radical ambivalence surrounding her relationship to her male lover and three female doubles/copies. Furthermore, repetition and circularity render the film's chronotope a poetic ritual, not a progressive narrative, making a conventional coupled resolution irrelevant.

Deren emphasizes the triangular relations of self, other, and self-image in *Meshes*. I argue that the film depicts the inseparable and simultaneous nature of the search for an other *and* a self. Deren's quest for self-representation refuses a coupled resolution, enmeshes identification and desire, and rejects linear narrative.

In *Meshes*, the protagonist dreams of a mirror-faced figure, her male lover, and three doubles of herself while occupying an intermediate, third space that encompasses lover and dream doubles, waking reality and dream. The dreamer also forms the interstices between these figures and spatiotemporal coordinates. Deren dreams three versions of herself, each of whom attempts to interact with a mirror-faced figure and fails, enters and investigates the dreamer's house, watches the other doubles through the window, and contemplates the dreamer herself. One result of this multiplication of same and different is that desires and identifications between and among the dreamer, her dreamed doubles and her male lover, are confounded, thus undercutting the issue of monosexual object choice, much less a permanent state of coupling. As the doubles watch one another as well as the dreamer, they are watching themselves as others.

Heterosexual desire is subverted in overt ways throughout the film. The male lover, for example, is an intruder in the dreamer's domestic and psychic (dreamed) space and is associated with violence. Early in the film, the dreamer sits down and caresses herself before falling asleep. She later awakens abruptly from a nightmare involving the aggressive dream doubles, and a rapid cut shows us that it is the male lover, not one of the dream doubles, who threatens her. As she reluctantly follows him upstairs to the bedroom, his insistence and her resistance become apparent. The earlier autoerotic caress is visually echoed by the male lover in a tension-charged moment. During his caress on the bed, the protagonist is unresponsive and visually fragmented.[20] Immediately afterward, she seizes a knife and stabs the man, disclosing this reality to be merely a dream within her dream: as she stabs him, the film frame itself cracks and reveals itself to be a mirror. The next shot depicts a mirror breaking on the beach. In the interaction between dreamer and lover, autoeroticism parallels heterosexuality and triumphs. Whereas the first caress initiates the protagonist's imaginative leap into a dream world of multiple selves, the lover's caress is explicitly distasteful to her, and she strikes out at him soon after he makes the gesture.

Like the male hero, the dream doubles are also associated with violence. The film circumvents any notion of unproblematic "woman identification."[21] It provides no "solution" to heterosexual difference and its limited choice of same or different; neither self-love nor lesbian sexuality offer refuge from the unstable heterosexual relationship. During the dream itself, the dreamer appears as herself—asleep in the chair near the living room window. The doubles engage in a complex set of repetitions with variation: chasing the mirror-faced figure, entering the house, climbing the stairs, and penetrating the domestic space. The three doubles converge at the dining room table and draw straws. The last of the doubles to enter the house draws the knife and approaches the dreamer, who is stirring restlessly in the chair. It is at this moment that the aggressive dream double is translated into the ominous male lover figure, who takes the dreamer upstairs. The conflation of double and lover is a mixture of self and other, male and female, which suggests that the pleasures and dangers of identification (based on self-love) and desire (love for another) function interchangeably.

In the final scene, the male lover returns home to find the protagonist asleep or dead in her chair, covered with mirror shards and seaweed; she has passed from her various dream worlds to one that is beyond representation. Interestingly, the collision of the dream state and reality has been so thoroughly explored in this film that one must question the reality of the final scene as well. The repetition and the violent imposition of one reality atop another suggest that dreaming and waking are interpenetrating both/and states; there is no space or time that can be categorized as exclusive, as entirely dream world or reality.

The subversion of coupling and multiplication of self and other in the film are connected to Deren's subversion of narrative. Without sequential reference points, the film cannot proceed according to cause-and-effect logic. Deren does not resolve the woman's victimization at the hands of dangerous doubles or a dubious lover by establishing a choice between self (liberatory solitude) or other (the lover, a double). The atemporal quality of the oceanic references and the protagonist's quasi-death merely confirm the importance of circularity and repetition: the dreamer may be dead and within the endless and therefore timeless cycle that the ocean waves evoke. At the very least, she is inaccessible to the reality represented by the lover's final (and perhaps only) entrance.

The bisexual aesthetic of *Meshes* grows out of the thematic rejection of a coupled conclusion, the conflation of various similarities and differences, and the recursive temporal structure. Deren refuses to construct an identity for her protagonist that is based on a relationship to an other. Although eroticism is invoked on many counts (the caresses, the upstairs bedroom, the flower motif), no stable object choice emerges. The dreamer's fluid relation to space, time, and otherness refuses to admit a number of binary and hierarchical distinctions, not least of which is monosexuality.

Position, Movement, and Power: *At Land*

In *At Land*, a woman (Deren) emerges from the ocean and infiltrates various social situations, including a dinner party and a chess game on the beach. Her emergence from the sea and ensuing sojourns among jarring geographies highlight the film's key device—editing. The editing in *At Land*, however, serves a distinctly different purpose than it does in *Meshes*. In this second film, editing yokes together the dissimilar, whereas in *Meshes*, editing infuses the domestic space with the danger of the dream world. In *At Land*, the spaces of same and different are made contiguous but do not interpenetrate, as they do in *Meshes*.

Furthermore, *At Land*'s central metaphor of a chess game signifies forms of difference that are choreographed by rules that are socially agreed on (color, location, mobility, gender) rather than by inner psychological realities. It also offers a quotidian means of avoiding narrative time—game time is also a form of suspended animation. The film casts the protagonist adrift in hostile social and natural environments but provides the character with the means to survive the inhospitable worlds she navigates—a multiplication of herself that produces sameness and difference. *At Land* is Deren's least personal and yet most individualistic film—ignored by many characters in the film, the protagonist is recognized and affirmed only by increasingly abstract, depersonalized, and spatially displaced versions of herself.

At Land's protagonist functions as an outsider, as an invisible intruder; she rejects the social activities available to her and prefers to identify with chess pieces rather than with other characters, male or female. After emerging from the ocean, she climbs a piece of driftwood on the beach. Her body is fragmented; successive shots depict her legs on the driftwood and her upper body at a banquet table populated by a number of guests. These two spaces (natural and social) are joined by her body and the camera, not by narrative logic. The protagonist crawls down the table, ignored by the guests, until she reaches a chess game in which the objects either move of their own accord or follow the protagonist's eye movements (it is unclear whether she is watching them or willing them to move).[22] The woman snatches a piece from the board, but it escapes her grasp, sending her on a chase across various landscapes for the remainder of the film.

Figure 31. *At Land* (1944). *At Land*'s protagonist (Maya Deren) crawls along a dinner table. She seems to be "at sea" even when she is on land, and yet she moves with purpose and direction. Courtesy of Tavia Ito.

The significance of the chess game in relation to Deren's concern with bodies and movement is played out across the film: position and movement establish one's role in the game. The power of each piece is determined by its ability to move and its pattern of movement. The oppositional win/lose character of the game is embodied in its black-and-white color scheme. The queen is the most versatile and mobile piece, arguably the most powerful; yet she is often sacrificed in order to protect the less mobile king, whose status determines the outcome of the game.

The protagonist's search for autonomy touches on each of the issues emanating from the chess game. The woman is highly mobile yet remains unseen by most of the other characters. When she interacts with male characters, they are hostile or threatening and attempt to limit her mobility. Women characters ignore her until she distracts them from their chess game by caressing their hair erotically; she then steals their chess piece. Her "liberation" of two chess pieces from men and women's games indicates her rejection of the rules defining individuals according to hierarchies of status, movement, color, and gender.

The woman becomes both an abstract subject and a multiplied version of herself—hovering between worlds of social interaction, game playing, and monosexualities. When she accompanies a man down a country road, the man fails to establish individuality, because three actors play the same character (Parker Tyler, John Cage, Alexander Hammid). Here Deren's editing highlights the woman's structural position relative to some larger, impersonal definition of "man" rather than to an individual man. Like the *Meshes* dream doubles, the man/men become increasingly hostile. The last man walks on ahead, finally deserting her outside a house. Inside, she encounters a sheet-draped man who starts at her, unmoving and unblinking. The protagonist, startled by a cat, turns and flees the house through a series of doorways. The woman's mobility—instigated by the cat—saves her from the stasis symbolized by the staring man.

The protagonist then encounters women playing chess on the beach; the women take no notice of her. The women's chess game is invested with an eroticism that the men's game is not. An outsider to both the (masculine) dinner party and (feminine) beach society, occupying a distinct but contiguous time and space, she steals a chess piece from each game. In the final scenes of the film, the camera revisits Deren's image in various locations (on the table in the first scene, on the beach searching for the pawn); her several doubles cheer her triumphant run down the beach with a chess piece held high.

Deren's protagonist, here multiplied in the self-observing selves of the concluding moments, occupies spaces contiguous with but not engulfed by the male and female worlds she encounters (which might stand in for masculine and feminine worlds or heterosexual and lesbian sexualities). The film's rhythmic and repetitive structure is inaugurated in the opening sequences, when the protagonist rolls in on an ocean wave. Throughout the film, she moves through time in a nonlinear manner that is tangential to the other times depicted in the film—the dinner party, the

Figure 32. *At Land* (1944). The female protagonist (Maya Deren) returns to the sea, triumphant, with the stolen chess piece. Courtesy of Tavia Ito.

game. She participates in the action of the other characters but remains unconstrained by their geographical locations or time frames. At the conclusion, the woman runs away alone, carrying her chess piece triumphantly, as if she holds the secret to their rule-bound game, a game overdetermined by oppositions such as mobility/immobility, masculinity/femininity, and heterosexuality/homosexuality.

While less psychologically complex and poetic than the dream-within-a-dream structure of *Meshes, At Land* nevertheless continues the project of resisting oppositional categories. The film presents the female protagonist with hostile heterosexuality and eroticized encounters with women. Yet she refuses relationships with other characters in favor of an identification with/desire for the chess piece and her multiplied self-others. In *At Land*, Deren again circumvents coupling, complicates identification, and suspends narrative time. Her protagonist is in process, defined in her resistance to the dualism represented by the game.

Dances of Difference: *Ritual in Transfigured Time*

In *Ritual in Transfigured Time* Deren evokes the liminal time and space of ritual—another form of suspended animation that circumvents cause and effect. In this film, Deren and her protagonist, dancer Rita Christiani, together defy coupling, heterosexuality, and ossification as objects of art. The two women forge a connection that ultimately subsumes self and other within larger forces such as motion and stillness; Deren's and Christiani's similarities and differences are not erased but drawn out by their visual merging. Their identification with and desire for each other are expressed in the final moments of the film in a sequence in which they merge and yet remain distinct. Because of this film's strong woman-centeredness, and somewhat surprising quasi-coupling, this film lends itself to a lesbian reading as well as a bisexual one. I would maintain its relevance to a bisexual reading because of the film's emphasis on the fluidity rather than the fixity of its protagonists' identities.

The film opens as dancer Christiani watches Deren unwind yarn several rooms away (see figure 11, p. 95). Christiani passes through a series of ritual portals, and the women unwind the yarn together. Slow-motion photography draws out their fluid dancelike motions; this space and time shared by the two women is distinct from that of the party Christiani later joins. Deren's yarn winder is an outsider to the contemporary social gathering, yet she occupies an unlikely proximity to the cocktail party. The connection forged between Deren and Christiani—evoked through gesture and movement—will reappear at the end of the film, as match-on-action editing creates the sense of the two women sharing a suspended space-time when they escape from a man who pursues them.

Through slow-motion and freeze-frame photography, Deren isolates the ritualistic nature of interaction at the cocktail party. Men and women

Figure 33. *Ritual in Transfigured Time* (1946). The dance in *Ritual* (also discussed by Turim and Holl) suggests a sense of fluid, relational identity rather than of one person and multiple roles. Though propelled by the male dancer, Frank Westbrook, none of the female dancers (Anaïs Nin, Maya Deren, or Rita Christiani, seen here) joins with him to form a classic couple; instead they remain in fluid combination. Courtesy of Catrina Neiman.

laugh, dance, talk, and drink—their actions are repetitious and their gestures exaggerated by the slow motion. Christiani is the alien intruder in this context; the only African American figure, she is dressed in what is either widow's weeds or a novitiate's garb and grows increasingly uncomfortable with the party's aggressive energy. The group of men and women seems to take on an identity of its own, as a mob distinct from individual characters.

Christiani, two other women (one of whom is Anaïs Nin), and a man (Frank Westbrook) escape from the party to a sculpture garden. Here the man occupies center stage as he flings the women around in a dance and they are frozen in a still shot—likening them to the static sculptures (see figures 6, 7, and 8, p. 87). Deren intervenes as a third term in the *danse macabre* or Roman Statues game controlled by Frank Westbrook, the dancer who has the power to turn the women into statuesque art objects. Deren is a means by which Christiani can reject the deadly game of aesthetics defined in male terms.

At the same time, the women's similarities are emphasized to the point of merging identities. A series of match-on-action shots forges an identification between Deren and Christiani as they escape from the game and run toward the ocean, finally plunging into the water. A movement begun by one woman is finished by the other; dancelike gestures represent a larger force—both internal and external—subsuming their separate identities. The final shot reveals the film negative of Christiani underwater, floating upward in a white gown. The rebirth in a fluid medium counters the danger of stasis and fixity represented by the Roman Statues game.

In *Ritual*, as in *Meshes* and *At Land*, Deren illuminates the structure of heterosexual interaction, using space and movement to lay bare the dangers of playing that game. At the party, Christiani is buffeted about by men and women intent on coupling, on terms that disadvantage women, as becomes clear in the sculpture garden. Unlike the two previous films, *Ritual* represents relationships among women as a potential means of transcending or escaping the stultifying rituals of aesthetic codification. Deren's singular protagonist, who heretofore has occupied the spaces of both/and rather than either/or (dream and reality in *Meshes*; beach and dinner party in *At Land*) now literally invites an other into her spacetime. Deren's and Christiani's identities are fractured and multiplied through each other—not through doubles of themselves. Matches on action are carefully composed to suggest the fluidity of the women's movements as they become each other and yet remain distinct. The oscillating shots of Deren and Christiani suggest a continuing process of

Figures 34–36. *Ritual in Transfigured Time* (1946). The two women (Maya Deren and Rita Christiani) descend into the ocean and merge into one character as the image changes from positive to negative. Figures 34 and 35 courtesy of the Anthology Film Archive. Figure 36 courtesy of Catrina Neiman.

34

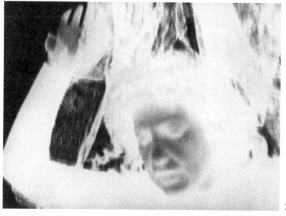

35

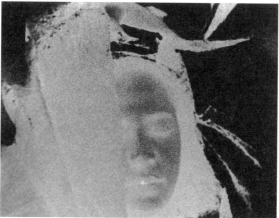

36

relational identity rather than a transformation from one identity to another.

This last of Deren's self-representation films may represent a modification of her prior rejection of monosexual coupled resolutions. I would argue that the doubling of Deren and Christiani does suggest a dyadic relation but that the dyad is based on the simultaneity of identification and desire, similarity and difference. The open-ended conclusion offers a number of interpretive possibilities, a few of which are that the two women merge as they escape Westbrook, that they are reborn in the ocean beyond the confines of static forms of art or identity, and/or that they have rediscovered the place and time of the *Meshes* protagonist, a region both imaginative and real.

The film's reliance on and return to the ocean only strengthens the poetic ambiance of the film and the trilogy as a whole. Their focus on ritual suspends time altogether. The suggestion of various means of escape (into interiority in *Meshes*, into individualism in *At Land*, and into an other/self in *Ritual*) is not so much a leap to transcendence as a transition to another realm already apparent within the films' spatial and temporal grammar.

Deren's self-representation films privilege neither heterosexual nor homosexual desire; in fact, in all the films, male and female figures are both eroticized and made ominous, even violent. Her protagonists wander through social landscapes unaccompanied but also experience sensual and erotic pleasure. They routinely reject narratives of romance, just as Deren rejects the romance of narrative. While the films seem to sanction the autonomy of the individual, the fragmentation (and multiplication) of characters undermines any claim that these films celebrate the narcissistic ego. The threat to the boundaries of the individual is posed by the complex play of similarity and difference that emanates from within as well as from the external environment. It may not be the lover who destroys the protagonist in *Meshes*, but her dreamed lover, or her mirror-image dream doubles. In *At Land*, the protagonist must navigate a game played by both men and women in order to expose and ultimately resist its hierarchical rules. In *Ritual*, the transfiguration of time and space is also a dangerous transposition of living women into statues when they are controlled by a man. The flight from this particular creative process is undertaken by women who remain distinct personas even as they share space and time—a couple occupying the both/and status accorded individuals who are also mythic figures.

In terms of a bisexual aesthetic, Deren's films allow one to imagine eroticism beyond the confines of the coupled resolution and to view sexuality as an engagement with both identification and desire, not merely one or the other. Furthermore, the films deconstruct presumptions about what exactly produces identification (similarities?) and desire (differences?). Finally, the films resist narratives of progress—whether beyond Oedipus toward a "mature" heterosexuality or a rejection/rewriting of prior experience in the homosexual coming-out narrative. They suggest that sexuality and identity are processes without resolution, only further unfolding. For Deren, the film medium's power is its ability to create new forms of time and space; her work expands the possibilities for viewing subjects who use her films to continue envisioning the implications of her experiments with temporal, spatial, and sexual fluidities.

Notes

1. Louise Heck-Rabi, *Women Filmmakers: A Critical Reception* (Metuchen, NJ: Scarecrow Press, 1984), p. 206.

2. Maya Deren, "Cinematography: The Creative Use of Reality," in *Film Theory and Criticism*, 4th ed., ed. Gerald Mast, Marshall Cohen, and Leo Braudy (New York and Oxford: Oxford University Press, 1992), p. 59.

3. Deren, "Cinematography," p. 65.

4. See, for example, the work of the classical feminist film theorists: Laura Mulvey's "Visual Pleasure and Narrative Cinema," in *Film Theory and Criticism*, pp. 746–57; Tania Modleski's *The Women Who Knew Too Much: Hitchcock and Feminist Theory* (New York: Routledge, 1988); Mary Ann Doane's "Film and the Masquerade: Theorizing the Female Spectator," in *Film Theory and Criticism*, pp. 758–72; and Gaylyn Studlar's *In the Realm of Pleasure: Masochism and the Perverse Pleasures of Cinema* (Urbana: University of Illinois Press, 1988). Recent work on identification encompasses

feminist, queer, and postcolonial film studies includes Anne Friedberg's "A Denial of Difference: Theories of Cinematic Identification," in *Psychoanalysis and Cinema*, ed. E. Ann Kaplan (New York and London: Routledge, 1990), pp. 36–45; Jackie Stacey's "Desperately Seeking Difference," in *The Sexual Subject: A Screen Reader in Sexuality* (London and New York: Routledge, 1992), pp. 244–60; Homi Bhabha's "The Other Question: The Stereotype and Colonial Discourse," in *The Sexual Subject: A Screen Reader in Sexuality* (London and New York: Routledge, 1992), pp. 312–31; and Kaja Silverman's *The Threshold of the Visible World* (London and New York: Routledge, 1996).

5. I draw on recent work on bisexual theory, much of it collected in Merl Storr's *Bisexuality: A Critical Reader* (London and New York: Routledge, 1999). I also have drawn from *RePresenting Bisexualities: Subjects and Cultures of Fluid Desire*, Hall and Pramaggiore, eds. (New York: New York University Press, 1996). This work grows out of my essay on Deren's paradoxical avant-garde/star persona: "Performance and Persona in the US Avant Garde: The Case of Maya Deren," *Cinema Journal* 36, no. 2 (1997): 17–40.

6. See, among others, Andrea Weiss, *Vampires and Violets: Lesbians in Film* (New York: Penguin, 1992); Alexander Doty, *Making Things Perfectly Queer* (London and Minneapolis: University of Minnesota Press, 1993); Teresa de Lauretis, *The Practice of Love: Lesbian Sexuality and Perverse Desire* (Bloomington: Indiana University Press, 1994); Chris Straayer, *Deviant Eyes, Deviant Bodies: Sexual Re-Orientation in Film and Video* (New York: Columbia University Press, 1996); and Jackie Stacey, *Star Gazing: Hollywood Cinema and Female Spectatorship* (London and New York: Routledge, 1994). A recent exception is Wayne Bryant's *Bisexual Characters in Film* (New York: Haworth Press, 1997). Rebecca Bell-Metereau's *Hollywood Androgyny* (New York: Columbia University Press, 1985) touches on bisexual representation but primarily through the trope of cross-dressing.

7. Storr, *Bisexuality*, pp. 3–5.

8. Certainly bisexuals may experience their sexuality in such a manner. However, bisexual "life stories" are often interpreted through an additive lens, with the result that ranges of experience are collapsed into sums. Note, for example, the contradictions in this short passage from Weinberg, Williams, and Pryor's *Dual Attraction: Understanding Bisexuality* (New York: Oxford University Press, 1994):

> In this book we show, for example, that the majority of bisexuals established heterosexuality first in their lives. Homosexuality was something they later "added on." They became bisexual over time, depending on a range of sexual and cultural experiences. And many did not define themselves as bisexual until years after their first dual attractions. (7)

Clearly, the issue of "becoming," acknowledging, and/or practicing any sexuality over time and through a range of cultural experiences is more complex than a mathematical model can accommodate.

9. Obviously, I have been intentionally vague. This formulation, however, allows for desires and practices that adopt the form of the couple and those that do not; it includes serial bisexuality ("oscillation" between and among variously sexed object choices); it includes fantasies of same and other sex relations; it includes the recognition that same and other sex friendships may be erotically charged. I am not arguing that everyone is bisexual, but I do want to argue for the specificity of bisexuality as more than, and different from, the addition of heterosexuality and homosexuality.

10. See my "Straddling the Screen: Bisexual Spectatorship and Contemporary Narrative Film," in *RePresenting Bisexualities: Subjects and Cultures of Fluid Desire* (New York: New York University Press, 1996), pp. 272–97.

11. I thank Lise Carlson, who first described these films to me as Deren's trilogy.

12. Thus, in Deren's films, ego idealization and scopophilic pleasures can both be satisfied, but not through the mechanisms Laura Mulvey discusses in "Visual Pleasure in Narrative Cinema," namely, active male characters who appeal to spectators' narcissism and passive women who are victims of fetishism and narrative sadism.

13. The phrase comes from the preface to Deren's *An Anagram of Ideas on Art, Form and Film* (New York: Alicat Book Shop Press, 1946), reprinted in *The Legend of Maya Deren*, ed. VèVè A. Clark, Millicent Hodson, and Catrina Neiman (New York: Anthology Film Archives, 1988), pt. 2. In *Divine Horseman: The Living Gods of Haiti* (New York: McPherson and Co., 1991 [1953]), Deren describes her experiences and observations in Haiti between 1947 and 1951. Deren won a Guggenheim Fellowship to study Haitian dance but abandoned that project when she became interested in Voudoun religious rituals and filmed these ceremonies. The footage was assembled but not edited before Deren's death in 1961.

14. The practice of determining sexuality according to object choice is clearly Freudian in origin, but it still serves as the dominant model of determining sexual identity.

15. One of the most prominent examples of characterizing lesbianism and, implicitly, women's bisexuality, as a stage appears in heterosexual pornography; see Judith Roof's *A Lure of Knowledge: Lesbian Sexuality and Theory* (New York: Columbia University Press, 1991).

16. See David Bordwell, Janet Staiger, and Kristin Thompson, *The Classical Hollywood Cinema* (New York: Columbia University Press, 1985), pp. 16–18, for a look at the sheer number of films that end in heterosexual coupled resolution.

17. René Girard, *Desire, Deceit and the Novel: Self and Other in Literary Structure*, trans. Yvonne Freccero (Baltimore: Johns Hopkins University Press, 1990).

18. Eve Kosofsky Sedgwick, *Between Men: English Literature and Male Homosocial Desire* (New York: Columbia University Press, 1985).

19. Marjorie Garber, *Vice Versa: Bisexuality and the Eroticism of Everyday Life* (New York: Simon and Schuster, 1995), p. 433. The cover to Garber's book suggests the play of meanings offered by bisexuality—it is a painting of three pears, a whimsical

suggestion of the subversion of the couple that bisexuality can, but does not necessarily, offer.

20. The shot of the autoerotic caress also fragments the protagonist's body, but the camera angle hints that we are sharing her point of view as she looks down at her own body, not that she is looked at from a distance, as the lover's caress shot suggests.

21. See Linda Williams, "A Jury of Their Peers: Questions of Silence, Speech and Judgment in Marleen Gorris's *A Question of Silence*," in *Multiple Voice in Feminist Criticism*, ed. Diane Carson, Linda Dittmar, and Janice Welsh (Minneapolis and London: University of Minnesota Press, 1994), pp. 432–44. Williams discusses the problem of assuming that "women's ways of knowing" permit women to form instantaneous and "natural" communities.

22. This animation of objects recalls several moments in *Meshes* when keys and knives seem to move of their own accord.

Barbara Hammer

Maya Deren and Me

Maya Deren's films, critical writing, and exhibition and distribution strategies have greatly influenced both my filmmaking and my professional life enormously.

I was a late bloomer of thirty when I entered film school at San Francisco State University. I'd tried many different vocations: bank teller, juvenile hall counselor, and playground director, but none of these fit. Recognizing that something inside wasn't being expressed, I decided to be an artist. Instead of painting, which I love dearly, I chose film, because the discipline included aesthetics as well as philosophical inquiry and politics.

In my film history course there were only a few women, but as budding feminists we were outspoken. Connie, Veronica, and I always sat together and criticized the ongoing academy of male filmmakers whose work we saw day in, day out. My arm grew tired of asking the questions: Where was Pudovkin's mother? Were there no women on Vertov's film train? And, why, oh why, was Lillian Gish portrayed as helpless?

Finally, toward the end of the course, there appeared on screen the black-and-white 16mm films of one Maya Deren. Something was radically different. The screen was filled with images that were created from a different sensibility, an aesthetic I intuitively understood. For the first time, a woman's cinema filled the screen in this dark, cavernous lecture hall. Until then, this "history of cinema" screen had been blank from a woman's point of view. I knew for certain that I would make film.

The physicality of Maya Deren's films impressed me. I could feel the director's energy in her presence behind the camera and in her movement on screen as an actor. Her invention of the concept of "creative geography," montaging vast expanses of time and space through the unifying image of a woman walking, impressed me.

Constrained by the limits of the rectangular film frame and screen projection, I created a more liberated space for my film *Available Space* (1978). Similar to Deren, I am the protagonist in the mise-en-scène, but instead of walking from space to space, I am seen literally pushing the edges of the window frame, the film frame, and spatial frame in eight different scenes. I built a table with wheels and a circular, rotating top for the 16mm projector and dubbed it an "active Annie" instead of a "lazy Susan." I moved the projections around the architectural space of the theaters and sometimes out of doors or windows, depending on the space. Not only was I able to place the film image within and around the corners, ceilings, floors, and walls of the room selectively, but I was also able to move my audience physically. They had to turn their heads and sometimes leave their seats to follow the projection. I believe that an active audience engaged perceptually, intellectually, and physically with cinema encourages its members to become more politically active in the world.

My film *Bent Time* (1983), a visual path across the United States beginning inside a linear accelerator in California and continuing through the Ohio Valley Mound sites to the Brooklyn Bridge, was also inspired by Deren's concept of "creative geography" as she walked from sand to weeds to pavement to a living room rug. Instead of using a single shot as Deren did, I used one frame of film per foot of physical space, bending time and space with an extreme wide-angle lens as I traversed locations of high energy.

Maya Deren's critical work as a theorist of her own cinema encouraged me to think deeply about my images and the formal manner in which I used them. The public humiliation she received from the male authorities (Dylan Thomas in particular) at the Cinema 16 film and

Figure 37. *I Was/I Am* (Barbara Hammer, 1973). Hammer's homage to *Meshes of the Afternoon*. The key, in this case, is to Hammer's motorcycle. Courtesy of Barbara Hammer.

poetry symposium angered me, and I identified with Deren's indefatigable commitment to continuing her theoretical explanations in the face of degrading put-downs. Her explanation of a "vertical cinema," a poetic cinema of feeling built by creating emotional layers and depths rather than linear stories, made perfect sense to me.

I entered avant-garde filmmaking at a time when structural cinema was the dominant aesthetic. I wanted to use some of the concepts of demystifying the apparatus and material used in filmmaking, but I also wanted to reenergize this rather academic approach by putting emotion back into film. In *Optic Nerve* (1985), I begin the film with images of the filmstrip itself, demonstrating the vertical nature of the projection system by pulling the filmstrip through the gate, with sprocket holes and frame lines showing. Through optical printing and editing I layered and manipulated present and past images with my own deliberate and repeated hesitancy in pushing a wheelchair in which my grandmother was seated through the door of a nursing home. Working intuitively with the printer, I found a way to communicate the emotional devastation of the act.

In 1978, at a conference on sexuality at York University in Canada, a representative of the Provincial Censor, Mary Brown, threatened to seize my film *Multiple Orgasms* (1977) if I projected it as scheduled. Not wanting to lose my print I devised a tactic that I believe would have made Maya Deren proud. At the microphone in the large auditorium I spent the seven minutes of what would have been screen time for the silent film to describe shot by shot the multiple vaginal contractions seen in the film.

Similarly, when a projectionist at the University of Florida, Orlando, turned off the projector in the middle of *Double Strength* (1978) because he was uncomfortable with the nudity, I entered the projection booth and in a controlled and assertive manner gave a minilecture on democracy and censorship to the poor fellow, who after some hesitation finally resumed the projection.

Maya Deren began the exhibition and distribution practices from which I have benefited. The college circuit still continues to be an excellent exhibition site, providing audiences and income for experimental filmmakers. I relish the opportunity to present my films and aesthetic views and to be adequately reimbursed in university settings. This gives me a chance to show my work as an experimental, but also lesbian-feminist, filmmaker to an audience often unfamiliar with experimental film. Education is one of the keys to preserving this maligned and underrated art form. I have shown my films to a third-grade class of eight-year-old children and found their reception of avant-garde cinema remarkable. I advocate the teaching of film in all its genres (experimental, documentary, narrative) in elementary schools.

In the late 1970s I didn't know that Maya Deren had confronted Jonas Mekas for his 1955 homophobic attack on experimental cinema when he named it "a conspiracy of homosexuality" in *Film Culture*, issue 3. I did know that Mekas had selected only two women, Maya Deren and Shirley Clarke, for his elite circle of important filmmakers called Essential Cinema. As a young woman filmmaker, I was aghast that a circle could be named, and once named would be so gender restrictive. I wrote Mekas a letter that today seems quite naïve in which I suggested that I could help him with his research to include more women in his circle. I remember mentioning the names of Sara Kathryn Arledge, Germaine Dulac, and Marie Menken. I never got a response.

Returning to my beginnings as an experimental lesbian-feminist film-maker, I remember one of my first invitations to screen on a college campus. Professor Jacqueline Zita invited me to Washington University in St. Louis, Missouri. After the projection, Zita asked to borrow the films to study them for an essay she later published in *Jump Cut* (March 1981). This was the first time someone had written about my films critically. Early in the morning I walked down the stairs from the second floor guestroom in Zita's house to the music of the soundtrack from *Dyke-tactics* (1974), my second 16mm film. I had the strange sensation of re-tracing Maya Deren's footsteps down the stairway of *Meshes of the After-noon*. These past thirty years have been an ongoing love affair with the moving image, a love affair, that, along with a Ukrainian heritage, I share with Maya Deren.

An Anagram of Ideas on Art, Form and Film

Maya Deren

PUBLISHER'S NOTE

Maya Deren's four 16 mm. films have already won considerable acclaim. Convinced that there was poetry in the camera, she defied all commercial production conventions and started to make films with only ordinary amateur equipment. Her first, MESHES OF THE AFTERNOON (1943), was made with her husband Alexander Hammid, whose films — FORGOTTEN VILLAGE, CRISIS, HYMN OF THE NATIONS (Toscannini) and others —reveal also that devotion to the poetry of vision which formed the common ground of their collaboration. When other work claimed his time, Maya Deren went on by herself — conceiving, producing, directing, acting, (being unable to afford actors) photographing (when she was not in the scene) and cutting. Through all the trials of such shoe-string production, which included carrying equipment for miles to the location, she had only the assistance of another woman, Hella Heyman, as camerawoman. Yet three more films were made: AT LAND, A STUDY IN CHOREOGRAPHY FOR CAMERA (with Talley Beatty(and RITUAL IN TRANSFIGURED TIME, thus proving that fine films could be made "for the price of the lipstick in a single Hollywood production." Her heroic persistence has just been rewarded by a John Simon Guggenheim Memorial Foundation Fellowship. Moreover, the reputation of the films has spread so that performances at the Provincetown Playhouse were completely sold out and they have also been shown in colleges and museums throughout the country.

In this pamphlet Maya Deren's approach to film reflects not the limited scope of a professional craftsman, but a broad cultural background—a profound interest not only in esthetics generally and in psychological insight, but in physics and the sciences as well. Russian-born, daughter of a psychiatrist, Maya Deren attended Syracuse University, where she first became interested in film, and received her B.A. from New York University and her M.A. from Smith College, both degrees in literature.

This is Number 9 of the "OUT-
CAST" Series of Chapbooks issued
by Oscar Baradinsky at the Alicat
Book Shop, 287 South Broadway,
Yonkers 5, N. Y. The edition con-
sists of 750 copies offered for sale.
Titles of other "OUTCAST" chap-
books will be found on the back cover.

AN ANAGRAM OF IDEAS ON ART, FORM AND FILM

by

MAYA DEREN

1946

THE ALICAT BOOK SHOP PRESS

Yonkers, New York

CONTENTS OF ANAGRAM

PREFACE

Any critical statement by an artist which concerns the field of his creative activity is usually taken to be a manifesto or a statement of the theories upon which the creative work is based. Art abounds in works designed to demonstrate principles and manifestos, and these are, almost without exception, inferior to those works from which the principles were derived.

In my case I have found it necessary, each time, to ignore any of my previous statements. After the first film was completed, when someone asked me to define the principle which it embodied, I answered that the function of film, like that of other art forms, was to create experience—in this case a semi-psychological reality. But the actual creation of the second film caused me to subsequently answer a similar question wth an entirely different emphasis. This time, that reality must exploit the capacity of film to manipulate Time and Space. By the end of the third film, I had again shifted the emphasis—insisting this time on a filmically visual integrity, which would create a dramatic necessity of itself, rather than be dependent upon or derive from an underlying dramatic development. Now, on the basis of the fourth, I feel that all the other elements must be retained, but that special attention must be given to the creative possibilities of Time, and that the form as a whole should be ritualistic (as I define this later in the essay). I believe, of course, that some kind of development has taken place; and I feel that one symptom of the continuation of such a development would be that the actual creation of each film would not so much illustrate previous conclusions as it would necessitate new ones—and thus the theory would remain dynamic and volatile.

This is not, therefore, to be taken as a manifesto. It is an organization of ideas in an anagramatic complex instead of in the linear logic to which we are accustomed.

An anagram is a combination of letters in such a relationship that each and every one is simultaneously an element in more than one linear series. This simultaneity is real, and independent of the fact that it is usually perceived in succession. Each element of an anagram is so related to the whole that no one of them may be changed without effecting its series and so effecting the whole. And, conversely, the whole is so related to every part that whether one reads horizontally, vertically, diagonally or even in reverse, the logic of the whole is not disrupted, but remains intact.

In this essay the element is not a single letter, but an idea concerned with the subject matter of its position in the anagram; that is, 2B, for instance, deals with the forms of art in reference to the mechanics of nature and the methods of man. In every other respect the principles governing an anagram hold. As printed, it proceeds from the general to the specific.

6

Those who prefer the inductive method may read the elements in reverse order. Or one may slice through on the diagonal, picking up the sides afterwards.

I recommend this form to anyone who has faced the problem of compressing into a linear organization an idea which was stimulating precisely because it extended into two or three different, but not contradictory directions at once.

It has seemed especially useful to me in this essay. In the effort to apply the currently accepted esthetic theories to the first new art form in centuries, I have found it necessary to re-examine and re-evaluate principles which had become so ''understood'' a quality of other arts as to have constituted, for the past century, the unquestioned premises of creative action. And so I have found myself involved in fields and considerations which seem far from my original concern with film. But I believe that these are not as irrelevant as they may, off-hand, seem.

Modern specialization has discouraged the idea of the whole man. One is timid to invade or refer to territories which are not, strictly speaking, one's own. In the need to do so, nevertheless—for to arrive at principles requires comparative analysis—it is possible that I have been inaccurate in various details. And in seeking for the principles of various concepts of art form, I have examined not those talents whose genius is to transcend all principles, but those lesser lights who, in failing to transcend them, illustrate them best. This may give, at times, the impression of a wholesale underestimation of modern art; and for this impression, which does not reflect my real evaluation, I must apologize. Whatever the errors of generalization or the weaknesses of critical omission, they are committed in the interest of showing film (in such a relatively short space) not as a localized, specialized craft but as an art form, sharing with other art forms a profound relationship to man, the history of his relation to reality, and the basic problems of form.

In an anagram all the elements exist in a simultaneous relationship. Consequently, within it, nothing is first and nothing is last; nothing is future and nothing is past; nothing is old and nothing is new . . . except, perhaps, the anagram itself.

AN ANAGRAM OF IDEAS ON ART, FORM AND FILM

1 A

At the moment, it has become fashionable, among all the self-appointed mentors of public conscience, to bemoan the inertia of the people towards the atom bomb, and to chastize this complacency with elaborate attitudes of righteous indignation, or pompous didacticism, or despair and silence. But inertia is, precisely, not a reaction—wrong or right;—it is the sheer persistence of an attitude already firmly habitual. The almost casual acceptance of the use of atomic energy is, if anything, testimony to man's complete adjustment to science; for him, it is merely the most recent in a long series of achievements, some of which, like electricity and the radio, have had far more the quality of miracle.

The anxiety of the scientists is based upon an intimate awareness of the destructive potential of the method which has been achieved. But ever since the curtains of specialization descended upon the methodology of of science, men have humbly accepted their inability to comprehend the detailed processes of such miracles, and have limited themselves to evaluating only the final results, which they have agreed to accept at their own risk. The gas piped through every kitchen simplifies the act of suicide; electricity can cause a strange death; cars can collide; airplanes can crash; tanks can explode. But man had come to terms with scientific disaster long ago, and remains consistent in his attitude.

What amazes him most, in the spectacle of current anxiety, is that the miracle-makers themselves, at this late date, seem to be attempting to reopen the first of all questions: to bite or not to bite of the forbidden fruit. Is not the public justified in its reluctance to become seriously involved in what is so obviously an academic discussion? And it is even possible that, pondering the force which can be contained in a fistful of matter, man might find poetic justice in an atomic bomb formed in the shape of an apple.

The distress of the scientists is, on the other hand, also justified. The occidental culture of the 17th century, where they began their specialized labors, had been homogeneous. All nature and reality, including man, had been previously accepted as a manifestation of the will of a central, absolute consciousness. In transposing that consciousness from the central position in the metaphysical cosmos to a location in man's own brain, the principle of conscious control and creative manipulation was, if anything, reasserted in science. It was logical to expect that this was true, as well, of all the other fields of activity.

But today the scientist emerges from the laboratory to discover himself part of a schizoid culture. The rationalism upon which he has predicated himself is an insular entity in a sociological structure which operates in terms of the most primitive motivations and non-rational procedures. And

8

this ambivalence is most strikingly evident in the existence of art forms which, claiming the scientific attitude toward reality as their source of inspiration, result in romantic or realistic exaltations of nature, and develop finally into the ecstasies of a sur-realism whose triumphant achievement consists in eliminating altogether the functions of consciousness and intelligence.

Presumably, man had enjoyed an age of reason in the 18th century. Yet today the concept of "reason" is as ambiguous as it had been during the 17th century, when ambiguity served to dis-simulate the actual revolution which was taking place. According to medieval concepts of absolute consciousness, the reason why a stone fell was because God willed that it do so. Reason was a function of the will of an inscrutable, immutable deity. Modern thought began with a most timid and subtle re-definition. When astronomical observations revealed the consistency of cosmic movement, it became necessary to account for this as a part of the nature with which the universe had been divinely endowed, which could henceforth function independently, (subject, of course, to divine intervention at will). In this way the divine will became a creator of laws, instead of functioning according to laws, as its consistency would have implied. The reason why a stone fell, now, was because such action was of its divine nature.

The following development was equally subtle. Reason was made a logical function, without a sacrifice of its metaphysical authority, by the simple device of attributing to the divine consciousness a rational character. When Milton wrote that it was more "reasonable" for the earth to revolve in the heavens than for the immense heavens to revolve their bulk around the earth, he was implying to deity the values of economy and efficiency—values relevant actually to the needs and conditions of man. From these "reasonable" terms to the "logical" terms of scientific cause and effect was but the last step in the achievement of a most critical intellectual revolution.

In the course of displacing deity-consciousness as the motive power of reality, by a concept of logical causation, man inevitably re-located himself in terms of the new scheme. He consciously distinguished himself from the nature which had now ceased to be divine, and proceeded to discover in himself, and within the scope of his manipulations, all the powers which he had previously attributed exclusively to deity. By the development of instruments of observation and discovery, such as the telescope, he achieved a measure of omnipresence. Through mathematical computations, he was able to extend his knowledge even beyond the reach of his instruments. From a careful analysis of causation and incidence, he developed the powers of prediction. And finally, not content to merely analyze an existent reality, he undertook to activate the principles which he had discovered, to manipulate reality, and to bring together into new relationships the elements which he was able to isolate. He was able to create forms according to his own intelligence. Thus he succeeded in usurping even the main attribute of divinity . . . fecundity. And although he was careful not to claim this, he had become himself God, to all intents and purposes, by virtue of the unique possession, among all natural phenomena, of creative consciousness.

I do not mean to imply that the exercise of consciousness originated in the 17th century. Previously, when man had considered himself a manifestation of divine consciousness, it was precisely through the exercise of consciousness that he could reaffirm his relationship with deity. The concerns of that relationship were moral, and up until the 17th century his activities —especially those of a philosophic and esthetic nature—consisted of moral (or ethical) ideas articulated in consciously creative and controlled forms.

Only when he relinquished his concept of divine consciousness did he confront the choice of either developing his own and accepting all the moral responsibilities previously dispensated by divinity, or of merging with inconscient nature and enjoying the luxurious irresponsibility of being one of its more complex phenomena. He resolved this problem by the simple expediency of choosing both; the forms of our modern culture are an accurate manifestation of this ambivalence. Man himself is a natural phenomenon and his activities may be either an extension and an exploitation of himself as a natural phenomenon, or he can dedicate himself to the creative manipulation and transfiguration of all nature, including himself, through the exercise of his conscious, rational powers.

Wherever he functions as a spontaneous natural phenomenon, he gives rise to forms typical of nature; wherever he functions as an analytical and creative intelligence, he achieves forms of an entirely different character. Nature, being unconscious, functions by an infinite process of inviolable cause and effect whose results are inevitabilities. But the forms of man are the results of a manipulation controlled according to motivation and intention. The forms of nature, springing from anterior causation, are often ambiguous both in their ''natural'' function and towards man. A mountain, created by the cooling of the earth's crust, is ambiguous in the first sense, since its incidence may or may not ''serve'' some purpose to the rest of the nature around it. A tree is ambiguous in its relation to man, in that its form and character are not intentionally designed, by nature, to serve any of the purposes to which man may put it. The forms of man, furthermore, are much more explicitly and economically determined by the function for which they are intended, even to the point of being limited, in their use, by that intention.

In these distinctions are implicit the moral attitudes which are respectively appropriate. The forms of nature, being inevitable, are amoral, and even at their most destructive, as in disease, cannot be considered morally responsible. The forms of man are, on the contrary, subject to moral evaluations in terms of the conscious intentions which they incorporate and they are not a priori exonerated from such judgment by their mere existence or even persistent survival.

All these basic distinctions, applied to the forms prevalent in modern culture, reveal its schizoid character. The achievements of science and industry are constituted of the forms and methods of man. The manifestations of much of our art (with which I am here specifically concerned) reveal, by and large, an effort to achieve the forms of nature.

Man's mind, his consciousness, is the greatest triumph of nature, the product of aeons of evolutionary processes, of infinite mutations, of merciless elimination. Now, in the 20th century, there are many among us who seek the long way back. In an essay on the relationship between art and the intellect, Charles Duits has given his commentary on sur-realism a profound

10

humor by referring to it in a terminology drawn from the medieval period. In the sense that the sur-realist esthetic reflects a state of mind which antecedes the 17th century, he is not only correct, but, if anything, too lenient. Their ''art'' is dedicated to the manifestations of an organism which antecedes all consciousness. It is not even merely primitive; it is primeval. But even in this effort, man the scientist has, through the exercise of rational faculties, become more competent than the modern artist. That which the sur-realists labor and sweat to achieve, and end by only simulating, can be accomplished in full reality, by the atom bomb.

2ᴀ

Total amnesia, although less spectacular than many other forms of mental disorder, has always seemed to me the most terrifying. A man so reduced to immediate perception only, has lost, in losing experience, all ability to evaluate, to understand, to solve and to create—in short, all that which makes him human. Moreover, in the process of evolving conscious memory man has had to forfeit those complex instinctual patterns which substitute, or rather, antecede, memory in animals. The infant kitten, out of itself—by a process of "vertical" inevitabilities—and through its own immediate experience of reality, will become a complete cat. But a human infant, out of itself, will not develop into its proper adulthood. It must learn beyond its instincts, and often in opposition to them, by imitation, observation, experimentation, reflection—in sum, by the complex "horizontal" processes of memory.

By "horizontal" I mean that the memory of man is not committed to the natural chronology of his experience—whether of an extended period, a single event, or a compulsive reaction. On the contrary, he has access to all his experience simultaneously. He can compare the beginning of a process to the end of it, without accepting it as a homogeneous totality; he can compare similar portions of events widely disparate in time and place, and so recognize both the constancy of elements and their variable functions in one context or another; and he is able to perceive that a natural, chronological whole is not immutable, but that it is a dynamic relationship of functioning parts.

So he is able to understand fire separate from the pain of his own burns.

For an animal, all experience remains immediately personal. Man's first step, accomplished through reflective recollection, is to depersonalize, to abstract from his personal experience.

Nowhere is the method more clearly epitomized than in mathematics. In order even to measure, it has first to abstract from the experience of space to a number. The concept of subjectivity, to which esthetic criteria have such frequent reference today, originated not in reference to art but, precisely, to science.

When man undertook to analyze the causes and effects of nature, on the basis of his observation, he became aware of the distorting window-glass of his subjectivity. At first he devoted himself to the development of instruments designed to "correct" his vision and to compensate for the limitations of his subjective perceptions—the sun-dial, the stable weight, the microscope, the telescope.

But even this was not enough. He became eventually aware of his subjective position. He understood that when, across a large distance, or in a reverse wind, the sound followed long after the image of an action—that this discrepancy was not due to an inaccuracy of observation because of a failure of his senses, but that it was a condition of his subjective position, one which would exist regardless of the presence of minds or senses to perceive it.

The theory of relativity is the latest triumph in the development of theoretical computations designed to overcome and compensate for the inalienability of subjective position. And if science has found it necessary to arrive at all these instruments and calculations in order to analyze reality realistically, how can the artist "realist" presume to cover the same ground on the basis of his personal powers of perception? Is not the relative poverty of contemporary art at least partly due to the fact that, in taking realism (which is not at all the same as objectivity) as its ambition it has basically denied the existence of art and substituted science?

The realist describes his experience of reality. He denies the value of the original, artificial reality created by the rigours and disciplines of the art instrument. But he is unwilling, also, to submit to the rigours and disciplines of the scientific instrument in objectively analyzing the existent reality. And so he moves among the optical illusions of that which really is, and the shadowy dreams of that which, by art, might be. He is tortured both by the anxieties of "truth," and the demands of that most precious of man's qualities—the vanity of the creative ego.

For man it has never been enough to merely understand the dynamics of a reality which would continue, in any case, to exist independently of his analysis. If all men had agreed, with the realists and the romantics, to describe, exalt, and extend the "natural condition" there would be no such thing as science, philosophy or art.

Even in science—or rather, above all in science, the pivotal characteristic of man's method is a violation of natural integrity. He has dedicated himself to the effort to intervene upon it, to dissemble the ostensibly inviolate whole, to emancipate the element from the context in which it "naturally" occurs, and to manipulate it in the creation of a new contextual whole— a new, original state of matter and reality—which is specifically the product of his intervention.

Once a natural integrity has been so violated, by the selection of elements from the original context, all subsequent integrations are no longer natural or inevitable. The task of creating forms as dynamic as the relationships in natural phenomena, is the central problem of both the scientist and the artist.

The most simple and primitive of artificial wholes is the arithmetical whole, which is the sum of its parts. The next step is the construction of a whole which consists of the sum of its parts in a certain arrangement, either in space or in time. A machine is such a whole, and standardization is possible because the parts are interchangeable with their equivalents. That is, a bolt or wheel may be replaced by similar bolts or wheels; a like organization of bolts, wheels, pulleys, etc., will result in a like machine. In such constructions the parts remain themselves; and although they may be designed to function in a certain manner, they are not transformed in the process of functioning. Consequently, such wholes are initially predictable from a knowledge of their parts.

But man's great dream is to achieve a whole whose character is far more mysterious and miraculous—that dynamic, living whole in which the inter-action of the parts produces more than their sum total in any sense. This relationship may be simple—as when water emerges from the inter-action of hydrogen and oxygen. But let a third element be added, which transfigures both; and a fourth, which transforms the three—and the difficulties of analysis and creation become incalculable.

The entire alphabet is insufficient to describe the infinite complex of variables which the theoretical formula of life or great art would involve. For the inter-action of the parts so transforms them into function that there are no longer parts, but a simple, homogeneous whole which defies dissectional analysis, and in so sublimating the complex history of its development, seems an instantaneous miracle.

All of living nature is constituted of such forms, and the nature in man may occasionally fuse all his resources into a moment of such miracle. Yet in creating man's consciousness—the capacity for conscious memory— nature created an impatience which will not wait the necessary aeons until a million conditions coincide to produce a miraculous mutation.

Memory makes possible imagination, which is the ability to so accelerate real, natural processes that they become unreal and abstract. It can tele-scope into a moment's thought an evolution which might take centuries and fail to occur altogether. It can arrange desirable conditions which, in nature, would have to occur as rare coincidence. Invisibly, and without the critical failures of actuality, man, in his mind, shuffles and re-shuffles the elements of his total experience—sensations, ideas, desires, fears—into a million combinations. In works of fantasy we can see the process as it occurs: the curious and often fascinating energy of a mind at work.

But should that triumphant moment—when the elements of a man's experience suddenly fuse into a homogeneous whole which transcends and so transfigures them—be left to the rarities of natural coincidence? Or should the artist, like the scientist, exercize his imaginative intelligence—the command and control of memory—to consciously try, test, modify, destroy, estimate probabilities, and try again . . . always in terms of the instrument by which the fusion will be realized.

3A

In a world so intimately overwhelmed by scientific discovery, revelation and invention—where even the most desolate island becomes a fueling station for the globe-circling airplane—it is impossible to justify a neglect or ignorance of its realities. Yet the schizophrenic solution is precisely this: to dispute nothing, to resolve no conflicts; to admit to everything and to disguise, under the homogeneity of this unassailable tolerance, the most insiduous contradictions. The popularized notion of Dr. Jekeyll and Mr. Hyde fails to comprehend that very element which makes the actuality possible: that the face of the man and the beast are one and the same.

Today the ostensible aspect of all man's endeavors is a scientific justification and the midnight hour when the true flesh becomes distinguished from the skillful mask has not yet been proclaimed. The "realist" presumes as the scientific observer. The sur-realist, disguised as the "sub-conscious" itself, demands the moral clemency which man has always graciously extended to that which cannot help itself (albeit from a superior position and with an undertone of condescension).

Such borrowing of scientific terms serves to create the illusion that the actual informations of that field are being put to a creative use. The work of art is thereby graced with the authority granted the science; and the principled proceedure of the former escapes investigation since the specialized proceedure of the latter is beyond popular comprehension. Unfortunately, it is not always that the art gains, as that the science loses, eventually, its popular prestige. The sur-realist exploitation of the confessional for its own sake has served to minimize the therapeutic intentions of disciplined, responsible psychiatry and has inspired the notion that anyone can be an analyst, particularly in art criticism. Yet such labors most often display an abysmal ignorance of both psychiatry and art.

One of the most revealing borrowings from science is the term "primitive," from anthropology. An age like ours, obsessed with a sense of evil, guilty failure, will seek redemption in devious ways. Although anthropology would be the last to support such a notion, it has pleased certain critics to imagine that the moral character of primitive societies is innocence; and so it pleases them the more to imagine that they discover, in the professional ignorance of the "modern primitive" painter, some archeological moral fragment, well preserved, of that idyllic time. Even if they are not dismayed by such a confusion between an intellectual and a moral quality, how can they imagine it desirable for men to think as if the discoveries and inventions of the past centuries had not intervened,—to effect, even if it were possible, a total cultural amnesia at will?

I am certain that thoughtful critics do not use the term "primitive" without definition and modification. But its general usage, and as a category title for exhibits, reveals a comparative ideal based on the superficial similarity between the skilled simplicity of artists whose culture was limited in informations and crude in equipment; and the crude simplifications of artists whose culture is rich in information and refined in its equipment.

The artist of a primitive society was far from its most ignorant and isolated member. On the contrary, since his function was to represent, towards the community, the "advanced" principles of the highest moral, political and practical authorities—both human and divine—he had almost to be best informed of all.

He had to create masks, garments, patterns of dance movement—real forms which would have super-natural authority, a most difficult accomplishment. The "lucky" symbol on the war-weapon must transcend, through form, the mortality of the natural source from which it was drawn. The tapestries and wall paintings must be the comforting presence of protective powers in the home. He must compose a chant seductive enough to invoke the favor of one god, or threatening enough to exorcise the evil spirit. He stood half in the human world and half in the world of the super-natural powers; much was demanded of him by both; he could not afford the luxury of ignorance or impressions.

That that mythology is, today, an imaginative exercise for us, should not obscure the reality it had for those who lived by it. And since the greater part of the knowledge of primitive societies was a mythological knowledge, the art was an art of knowledge. But today, the distinction of the "modern primitive" is that he is unhampered by the facts which so often inhibit the imagination of his contemporaries, and so is freer to pursue the utterly imaginative concept.

It is not only in the discrepency of intellectual attitude that the real primitive and the "modern primitive" differ, but also, and necessarily, in the forms of the art.

Two-dimensionalism, and similar conventions, on the basis of which "modern primitives" are so called, does not, in the art of primitive societies, derive from an inability to comprehend or to realize the three-dimensional perspective. Various theories have been advanced for the consistent use of abstracted and simplified form in primitive art. T. E. Hulme suggests that when man is in conflict with a nature which he finds dangerously uncontrollable, he attempts to order and control it, vicariously, by doing so in his art; whereas when he has an aimable, confident relationship to nature he is pleased to repeat such sympathetic forms. It is an interesting and perhaps valid theory.

In any case, an absolutism of art forms seems highly appropriate to societies which, subject to natural disaster, rigidly localized by geographic and material restrictions, must place the unity of the tribe above all else and thus evolve an absolutism of political, moral and economic authority and an absolutistic concept of time and space.

Thus the art works of primitive cultures comprehend and realize a whole system of ideas within their forms. For this reason they have always an authoritative and sober aspect, and even at their most delicate and

16

refined, they seem somehow weighted with dimensions of destiny and meaning. However mysterious the complexities and configurations may be, they never are fanciful or fantastic (except to the fanciful and fantastic). Certainly its intent is never casual, personal or decorative. The shield which was originally conceived primarily to protect, by material and magical means, is today of value on the basis of its sheer beauty, alone. Can anything testify better to the skill with which the primitive artist was able to fuse all functions (mythological, material and esthetic) into a single form? But does the "modern primitive" even aspire, much less achieve such fullness of dimension?

At its most sincere, as with Rousseau, contemporary primitive painting is a style of personal expression, a curiously naive and individual system of ideas. Sometimes, as in such creative talents, it can be sustained in the face of the informations of modern culture. But this is not often the case.

Creativity consists in a logical, imaginative extension of a known reality. The more limited the information, the more inevitable the necessity of its imaginative extension. The masks of primitive ritual extend the fierce grimace of the uncontrolled animal; the astronomical, literary voyages of the 17th and 18th centuries extended the suggestions of the telescope. The contemporary "primitive" may achieve some extraordinary effects by imaginatively extending some immediate, simple knowledge. But imagine his embarrassment at suddenly confronting fields of knowledge whose real discoveries make redundant his extensions, and are often even more astounding and miraculous. His knowledge is invalidated and ceases to serve as a springboard for creative action. Adjusted to the stable, absolute concepts of his own small world he cannot, in a moment, readjust his imagination to extend the new, miraculous realities of the airplane, the telephone, the radio. Nor can he make the philosophical and psychological adjustment necessary to relocate himself in the strange relativisms of time and space which these instruments introduce into his life.

As the art dealers know very well, the "modern primitive" must be a zealously guarded recluse. But if this is so, he differs from the true primitive not only in being less informed of his own culture (in meaning if not in actual fact) and in creating forms irrelevant to its informations, but in creating them also in isolation, rather than in functional relation to that culture. Failing of a mythological authority for his ideas, his point of view on reality, however charming, must stand comparison with our knowledge of reality. All this conspires to make of the "modern primitive" a singular curiosity which must, at best, be evaluated not by the pseudo-scientific approach implied in the word "primitive," but as a personal style which stands or falls, as all art does, by the creative genius of the artist.

I hope that in using the exaggerations of the special category of the "modern primitive" I have not weakened my essential point. In its ambiguous implications, and in the possibility of contrasting it to its namesake, it afforded a convenient opportunity to point out a common failure of modern thought to understand that <u>art must at least comprehend the large facts of its total culture, and, at best, extend them imaginatively.</u>

As I suggest elsewhere, the distinctions between the romantic, the realist and the sur-realist are not as great as each of them would like to believe. To invade (as they all do) the province of science—the analysis of the nature of reality—with the minimal instruments of personal perception is surely not the same as to benefit by the discoveries arrived at by refined, scientific methods. To be a deliberately primitive scientist is today, of all ambitions, the most senseless. And to substitute such redundant, exploratory activity for that of creating an art reality is to fail entirely to add to the variety and richness of one's culture.

Art is the dynamic result of the relationship of three elements: the reality to which a man has access—directly and through the researches of all other men; the crucible of his own imagination and intellect; and the art instrument by which he realizes, through skillful exercize and control, his imaginative manipulations. To limit, deliberately or through neglect, any of these functions, is to limit the potential of the work of art itself.

The reality from which man draws his knowledge and the elements of his manipulation has been amplified not only by the development of analytical instruments; it has, increasingly, become itself a reality created by the manipulation of instruments. The reality which we must today extend—the large fact which we must comprehend, just as the primitive artist comprehended and extended his own reality—is the relativism which the airplane, the radio and the new physics has made a reality of our lives.

We cannot shirk this responsibility by using, as a point of departure, the knowledge and state of mind of some precedent period of history. My repeated insistence upon the distinctive function of form in art—my insistence that the distinction of art is that it is neither simply an expression, of pain, for example, nor an impression of pain but is itself a form which creates pain (or whatever its emotional intent)—might seem to point to a classicism. If so, I must remind the reader that I have elsewhere characterized the ''ritualistic'' form (in which I have included classicism) as an exercise, above all, of consciousness. The reality which such consciousness would today comprehend is not that of any other period. In this, and in the invention of new art instruments, lies the potential originality of the art of our time.

18

1B

Accustomed as we are to the idea of a work of art as an ''expression'' of the artist, it is perhaps difficult to imagine what other possible function it could perform. But once the question is posed, the deep recesses of our cultural memory release a procession of indistinct figures wearing the masks of Africa, or the Orient, the hoods of the chorus, or the innocence of the child-virgin . . . the faces always concealed, or veiled by stylization —moving in formal patterns of ritual and destiny. And we recognize that an artist might, conceivably, create beyond and outside all the personal compulsions of individual distress.

The evidence accumulates, and presses, in the occident, towards the 17th century. And it becomes important to discover how and why man renounced the mask and started to move towards the feverish narcissism which today crowds the book-stores, the galleries, and the stage.

The change was subtle. The relationship of thought and art on the one hand and discovery and invention on the other, is not a settled marriage, grown steady with agreement and adjustment. It is more like a passionate flirtation, full of defiance, reluctance, anticipation and neglect. It is true that in his treatment of personality Shakespeare anticipates that amalgam of romanticism and realism which reached its peak in the 19th century and has not yet spent its force. But the formal whole in which the characters of his dramas expounded their personal emotions, was as stringent a destiny as that of classicism. Perhaps the secret of his art lies, precisely, in the impact of the intensely romantic personality upon a universe still absolute in structure.

In the 17th century man, along with nature, ceased to be a manifestation of the absolute divine will, and accepted, in the first pride of his newfound, individual consciousness, the moral responsibilities which he had, until then left to the dispensation of the deity. All this was reflected in the classicism of the early 18th century, and it seems to me evident that if a period of classicism could occur in the full flush of this exhilarating belief that man was, to all intents and purpose, the dominant figure of the universe, then it must be a form predicated not upon absolutism, but upon the idea of consciousness. Whether this consciousness is a manifestation of deity in man, or whether it is of man's own nature becomes important only at the moment that its powers are put to a test and found wanting. It was exactly such a failure which the violences, confusions, and reversals which followed seemed to indicate.

For man, in his political and social activities, did not pause to develop instruments and methods equivalent to those which the scientist, in his province, labored to perfect. Nor did he stop to realize that invention anywhere could successfully follow only upon cautious preparations and analyses. His repeated failure to invent a social organization which would be immediately successful and appropriate to his new concept of the universe was a critical blow to his newly acquired self esteem and seemed to be a failure of consciousness itself. Nor was he experienced enough a scientist to be consoled by the long history of failure which, in scientific experiment, precedes any achievement. Even if he were aware of this, his central position in the universe endowed his problems, pains and disappointments with an importance to which the impersonal, experimental failures of science could not presume to compare. He could not now endure those troubles which, as a more modest element of the universe, he had previously accepted in the firm conviction that even misfortune contained some benediction according to the inscrutable will of God.

His adjustment to this complex of conditions was most dextrous. As a realist, conversant with scientific causation, he relinquished the principle of control and "acknowledged" the forces of reality as beyond the scope of his individual, moral responsibility. But as a romantic, he retained his exalted position in center of the universe and so was entitled to give full expression to his individual concerns and agonies. In this way he could be both nature and deity, except that, as part of nature, he could not be held responsible as a divine will. Once this principle was established, it was simple to accomplish, eventually, the shift of emphasis from self-expression to self-exaltation as a phenomenon of nature whose actions and reactions, being inevitable, were, like nature, outside the law of moral responsibility; and, finally, encouraged by the dignified benediction of psycho-analysis, as a science, he could indulge in the ecstasies of sur-realist confessional. Since to confess to some banality is to lose the advantage of confessional, even those artists who are reasonably happy find it necessary to pretend to horrors in the effort to present a "truth which is stranger than fiction."

The romantic and the sur-realist differ only in the degree of their naturalism. But between naturalism and the formal character of primitive, oriental and Greek art there is a vast ideological distance. For want of a better term which can refer to the quality which the art forms of various civilizations have in common, I suggest the word ritualistic. I am profoundly aware of the dangers in the use of this term, and of the misunderstandings which may arise, but I fail, at the moment, to find a better word. Its primary weakness is that, in strictly anthropological usage, it refers to an activity of a primitive society which has certain specific conditions: a ritual is anonymously evolved; it functions as an obligatory tradition; and finally, it has a specific magical purpose. None of these three conditions apply, for example, to Greek tragedy. On the other hand, they are, in a sense, exterior to the ritual form itself, since they refer to its origin, its preservation and its function. Moreover, it is hardly beside the point that all art forms were originally a part of such rituals and that the form itself, within itself, has remained strikingly intact in general outline, in spite of the changes in these exterior conditions. It is to these constant elements, which seem to me of major importance since they exist simultaneously in unrelated cultures, to which I have reference.

20

Even when it is not the anonymous primitive ritual, the ritualistic form is not the expression of the individual nature of the artist; it is the result of the application of his individual talent to the moral problems which have been the concern of man's relationship with diety, and the evidence of that privileged communication. It is never an effort to reveal a reality which, in the face of divine omniscience and power, man could not presume to know.

The ritualistic form reflects also the conviction that such ideas are best advanced when they are abstracted from the immediate conditions of reality and incorporated into a contrived, created whole, stylized in terms of the utmost effectiveness. It creates fear, for example, by creating an imaginative, often mythological experience which, by containing its own logic within itself, has no reference to any specific time or place, and is forever valid for all time and place. How different is the customary modern method, which induces fear by employing some real contemporary figure which, in reality, inspires it; or reconstructs some situation which might be typical of the contemporary experience of some cultural majority. Such a method may be temporarily effective, but the conditions of life, and so the "real" experience of men, changes with a rapidity which can date such "realism" in a few years. That which was frightening today is no longer frightening tomorrow.

Above all, the ritualistic form treats the human being not as the source of the dramatic action, but as a somewhat depersonalized element in a dramatic whole. The intent of such depersonalization is not the destruction of the individual; on the contrary, it enlarges him beyond the personal dimension and frees him from the specializations and confines of personality. He becomes part of a dynamic whole which, like all such creative relationships, in turn, endow its parts with a measure of its larger meaning.

If it can be said that, in romanticism, the tragedy results from the destructive, tragic nature of its central figure, then it must be said, by contrast, that in ritualistic form the tragedy confers often upon an unsuspecting person, the heroic stature of the tragic figure.

In its method—a conscious manipulation designed to create effect, in contrast to the spontaneous compulsions of expression—and in its results—the new, man-made reality, in contrast to the revelation or recapitulation of one which exists—the ritualistic form is much more the art equivalent of modern science than the naturalism which claims to be so based.

Today it would decline to concern itself with a revelation of reality not because man is incapable, but because science is more capable than art in that capacity. And it would be predicated upon the exercize of consciousness, not as the instrument by which divine will is apprehended, but as the human instrument which makes possible a comprehension and a manipulation of the universe in which man must somehow locate himself.

2ᴮ

The impulse behind my insistent concern with the triumphant achievements of science is most elemental: I believe simply that an analysis of
any of man's achievements may reveal basic principles of methodology
which, properly adjusted to the immediate conditions of other problems,
may lead to similar triumphs. I do not claim this to be an original attitude,
for naturalism is presumably just such a transcription from the methods of
science to those of art. My argument is that if such a procedure is to have
any value, then it must be based on a thorough observation of the whole
method, and not a tangential development of some portion of it. If the
complex specialization of science in the 18th and 19th centuries obscured the
basic design of its method, then it might even have been better to follow,
as example, some other field of achievement altogether.

Just as the varying use of the word reason reflected the development of
the concept of reason in the 17th century, so the current use of the word
consciousness reveals the underlying concept of its function. In art, today
a state of consciousness is understood as synonymous with a capacity for
obervation. This capacity may range, in degree, from the most simple sen-
sory perception to the most complex analysis or the acute, associational
insight. These are then recorded in a style of notation which may range
from the defiantly awkward (proof of the fact that the original impression
of a truth has not been tampered with) to the decoratively graceful (the
flirtatious pirouette of the artist around his subject).

In such a concept of art, the role of the artist has degenerated into a
basic passivity. He functions as an often inaccurate barometer, scaled in
emotional degrees, whose nervous fluctuations are recorded by a frequently
defective mechanism, in a code whose key is often inconstant and sometimes
even unknown. His achievement, if any, consists in a titilating reproduction
of a reality which can be enjoyed in air-conditioned comfort by an audience
too comatose to take the exercise of a direct experiece of life.

The essential irony of such a concept is that, in undertaking to reveal
the nature of reality, the artist enters the province of science, lacking the
very weapons, skills and strategems with which the scientist has carefully
equipped himself; and worst of all, he has no concept for the function of
his discoveries, except to stuff, mount and exhibit the more impressive and
presentable portions (or, with the sur-realists, the more gruesome and
shocking) on the walls of his house, as proof of his capacity for extravagant
emotional adventure.

In science, the findings, no matter how painfully accumulated, are but
the raw materials of an ultimate creative action. The first step of creative
action is the violation of the ''natural'' integrity of an original context.

22

But much of the art of our time, and of the period immediately preceeding it, has, as its avowed purpose, the representation or projection of some natural integrity in terms of its own exaltedly "inalienable" logic of inevitabilities. This is equally true of the various "schools" who imagine themselves in fundamental opposition. Nor should the basic method be obscured by those singular talents who, in the process of creating, transcend all theoretical principles.

The "realists," critical of the esoteric aspects of sur-realism, propose an art form constituted of "common, recognizable emotions" occurring in a "common, realistic" frame of reference, and presented in the "common language of every day speech." They regard this as a guarantee of communicability and "mass appeal." Yet the precedents of our cultural history do not support such a theory. On the contrary, the most popular theaters—the Elizabethan and the Greek—dealt with emotions universal only by generalization, but extraordinary in their immediate quality (Hamlet and Oedipus), resulting from extraordinary circumstances, and articulated in a most uncommon, highly stylized speech.

It is at least to the credit of the sur-realists that once they accepted the forms of nature as model, they were relentless and uncompromising in the logical pursuit of this principle. In atomizing the human being, they even anticipated, in a sense, a scientific destiny. Many of their paintings, if they were not presented as works of the imagination, might easily pass for emotionally heightened reportorial sketches of Hiroshima (of the kind which Life Magazine reproduces): the nightmare of oozing blood, the horror of degenerative death from invisible, inner radiations, the razed landscapes reduced to its primeval elements, the solitary, crazed survivors. But even if one were not to find such a point of exterior reference, the sur-realists are self-avowedly dedicated to externalizing an inner reality whose original integrity has been devotedly preserved.

Both the "realists" and the "sur-realists" have a very righteous contempt for the group loosely characterized as the "romantics." The realists criticize them for "escaping" from reality, whereas the sur-realists criticize them for the sentimentality with which they idealize reality. But one consistent motivation of the creative act is the conviction of one's originality; the entire personal justification of whatever effort is required is that the result does not duplicate (at least in its particular aspects) the achievements of another artist. Taken in terms of the representation or the expression of natural reality, the originality of achievement becomes, then, an originality of discovery, a pursuit of the exotic, novel condition, exterior or interior, the search for the "truth which is stranger than fiction."

Thus the argument between the "realists," the "sur-realists" and the "romantic escapists" is not one of form, nor even of the method of art, but merely a disagreement as to which landscape is of most consequence: the familiar, drug-store around the corner, the inner chamber of horrors, or the island utopias of either an inner or outer geography.

Before psychiatry, as a science, began its investigation of emotional realities, or photography its immaculate observation of material reality, the artist was often concerned with either or both of these. But he did not always indulge in the simple expediency of representation as he does today.

That which was, in reality, a result of natural, inevitable processes had to emerge, in the work of art, as the effect of a controlled, artificial manipulation. The configurations and colors of a landscape are a part of an infinite complex of climatic, chemical, botanical, and other elements. In a painting of such a landscape, the harmony, brilliancy, etc., had to be achieved through the manipulation of paint, line, color, shape, size. The least requirement of such a transcription was professional skill and an understanding of one's chosen medium.

The art world today is overwhelmed by the products of arrogant amateurs and dilletantes who refuse to respect their "profession" by even so much as a dedication to its skills and techniques. The emphasis is upon spontaneity in the act of creation, although this is the last possible means by which inevitability can be created in the work itself. It is revealing that the exercise of skill—professionalism in its highest sense—is at an apparent all-time low in art. The prevalent feeling is that you, too, can be an artist in three easy lessons, providing you are "sensitive" or "observant," and so can discover, in the world outside or in the microcosmos of your own tortures, some bit of reality which has not already been exploited. The central problem is to represent it with a fair degree of fidelity.

But why would one exalt the integrity of nature or any part of it, in its own terms, or seek to fashion an art form out of its "intrinsic values" and inalienable logics, when our age has arrived at the ultimate recognition of relative relationships in the discovery that all matter is energy? If the achievements of science are the result of a violation of natural integrity, in order to emancipate its elements and re-relate them, how can an artist be content to do no more than to perceive, analyze and, at most, recreate these ostensibly inviolable wholes of nature?

To renounce the natural frame of reference—the natural logic and integrity of an existent reality—is not, as is popularly assumed, an escape from the labor of truth. On the contrary, it places upon the artist the entire responsibility for creating a logic as dynamic, integrated and compelling as those in which nature abounds. To create a form of life is, in the final analysis, much more demanding than to render one which is ready-made.

The intent to create a new set of relationships effects, first of all, the selection of elements. In a naturalistic form, an element is selected in terms of a presumed "intrinsic" value; actually, this value is not intrinsic but is conferred upon it by the context in which it "naturally" occurs. In creating a new form, the elements must be selected according to their ability to function in the new, "un-natural" context. A gesture which may have been very effective in the course of some natural, spontaneous conversation, may fail to have impact in a dance or film; whereas one which may have passed unnoticed may be intensely moving if it lends itself to a climactic position in art context.

On the face of it, such considerations may seem obvious. Yet much of naturalistic art relies precisely on the "intrinsic" value of the element. Here it is not the context of the work which endows the element with value, but the associational process by which the audience refers that element to its own experience of reality. To rely upon such reference is to limit communicability to an audience which shares, with the artist, a common ground of experience.

24

Such "timely" art stands in great contrast to, for instance, the Greek drama, which has survived precisely because the elements which it employed had only a coincidental reference to the reality of the period in which it was created. Actually, these elements were emancipated from all immediately recognizable contexts, and so were never dependent upon being confirmed by personalized references of the audience. Their value derives from the integrated whole of which they are a part, and this whole is not a familiar, but a new experience. Being new, it illuminates emotions and ideas which may have escaped our attention in the distracting profusions of reality, and so becomes educational (in the finest sense of the word). The lavish fecundity of nature, without which it could not survive all material disasters, gives way, in art, to a concept of economy. Out of the wealth of remembered experience, the elements are selected with discrimination, according to their compatibility with the other elements of the intended whole.

In speaking of the relationships which are created in scientific forms, I listed those wholes which are the sum total of parts, and those which are the sum total of parts in a certain arrangement (as in a machine), and finally that "emergent whole" (I borrow the term from Gestalt psychology), in which the parts are so dynamically related as to produce something new which is unpredictable from a knowledge of the parts. It is this process which makes possible the idea of economy in art, for the whole which here emerges transcends, in meaning, the sum total of the parts. The effort of the artist is towards the creation of a logic in which two and two may make five, or, preferably, fifteen; when this is achieved, two can no longer be understood as simply two. This five, or this fifteen—the resultant idea or emotion—is therefore a function of the total relationships, the form of the work (which is independent of the form of reality by which it may have been inspired). It is this which Flaubert had reference to in stating that "L'idee n'existe qu'en vertu de sa forme."

One of the most unfortunate aspects of the dominance of the naturalist tradition in art today is the existence of an audience unaccustomed to the idea of the objective form of art. Instead, accustomed to a work of art as a reference to nature, they anticipate a re-creation of their own experience. They take issue with any experience which does not conform with their own, and characterize it as a personalized distortion. On the other hand, they may, coincidentally, concur with that observation, in which case it is not a distortion, but an "acute insight into reality." The development and decline of the vogue for sur-realism is almost a graph of the fluctuation of such coincidences.

Yet, as I have pointed out elsewhere, the most enduring works of art create a mythical reality, which cannot refer to one's own personal observations.

Even antiquity does not always protect such works from dismemberment by the subjective audience. But in contemporary art, and especially when the elements are drawn from reality, the audience is certain to approach the work as if it were altogether a natural phenomenon. They isolate from it those elements which they find most personally evocative, and interpret them according to their personal context of experience. Such an individualism implies a complete refusal to recognize the intention of the artist in creating a specific context, and the meaning which is conferred upon the elements by this context. It results in the incredible platitude, intended always as a compliment, that in the great works of art every one can read his own personal meaning. Or, as I treat in detail elsewhere, the dismemberment may be achieved by the instrument of an alien system, such as Freudianism.

A work of art is an emotional and intellectual complex whose logic is its whole form. Just as the separate actions of a man in love will be misunderstood, or even thought "insane," from the logic of non-love, so the parts of a work of art lose their true meaning when removed from their context and evaluated by some alien logical system. And just as an analysis of the reasons for love may follow upon the experience, but do not explain or induce it, so a dis-sectional analysis of a work of art fails, in the act of dismemberment, to comprehend the very inter-active dynamics which give it life. Such an analysis cannot substitute, and may even inhibit, the experience itself, which only an unprejudiced receptivity, free of personal requirements and preconceptions, can invite.

In the effort to protect their art from dismemberment, many painters have become abstractionists. By eliminating recognizable form, they hoped to eliminate exterior reference. It is my impression that music, being by nature abstract, is less subject to such dismemberment, although I have heard the most gruesome tales of what has been done even to Mozart. But language is, by its own nature, recognizable. For this reason we have developed, in connection with poetry, a phenomenal quantity of interpretative literature. Many writers compose more creatively in their commentaries upon other writers than they do in their art proper. Poetry has suffered most at the hands of the subjective reader, for each word can be pried from its context and used as a springboard for creative action in terms of some personal frame of reference and in all art, the more integrated the whole, the more critically it is effected by even the most minute change.

When Marcel Duchamp drew a mustache on the Mona Lisa, he accepted the painting as a ready-made reality out of which, by the addition of a few well-placed lines, he created a Duchamp, which he thereafter exhibited under his own name. And the subjective spectator who adds his personal mustaches to works of art should have the courage and the integrity to thereafter assume responsibility for his creative action under his own name.

3B

As in science, the process of creative art is two-fold: the experience of reality by the artist on one side, and his manipulation of that experience into an art reality on the other. In his person he is an instrument of discovery; in his art he exercizes the art-instrument of invention.

Contemporary art is especially characterized by an emphasis upon the artist as himself instrument of discovery and the role of the art instrument has, for the most part, degenerated into a mere means of conveying those discoveries. In other words, the emphasis is upon reality as it exists, obvious or obscured, simple or complex.

The incidence of naturalism in art is in almost direct proportion to the extent to which the elements of reality (the experience of the artist) can serve also as the elements of the work of art; and to the extent to which the natural, contextual logic in which they occur can be simulated or reconstructed in the art work. Thus, naturalism has been most of all manifest in the plastic forms, where the art elements—lines, colors, masses, perspectives, etc.—can be immediately derived from reality.

Language, on the other hand, consists of elements which are themselves un-natural and invented. Here it is possible to be naturalistic in reference to a language reality: that is, a conversation, being already a transcription of ideas and emotions into verbal patterns, can be itself reproduced as an intact reality in literature. One has only to compare the dialogues of classic literature to the conversations of naturalistic novels and dramas, or, further, to the word-doodling of some sur-realist ''poetry,'' to see the difference in the approach to language.

Even in naturalism, a departure from ready-made conversational reality, or from word-ideas, may inspire a creative exercize on the part of the writer. A verbal description, however accurate, is not the reality itself of a chair, for instance, since the chair exists in spatial terms; just as a painting becomes ''literary'' when it is based upon an effort to illustrate, in spatial terms, ideas which are essentially verbal.

Flaubert is thought of as a prime example of an artist dedicated to the accurate description of reality. Yet his linguistic diligence indicates that he thought, actually, of creating, in verbal terms, the equivalent of the experience which he had of spatial reality. He succeeded in creating a verbal reality whose validity is not at all dependent upon the degree of accuracy which it achieves in reference to the reality by which it was inspired. In Flaubert it is completely irrelevant whether there ever existed, in reality, the chair which exists in the novel. But in many of those writers which claim to his tradition it is, on the contrary, important for the reader to decide: are these things really true in the world?

The chair which Flaubert creates by the exercise of his art instrument—language—is not a visual image, it is a verbal image. Moreover, it is, precisely, an independent verbal image and not a symbol. (I elaborate on this distinction, in another respect, elsewhere.) For if it were a symbol, its meaning would reside outside the work, in whatever reality—object or event—it represented as substitute or had reference to. I stress this independence of an image created by the work of art itself because there is a tendency, today, to regard all images as symbols: to insist that nothing is what it is but that it must "stand for" something else.

In view of the currently loose, casual usage of the word "symbol," it would seem important to re-ascertain its more explicit meaning. In speaking of the direct, immediate meaning of an "image," I do not intend to exclude the process of generalization. On the contrary, the individual moment or image is valuable only insofar as its ripples spread out and encompass the richness of many moments; and certainly this is true of the work of art as a whole. But to generalize from a specific image is not the same as to understand it as a symbol for that general concept. When an image induces a generalization and gives rise to an emotion or idea, it bears towards that emotion or idea the same relationship which an exemplary demonstration bears to some chemical principle; and that is entirely different from the relationship between that principle and the written chemical formula by which it is symbolized. <u>In the first case the principle functions actively; in the second case its action is symbolically described, in lieu of the action itself.</u> An understanding of this distinction seems to me to be of primary importance.

All works employing figures of mythology are especially proposed as evidence of the "symbolic" method. Yet to say this is to imply that a Greek tragedy would fail to convey its values to one ignorant of the complex genealogy and intricate activities of the pantheon.

It may be argued that the references which would, today, be ascertained only by scholarly research were, at the time of the creation of the work, a matter of common knowledge. But I have pointed out elsewhere, and it is relevant here, that an integrated whole emerges not from some intrinsic value of its elements, but from their function in dynamic relationship to all the others. Consequently, even when an object may have also some exterior symbolic reference, it functions accordingly in the whole, and so is redefined by its own immediate context. Zeus is a great power in the mythological pantheon. But Zeus also functions as a great power whenever he is introduced as a dramatic element in a theatrical creation—to the extent that the author believed in the mythology. Consequently we can know his power from the work of art where it is re-created by the art instrument, without knowing anything else. In this way it is possible for an image to "mean" much directly, and not by virtue of an indirect, symbolic representation.

It may be possible that some esoteric research into the domestic complications of the pantheon would reveal some second level of meaning, as symbolic reference. But it is a question as to whether appreciation is ever intensified by such effort. And I doubt that such works of art, dedicated to the creation of an experience which should illuminate certain ethical or moral principles, would entrust their primary ideas to a second or third level of diagnosis.

For similar reasons, I cannot see what is to be gained by the current tendency to regard all the images of a work in terms of Freudian symbolic reference. A competent artist, intent on conveying some sexual reference, will find a thousand ways to evade censorship and make his meaning irrevocably clear. Even the incompetants of Hollywood daily achieve this; should we deny at least a similar skill in our more serious artists?

My contention is that whenever an image is endowed with a certain meaning-function by the context of the work of art—the product of an art instrument itself—then that is the value proper of the image in reference to the specific work. When an author is delicate in reference to love or sex, it very well may be that he intends it as a delicate experience (as contrast and deliberate counter-point to other experiences in the work); or, as artist, he may prefer to leave such lyric, exalted experience to the imagination of the audience, rather than confine and limit it by the crudities of his technique. And what right have we then to shout out that which he intended to have the qualities of a whisper; or destroy his counter-points; or to define that which he, in considered humility, found, himself, undefinable? To do so would be to destroy the integrity which he has carefully created—to destroy the work of art itself.

One could, perhaps, psycho-analyze the artist as a personality . . . why does he think love to be a delicate and magical experience? But to the extent that the artist manipulates and creates consciously according to his instrument, the instrument acts as a censor upon the free expression which psycho-analysis requires, for he selects, from his associational stream of images, those which are appropriate to and compatible with the other elements.

Psycho-analysis, while valid as a therapy for mal-adjusted personality, defeats its own purpose as a method of art criticism, for it implies that the artist does not create out of the nature of his instrument, but that it is used merely to convey some reality independent of all art. It implies that there is no such thing as art at all, but merely more or less accurate self-expression. In an essay on La Fontaine's "Adonis," Paul Valery makes some very penetrating observations on the difference between the personal dream and the impersonal work of art, which are very relevant to this whole discussion.

It is customary today to refer to the sensitivity or perception of an artist as a primary value; and to the extent that the artist seeks to reveal the nature of reality, it is entirely appropriate to consider him, by inference, an instrument of discovery. But if such is his function, then he cannot protest a comparison with the other instruments of discovery, such as the telescope or the microscope, and, in the provinces of his frequent concerns, the instruments and methods of the sociologist and the psychologist. Nor can he protest an evaluation of the "truths" at which he arrives, not only in comparison to our own personal impressions as audience, but also according to the extent that these "truths" conform to the revelations of specialists who devote themselves to the same material. We tend to approach a work of art with a certain sentimental reverence, but if we are able to avoid this prejudice in comparing, for example, one of the "psychological" novels to the meticulous observations of a well-documented case history, I, for one, find the latter to be by far a more stimulating, revealing experience of reality.

Such psychological novels (I except, obviously, such masters as Dostoevsky, James, etc.) often fail not only in the accuracy of their observation, but, in their determined efforts to analyze the personality, frequently contradict the fundamental principle of effectiveness in art: they fail to so present their observations as to make a certain conclusion inevitable to the reader, and they substitute, instead, a statement of their own conclusion. All is understood for us, and we are deprived of the stimulating privilege of ourselves understanding.

The decorative "artistic" periphery of such "analytical" works of art fails to disguise their essentially uncreative nature and serves, most frequently, to simply obscure that very truth which the artist undertakes to reveal. There are also other disadvantages to art as scientific observation. Gertrude Stein has somewhere stated that "the realism of today seems new because the realism of the past is no longer real." And if the validity of a work depends upon either the accuracy of its revelations or the novelty of its discoveries it is subject to the failure here implied, of becoming, one day, dully past. If the importance of "Paradise Lost" had been predicated upon the "truth" of its medieval cosmography, the astronomical discoveries of the 17th century would have invalidated the entire work.

Unlike the inventions of science, which are valuable only until another invention serves the purpose better, the inventions of art, being experiences of emotional and intellectual nature, are, as such, valid for all time. And unlike discoveries, which are confined by the fixed limits of human perception, or advanced in a different manner by scientific instruments and knowledge, the collaboration between imagination and art instrument can still, after all these centuries, result in marvelous new art inventions.

1c

My extended analysis and criticism of the naturalistic method in art is inspired by my intimate awareness of how much the very nature of photography, more than any other art form, may seduce the artist (and spectator) into such an esthetic.

The most immediate distinction of film is the capacity of the camera to represent a given reality in its own terms, to the extent that it is accepted as a substitute proper for that reality. A photograph will serve as proof of the "truth" of some phenomenon where either a painting or a verbal testimony would fail to carry weight. In other art forms, the artist is the intermediary between reality and the instrument by which he creates his work of art. But in photography, the reality passes directly through the lens of the camera to be immediately recorded on film, and this relationship may, at times, dispense with all but the most manual services of a human being, and even, under certain conditions, produce film almost "untouched by human hands." The position of the camera in reference to reality can be either a source of strength, as when the "realism" of photography is used to create an imaginative reality; or it can seduce the photographer into relying upon the mechanism itself to the extent that his conscious manipulations are reduced to a minimum.

The impartiality and clarity of the lens—its precise fidelity to the aspect and texture of physical matter—is the first contribution of the camera. Sometimes, because of the physical and functional similarity between the eye and the lens, there is a most curious tendency to confuse their respective contributions. By some strange process of ambiguous association (which most photographers are only too willing to leave uncorrected) the perceptiveness and precision of a photograph is somehow understood to be an expression of the perceptiveness of the eyes of the photographer. This transcription of attributes is more common than one might imagine. When the primary validity of a photograph consists in its clarity or its candidness (and these are by far the most common criteria) it should be signed by those who ground the lens, who constructed the fast, easily manipulated camera, who sweated over the chemistry of emulsions which would be both sensitive and fine-grained, who engineered the optical principles of both camera and enlarger—in short, by all those who made photography possible, and least of all by the one who pushed the button. As Kodak has so long advertized: "You push the button, IT does the rest!"

The ease of photographic realism does not, however, invalidate the documentarist's criticism of the "arty" efforts (characteristic of a certain period of film development) to deliberately muffle the lens in imitation of the myopic, undetailed, and even impressionistic effects of painting where, precisely, the limitations of human vision played a creative role in simplifying and idealizing reality.

On another level, the realists are critical, and again justifiably so, of the commercial exploitation of film as a means of reproducing theater and illustrating novels . . . almost as a printing press reproduces an original manuscript in great quantity. Out of respect for the unique power of film to be itself a reality, they are impatient with the painted backdrops, the "furnished stages," and all the other devices which were developed as part of the artifice of theater and drama. If it is possible, they say, to move the camera about, to capture the fleeting, "natural" expression of a face, the inimitable vistas of nature, or the unstageable phenomenon of social realities, then such is the concern of film to be exploited, as distinct from other forms.

Such a concept of film is true to its very origins. The immediate precursor of movies was Mary's photographic series of the successive stages of a horse running. Between this first record of a natural phenomenon, and the more recent scientific films of insect life, plant life, chemical processes, etc., lies a period of increasing technical invention and competency, without any basic change in concept.

In the meantime, however, a concern with social reality had branched off as a specific field of film activity. The first newsreels of important historical events, such as the coronation, differ from the newsreels of today only in terms again of a refined technique, but from them came the documentary film, a curious amalgamation of scientific and social concerns. It is not a coincidence that Robert Flaherty, who is considered the father of the documentary film, was first an explorer, and that his motivation in carrying a camera with him was part anthropological, part social, and part romantic. He had discovered a world which was beyond the horizon of most men. He was moved both by its pictorial and its human values; and his achievement consists of recording it with sympathetic, and relative accuracy. The documentary of discovery—whether it records a natural, a social, or a scientific phenomenon—can be of inestimable value. It can bring within the reach of even the most sedentary individual a wealth of experience which would otherwise come only to the curious, the painstaking, and the heroic.

But whenever the value of a film depends, for the most part, upon the character of its subject, it is obvious that the more startling realities will have a respectively greater interest for the audience. War, as a social and political phenomenon, results in realities which surpass the most violent anticipations of human imagination. Because it also played an immediate role in our lives, we were obsessed with a need to comprehend them. And so, since the reality itself was more than enough to hold the interest of the audience (and so required least the imaginative contributions of the film maker) the war documentaries contain passages which carry naturalism to its farthest point.

I should like to refer to two examples which are strikingly memorable but essentially representative. In a newsreel which circulated during wartime, there was a sequence in which a Japanese soldier was forced from his hideout by flame throwers and ran off, burning like a torch. In the

32

documentary "Fighting Lady" there is an exciting sequence in which the plane which carries the camera swoops down and strafes some enemy planes on the ground. This latter footage was achieved by connecting the shutter of the camera with the machine gun so that when the gun was fired the camera would automatically begin registering.

An analysis of these examples can serve to illuminate the essential confusion, implicit in the very beginnings of the idea of the natural form in art, between the provinces and purposes of art and those of science, as well as the distinctions between those art forms which depend upon or extend reality, and those which themselves create a reality. The footage of the burning soldier points up the reliance upon the accidents of reality (so prevalent in photography) as contrasted to the inevitabilities, consciously created, of art. The essential amorality and ambiguity of a "natural" form is also apparent here; for were we not prepared by previous knowledge,—by an outside frame of reference—we would undoubtedly have deep compassion for the burning soldier and a violent hatred for the flame thrower.

In the case of the camera which is synchronized with the machine gun, the dissociation between man and instrument, and the independent relationship between reality and camera, is carried to an unanticipated degree. If this film can be said to reflect any intention, it must be that of death, for such was the function of the gun. In any case, the reality of the conflict is itself entirely independent of the action of the camera, rather than a creation of it, as is true of the experience of an art form.

Nor is it irrelevant to point out here that the war documentaries were achieved with an anonymity which even science, the most objective of professions, would find impossible. These films are the product of hundreds, even thousands, of unidentified cameramen. This is not another deliberate effort of the "top brass" to minimize the soldier-cameraman. It is a reflection upon a method which, unrestricted by budgetary considerations of film or personnel, could be carried to its logical conclusion. These cameramen were first instructed carefully in the mechanics of photography—(not in the form of film)—and were sent out to catch whatever they could of the war, to get it on photographic record. The film was then gathered together, assorted according to chronology or specific subject, and put at the disposal of the film editors. If the material of one cameraman could be distinguished from another, it was in terms of sheer technical competence; or, perhaps, occasionally a consistent abundance of dramatic material which might testify to an unusual alertness and a heroic willingness to risk one's life in order to "capture" on film some extraordinary moment.

This whole process is certainly more analogous to the principle of fecundity in nature than to that of the economical selectivity of art. Of all this incalculably immense footage, no more than a tiny percentage will ever be put to function in a documentary or any other filmic form.

Let me make it clear that I do not intend to minimize either the immediate interest or the historical importance of such a use of the motion-picture medium. To do so would require, by logical analogy, that I dismiss all written history, especially since it is a much less accurate form of record than the film, and value only the creative, poetic use of language.

But precisely because film, like language, serves a wide variety of needs, the triumphs which it achieves in one capacity must not be permitted to obscure its failures in another.

The war years were marked by a great interest in the documentary, just as they were characterized by the overwhelming lionization of foreign correspondents, and for the same reason. But such reportage did not become confused in the public mind with the poem as a form, simply because they both employed language. In spite of the popularity and great immediate interest in journalism, the poem still holds its position (or at least such is my fervent hope) as a distinguished form of equal, if not superior, importance in man's culture; and although it may, in certain periods, be neglected, there is never an implication that, as a form, it can be replaced by any other, however pertinent, popular, or refined in its own terms.

I am distressed, for this reason, by the current tendency to exalt the documentary as the supreme achievement of film, which places it, by implication, in the category of an art form. Although an explicit statement of this is carefully avoided, the implication is supported by an emphasis upon those documentaries which are significant not for their scientific accuracy, but for an undertone of lyricism or a use of dramatic devices— values generally associated with art form. Thus the campaign serves not so much to point up the real values of a documentary—the objective, impartial rendition of an otherwise obscure or remote reality—but to cast suspicion upon the extent to which it actually retains those documentary functions. A work of art is primarily concerned with the effective creation of an idea (even when that may require a sacrifice of the factual material upon which the idea is based), and involves a conscious manipulation of its material from an intensely motivated point of view. By inference, the unconsidered and unmodified praise which has recently attended the documentarist requires of him, again by inference, that he function also in these latter terms.

In this effort he has not failed altogether. When the reality which he seeks to convey consist largely of human and emotional values, the perception of these and their rendition may require of the documentarist a transcription similar to that which I discuss elsewhere, when the art reality becomes independent of the reality by which it was inspired. ''Song of Ceylon'' (Basil Wright and John Taylor), sections of ''Forgotten Village'' (Steinbeck, Hackenschmied and Klein), ''Rien Que Les Heures'' (Cavalcanti), ''Berlin'' (Ruttman), the Russian ''Turksib'' and the early work of Dziga Vertov are among those documentaries which create an intensity of experience, and so have validity quite irrespective of their accuracy. They are the counter-part, in literature, of those travel-journals which inform as much of the subtleties of vision as of the things viewed or of those impassioned reportages which convince as much by the sincere emotion of the reporter as by the fact reported.

But the documentary film maker is not permitted the emotional freedom of other artists, or the full access to the means and techniques of this form. Since the subjective attitude is, at least, theoretically discouraged as an impediment to unbiased observation, he is not justified in examining the extent of his personal interest in the subject matter. And so he finds himself occupied, to an enervating degree, with material which does not inspire him. He is further limited by a set of conventions which originate in the methods of the scientific film. He must photograph "on the scene" (often a very primitive one) even when material circumstances may hamper his techniques, and force him to select the accessible rather than the significant fact. He must use the "real" people, even if they are camera-shy or resentful of him as an alien intruder, and so do not behave as "realistically" as would a competent professional actor. If I were to believe in many of the documentaries which I have seen, I would deduce that most "natives" are either predominantly hostile, taciturn or simply ill-humored, and capable of mainly two facial expressions: a blank stupidity punctuated by periods of carnival hysteria. Even in our urban, sophisticated society, the portrait photographer inspires an uneasy rigidity. It would be a rare native indeed who, confronted by the impressive and even ominous mechanism of the camera and its accoutrements (and that in the hands of a suspect stranger), could maintain a normally relaxed, spontaneous behavior. These are but some of the exterior conditions rigidly imposed upon the documentary film maker, in addition to the creative problems within the form itself.

Yet the products created under these conditions are made subject, by the undefined enthusiasms of their main "appreciators," to an evaluation in terms usually reserved for the most creative achievements of other art forms. And so the documentarist is driven to the effort of satisfying two separate demands, which are in conflict. He fails, in the end, to completely satisfy either one or the other.

I am sure that few, if any, of the so-called documentaries would be acceptable as sufficiently objective and accurate data for either anthropologists, sociologists or psychologists. On the other hand, few, if any, are comparable in stature, authority, or profundity, to the great achievements of the other arts.

The documentarist cannot long remain oblivious of his ambiguous position. The greater his understanding of truly creative form, the more acute is his embarrassment at finding his labors evaluated in terms which he was not initially permitted or presumed to function. Whereas, formerly, he might have been able to maintain some middle ground, the insistence of the current campaign precipitates the basic conflicts, and forces upon him the necessity of a decision. It will succeed, in the end, in driving the more creative workers, embarrassed by the exaggerated, misdirected appreciation, out of the field. And it will be left in the hands of skilled technicians where, perhaps, it rightfully belongs.

Since these ideas are in opposition to the current wave of documentary enthusiasm, and would, perhaps, be ascribed to the prejudice of my own distance from that form, I should like to quote from an article by Alexander Hammid. He has been recognized as an outstanding talent in documentary film for 18 years, both here and abroad. He is the director of the "Hymn of the Nations" (the film about Toscanini) and other films for the OWI, and (as Alexander Hackenschmied) photographed and co-directed "Forgotten Village," "Lights Out in Europe," "Crisis," and a multitude of documentaries which have been circulated only in Europe. It therefore must be admitted that he would be at least "conversant" with the problems of his field.

It is revealing that Mr. Hammid devotes considerable space to the fact that, in order to achieve a "realism" of effect, it is often necessary to be imaginative in method.

"In their (the early documentarists) drive towards objectivity, they brushed aside the fact that the camera records only in the manner in which the man behind it chooses to direct it. I believe that the necessity of subjective choice is one of the fundamentals of any creation. In other words, we must have command of our instrument. If we leave the choice to our instrument, then we rely upon the accident of reality which, in itself, is not reality. The necessity of choice and elimination which eo ipso are a denial of objectivity, continues throughout the entire process of film making; . . . Many people believe that if there is no arrangement or staging of a scene, they will obtain an unadulterated, objective picture of reality . . . But even if we put the camera in front of a section of real life, upon which we do not intrude so much as to even blow off a speck of dust, we still arrange: by selecting the angle, which may emphasize one thing and conceal another, or distort an otherwise familiar perspective; by selecting a lens which will concentrate our attention on a single face or one which will reveal the entire landscape and other people; by the selection of a filter and an exposure . . . which determine whether the tone will be brilliant or gloomy, harsh or soft . . . This is why, in films, it becomes possible to put one and the same reality to the service of democratic, socialist or totalitarian ideologies, and in each case make it seem realistic. To take the camera out of the studio, and to photograph real life on the spot becomes merely one style of making films, but it is not a guarantee of truth, objectivity, beauty or any other moral or esthetic virtue. As a maker of documentary films I am aware of how many scenes I have contrived, rearranged or simply staged . . . These films have been presented in good faith and accepted as a "remarkably true picture of life." I do not feel that I have deceived anyone, because all these arrangements have been made in harmony with the spirit of that life, and were designed to present its character, moods, hidden meanings, beauties and contrasts . . . We have not reproduced reality but have created an illusion of reality."

And Mr. Hammid pursues his observations with relentless logic—right out of the documentary field, as it is generally understood.

"I believe that this reality, which lives only in the darkness of the movie theater, is the thing that counts. And it lives only if it is convincing, and that does not depend upon the fact that someone went to the great trouble of taking the camera to unusual places to photograph unusual events, or whether it contained professional actors or native inhabitants. It lies rather in the feeling and creative force with which the man behind the camera is able to project his visions."

If we accept the proposition that even the selected placing of the camera is an exercise of conscious creativity, then there is no such thing as a documentary film, in the sense of an objective rendition of reality. Not even the camera in synchronization with the gun remains, for it could be argued that such an arrangement was itself a creative action. And, many documentarists, confronting in the principle of objectivity an implication of their personal, individual uselessness, salvage their ego and importance by a desperate reversal. They attempt to establish, as the lowest common denominator of creative action, the exercise of even the most miniscule discrimination.

If such a low denominator is not acceptable, does it become so according to the degree and frequency of selectivity? Such a gradation can be enormous, as Mr. Hammid's reference to angles, lenses, filters, lighting, suggests. In the final analysis, is creative action at all related to elements and the act of selection from them? For would not such a concept make creativity commensurate with the accessibility of elements, so that a man of broad experience would have a high artistic potential, whereas the shy, retiring individual would not? Or does it begin, as Mr. Hammid last implies, on a level different entirely, where the elements are re-combined, not in an imitation of their original and natural integrity, but into a new whole to thus create a new reality.

2c

For the serious artist the esthetic problem of form is, essentially, and simultaneously, a moral problem. Nothing can account for the devoted dedication of the giants of human history to art form save the understanding that, for them, the moral and esthetic problems were one and the same: that the form of a work of art is the physical manifestation of its moral structure.

So organic is this relationship that it obtains even without a conscious recognition of its existence. The vulgarity and cynicism, or the pompousness and self-conscious ''impressiveness'' of so many of the films of the commercial industry—these ''formal'' qualities are their moral qualities as well. Our sole defense against, for example, the ''June-moon'' rhymes and the empty melodies of Tin Pan Alley lies in the recognition that the ''love'' there created has nothing in common with that profound experience, known by the same name, to which artists have so desperately labored to give adequate, commensurate form.

And if the idea of art form comprehends, as it were, the idea of moral form, no one who presumes to treat of profound human values is exonerated from a moral responsibility for the negative action of failure, as well as the positive action of error.

Least of all are the documentarists exonerated from such judgment, for in full consciousness they have advanced, as the major plank of their platform, not an esthetic conviction but a moral one. They have accepted the burden of concerning themselves with important human values, particularly in view of the failure of the commercial industry to do so adequately. They stand on moral grounds which are ostensibly impregnable.

Yet it is my belief, and I think that I am not alone in this, that the documentaries of World War II illuminate precisely how much a failure of form is a failure of morals, even when it results from nothing more intentionally destructive than incompetency, or the creative lethargy of the ''achieved'' professional craftsman.

Surely the human tragedy of the war requires of those who presume to commemorate it—film-maker, writer, painter—a personal creative effort somehow commensurate in profundity and stature. Surely the vacant eyes and the desolated bodies of starved children, deserve and require, in the moral sense, something more than the maudlin cliches of the tourist camera or the skillful manipulations of a craftsman who brings to them the techniques developed for and suitable to the entertaining demonstration of the manufacture of a Ford car. Is it possible not to be violently offended to discover that all these inarticulate animal sounds of human misery, all the desperate and final silences can find no transcription more inspired and

38

exalted than the professional fluency of a well-fed voice and commentary. And how can we agree that the heroism of a single soldier is in the least celebrated by the two-dimensional record of his falling body; or that the meaning of his death is even remotely comprehended by whoever is capable of exploiting the ready-made horror of his mangled face, which he can no longer protect from the cynical intimacy, the mechanical sight of the camera.

Whether there will ever appear a spiritual giant, of the stature of a Da Vinci, who can create, out of his individual resources, the form of such gigantic tragedy is a question. Short of such achievement, the least requirement is a profound humility, and a truly immense, dedicated, creative effort which would begin with the conviction that any skill or technique which has served a lesser purpose is a priori inadequate for this one. Where even such considerations are absent—and they are absent from all the war documentaries which I have seen—the result is nothing less than a profanity in a profoundly moral sense.

During the war, the documentarists interpreted the great public interest as a triumph for their form. But after the photographs of skeletonized children, the horrors of Dachau, the burning Japanese soldier, the plunge into the very heart of fire—after all the violences of war—even the best intentioned reportages of matters perhaps equally important but less dramatic and sensational cannot but seem anti-climactic and dull.

On the other hand, the extension of realism into sur-realism, as a spontaneous projection of the inner reality of the artist—intact in its natural integrity—is impossible. Since it is the camera which actually confronts reality, one can theoretically achieve, at most, a spontaneity of the camera in recording, without conscious control or discrimination, the area that it is fixed upon. This naturalism is preserved only if the pieces of film are conscientiously re-combined into the relationship of the reality itself, as in documentaries. Moreover, since the camera records according to its own capacity, even the most personalized editing of this material cannot be taken as a free expression of the artist. Thus, while film may record a sur-realist expression in another medium, "film spontaneity" is impossible.

The Hollywood industry, its shrewdnes undiverted by esthetic or ethic idealisms, knew (even before the war had ended) that only the imaginatively contrived horror or the fantastically artificial scene could capture the attention of a public grown inured to the realities of war.

To these ends, Hollywood had been itself primarily responsible for increasing the catalogue of elements which film has at its disposal for creative manipulation. In the spatial dimension it had access to the source material of the plastic arts. In the temporal dimension it had access to all movement, which could also be used to round out a two dimensional shape so that it functioned as a three-dimensional element. When sound was added, the linguistic elements upon which literature is founded, and also natural sound and music, were made available. Now, with the rapid development of color processes, still another dimension of elements is being proffered film.

My insistence upon the creative attitude, and the "un-natural" forms to which it gives rise, might seem to comprehend Hollywood films, which are obviously artificial in form. But film has access not only to the elements of reality but also, and as part of reality, to the ready made forms of other arts. And Hollywood is as realistic in reference to these art realities—literature, drama, dance, etc.,—and as faithful to their original integrities, as the documentary is in reference to social reality. This is, moreover, a tendency which has grown with time.

The film producer, responsible for the success of a project in which increasingly enormous sums are usually invested, avails himself of material, methods and personnel which are already "tested and approved." Consequently, most films make use of the elements of reality not according to the film instrument, but as elements already part of an integrated art form.

As the film industry became secure and also subject to the scrutiny of French, British and German cultural criteria, it became culturally defensive, and interested in achieving "class" on an intellectual level. In typical "nouveau-riche" fashion, the studios began to buy some of the more "intellectual" writers almost in the way that a piano, prominently displayed, is widely used to lend an aspect of refinement to a home. And just as piano lessons are rarely pursued to the point of any real musical accomplishment or understanding, so I doubt that there has ever been any real intention to make use of the real capacities of the best writers. The Hollywood writer cannot be blamed for a reluctance to recognize or admit the humiliating, decorative purpose for which he receives his irresistible salaries and so is angry and bewildered at being forced to function in films on a level far below that which ostensibly induced the original bargain. There are times when this situation creates an impression of Hollywood as no less than a Dantesque purgatory from which rise, incessantly, the hysterical protests of violated virgins.

Nevertheless, the literary approach, encouraged by the use of verbal expression in sound, has set the pattern of film criteria in much the same way that token music lessons set the pattern of musical taste and account for the notion that the "light classic" composition is the "good music." It might have been better for films if the industry was never able to afford the cultural pretension of employing writers or buying literary works but were forced to continue in the direction of some early silent films. These emphasized visual elements and even sometimes, as in the comedies of Buster Keaton, displayed a remarkable, intuitive grasp of filmic form.

I do not intend to minimize the importance of literature or drama or of any of the art forms which film records; nor even to minimize the value of such records. On the contrary, just as I am deeply grateful to some documentaries for showing me a world which I may have been otherwise denied, so I am grateful to those films which make it possible for me to see plays which I could not have attended or the performances of actors now retired or dead.

But just as I do not consider documentary realism a substitute for the creative form of film proper, neither do I feel that this is accomplished by an extension of the recording method to cover the forms of any or all the other arts. The form proper of film is, for me, accomplished only when the elements, whatever their original context, are related according to the special character of the instrument of film itself—the camera and the editing—so that the reality which emerges is a new one—one which only film can achieve and which could not be accomplished by the exercize of any other instrument. (If, on the face of it, this seems a stringent, purist or limiting requirement, then I can only point out that, far from inhibiting the other art forms, such a principle, in terms of their respective instruments, is most manifest in the greatest of their achievements.)

This critical relationship between form and instrument is the special concern of the section dealing with instruments; but it is impossible to make clear how a fiction film remains, even on film, a literary form, without reference to the manner in which instruments operate in creating a form.

In discussing the formal emergent whole of a work of art, I pointed out that the elements, or parts, lose their original individual value and assume those conferred upon them by their function in this specific whole.

Such redefined elements are then pre-disposed towards functioning in the respective form from which they derive. Consequently, even when a Hollywood writer aspires to film as a distinct medium, he usually begins with the literary and verbal elements to which he has been previously devoted. These encourage, if not actually impose, the creation of the very literary form which he has ostensibly refuted, as a principle, in film. For this reason it is usually impossible to distinguish whether film is an ''original'' (conceived specifically for filming) or an ''adaptation'' of a novel, or a novel preserved more or less intact.

The special character of the novel form is that it can deal in interior emotions and ideas—invisible conflicts, reflections, etc. The visual arts—and film is, above all, a visual experience—deal, on the contrary, in visible states of being or action. When a fictional character, whose meaning has been created by the development of his interior feelings and ideas, is to be put into a film, the first problem is: what should he do to show visibly what he thinks or feels—what is the activity best symptomatic of his feelings? This ''enactment'' must not take an undue length of time, and so certain ''symptom-action'' cliches are established. We have come to accept a kiss as a symptom-action of love, or a gesture of the hands thrown back as a symptom-action of an inner fear, etc.

Thus the Hollywood fiction film has created a kind of visual shorthand of cliches with which we have become so familiar that we are not even aware of the effort of transcription. As we watch the screen we continually ''understand'' this gesture to stand for this state of mind, or that grimace to represent that emotion. Although the emotional impact derives not from what we see, but from the verbal complex which the image represents, the facility with which we bridge the gap and achieve this transcription deceives us, and we imagine that we enjoy a visual experience. Actually, this has nothing in common with the directness with which we would experience a truly visual reality, such as falling, whose ''symptomatic sensations'' would have to represent it in a literary form.

The visual cliche acts, therefore, as a symbol, in the way that the cross is a symbol for the whole complex of ideas contained in the crucifixion. When we react emotionally to a cross, it is not to the visual character of the cross proper but to the crucifixion, to which the cross leads as a bridge of reference. It is true that symbols have been used in many works of art, but they have been drawn, always, from a firmly established mythology.

Moreover, the artist rarely relies upon such an exterior frame of reference. He is usually careful to reaffirm, in the immediate context of his work of art, those values which the object, as symbol, might have in exterior reference. It is impossible to maintain, for instance, that a good painting of the Madonna would fail to convey its devotional, exalted emotion even to someone ignorant of the symbolism employed.

The rapidity with which so many Hollywood films cease to make sense or carry emotional weight is an indication of their failure to create meaning in the direct visual terms of their own immediate frame of reference. The shorthand cliches which they employ, to bridge back to the literary terms in which the film is actually conceived, are drawn not from a recognized mythology but from superficial mannerisms which are transitory and soon lose their referential value. If the great works of art have succeeded in retaining their value even long after their symbols have lost their referential power it is precisely because their meaning was not entrusted, in the first place, to the frail bridges of the symbolic reference.

It is also a common belief that when a literary work contains many ''images'' it is especially well suited to being filmed. On the contrary, the better the writer, the more verbal his images . . . in the sense that the impact derives not from the object or events described, but from the verbal manner of their description. I take, at random, the opening paragraph of ''The Trial'' by Franz Kafka.

''Someone must have been telling lies about Joseph K. for without having done anything wrong he was arrested one fine morning. His land-lady's cook, who always brought him his breakfast at eight o'clock, failed to appear on this occasion. That had never happened before. K. waited for a while longer, watching from his pillow the old lady opposite, who seemed to be peering at him with a curiosity unusual even for her, but then, feeling both put out and hungry, he rang the bell. At once there was knock on the door and a man entered whom he had never seen before in the house.''

In this paragraph the words are themselves simple; concrete; they describe a physical event in which both real actions and real objects are included. Yet I challenge anyone to create, in visual terms, the meaning which is here contained in no more than a moment's reading time.

In literature, when an image or an event is modified by the negative, as ''failed to appear'' or ''had never seen before'' they are endowed with a meaning impossible to achieve in visual terms by mere absence. Yet it is precisely this negative reference which is important in the paragraph quoted. In visual terms the time which would be required to first establish an expectation in order to disappoint it, would be so long and the action so contrived, as to contradict the very virtue of economy which is here achieved, and to unbalance, by the emphasis which time always brings to an event, the subtle structure of the work. Not only by the pathos and disappointment of negative modification, but by a thousand other verbal and syntactical manipulations, good literature remains verbal in its impact no matter how much it seems to deal with concrete situations and images. I would even go so far as to say that only that literature which fails to make creative use of its verbal instrument, could be made into a good film. And I would like to place this entire consideration before those writers who imagine that their

42

constant use of imagery in short stories and poetry would indicate an inhibited talent for film.

The comparative economy with which an emotion can be established in verbal or in visual terms is, as a matter of fact, a good indication of whether it is a verbal or a visual image for there are, on the other hand, visual moments, which contain such a rich complex of meanings, implications, over- and under-tones, etc., that only a labored and lengthy verbal description could begin to convey their impact. The immense difference between an accurate description of an experience and the experience itself must not be minimized.

In many films such indirection—the visual description of non-visual experiences—is concealed by a rococo of photographic ''effects.'' For example a static sequence will be photographed from a dozen different angles, even when such a shifty point of view is not, emotionally or logically, justified. But all the photographic virtuosity in the world cannot make a visual form out of a literary concept.

Theater, unlike literature, is concerned with an exterior physical situation in which a verbal activity takes place; and the sound film is able to retain theater intact in its original terms. Similarly, dance retains its stage logics in film, music is composed in concert terms and remains unrelated to the other sounds of film except in an ''accompanist,'' theatrical fashion. I think I have, perhaps, made my point which is, in any case, amplified in the section dealing with the film instrument.

And it seems to me that the development of a distinctive film form consists not in eliminating any of the elements—whether of nature, reality, or the artifices of other arts—to which it has access, but in relating all these according to the special capacity of film: the manipulations made possible by the fact that it is both a space art and a time art.

By a manipulation of time and space I do not mean such established filmic technique as flash-backs, parallel actions, etc. Parallel actions for instance—as in a sequence when we see, alternately, the hero who rushes to the rescue and the heroine, whose situation becomes increasingly critical— is an omni-presence on the part of the camera as a witness of action, not as a creator of it. Here Time, by remaining actually constant, is no more than a dimension in which a spatial activity can occur. But the celluloid memory of the camera can function, as our memory, not merely to reconstruct or to measure an original chronology. It can place together, in immediate temporal sequence, events actually distant, and achieve, through such relationship a peculiarly filmic reality. This is just one of the possibilities, and I suggest many others in a discussion of the instrument of film itself.

But it would be impossible to understand or appreciate a filmic film if we brought to it all the critical and visual habits which we may have developed, to advantage, in reference to the other art forms. On the other hand, since a film makes much use of natural reality, we may be inclined, by habit, to approach it as if it were, truly, a natural phenomenon, and proceed to select from it elements which we interpret according to some personal context, rather than the context which the film has carefully evolved. Or, accustomed to film as a record of another art form, we anticipate a literary-symbolic logic. Just as, in waiting anxiously for a specific friend, we fail to recognize or even see the other faces in a crowd, so, in watching for some familiar pattern of relationship in a film we may fail to perceive the reality which is there created.

Another habit is the current tendency to psycho-analyse anything which deals in an imaginative reality. The special conditions of film production, where it is the camera which perceives and records, according to its capacity, introduces a non-psychological censor. The spontaneous associational logics of the artist cannot be retained intact by an instrument which eliminates certain elements by virtue of its mechanical limitations and introduces other elements by virtue of its refined optics, its ability to remember details which the sub-conscious might not have considered significant, its dependence upon weather conditions, its use of human beings in their own physical terms, etc. As a matter of fact, the less the artist collaborates with the instrument, with full consideration to its capacities, the more he will get, as a result, film which expresses mechanics of the camera, and not his own intentions.

It is not only the film artist who must struggle to discover the esthetic principles of the first new art form in centuries; it is the audience, too, which must develop a receptive attitude designed specifically for film and free of the critical criteria which have been evolved for all the older art forms.

3c

Everything which I have said in criticism of film may create an image of severe austerity and asceticism. On the contrary, you may find me many evenings in the motion-picture theater, sharing with the other sleepers (for nothing so resembles sleep), the selected dream without responsibilities. The less the film pretends to profundity—the less it is involved in a mediocre compromise of ideas and emotions which might be otherwise important—and the more casually circus-like it is, the more it fills the role of an extremely economical, accessible divertissement; or, as with the documentary, a satisfaction of our curiosity about the world.

But in so well exploiting the reproductive potential of film, the makers have for the most part permitted this function to supplant and substitute for a development of film-form proper. The failure of film has been a failure of omission—a neglect of the many more miraculous potentials of the art instrument.

In directing my critical remarks at the Hollywood industry, I have made convenient use of familiar points of reference; but I do not concur in that naive snobbishness which places the European industries so far above it. It must never be forgotten that only the better foreign films are imported, and that we are therefore inclined to generalize from these, neglecting that the French neighborhood double-feature is on a much lower level. And because we see few foreign films, at long intervals, the acting and the camerawork seem exotically interesting and fresh. Actually, in terms of their own native soil, these films are often as cliche and conventionalized as ours, which incidently, seem fresh and exotic to Europeans. It is true that French films, for instance, sometimes create a more subtle, introverted intensity, particularly in romantic relationships, than ours do; but I feel that this is not so much an expressly filmic virtue as a filmic fidelity to a reality both of French life and art, just as a healthy buoyancy is characteristic of many American expressions.

Above all it must never be forgotten that film owes at least as much to D. W. Griffith and Mack Sennett as to Murnau and Pabst of Germany, Melies and Delluc of France, Stiller of Sweden and Eisenstein of Russia. It is not my intention to enter, here, upon a discussion of the various styles of film-making. There are already many historical volumes on the subject. In all of them the Russian films occupy an important position, one which has created, again on the basis of a mere handful of selected achievements, a legendary notion of the Russian film industry as a whole. Although Eisenstein and his compatriots must be credited with an intensely creative extention of ''montage'' and other conventions (for these originally inspired methods have fallen into conventionalized usage) it must be remembered that they were so inspired by its more casual, prior use by Griffith (to whom they themselves give due credit).

Even with montage, the all-over concept of the form as a whole of the Russian films is that of the literary narrative. And at the risk of seeming heretical, I feel that although "Potemkin" has sequences which are extremely impressive (Eisenstein is nothing if not impressive, usually ponderously so), for sheer profundity of emotional impact and for an intensely poetic concept of film, I find nothing there to equal various sequences in the much less publicized works of Dovzhenko, such as "Frontier" or "Ivan."

It is disappointing to find, even in the "experimental" field, that the infinite tolerance of the camera—its capacity to record whatever is put before it under many modifying conditions, is too great a temptation. The painter who has an earnest interest in spatial manipulations often continues, as a film-maker, to function according to his original plastic concepts. Using chiffon and other devices he may conscientiously restore to the laboriously perfected optics of the lens all the limitations which characterize human vision, so that he can then proceed to create again as a painter. He may compose his frame as one does a canvas, in the logics of simplified masses, lines and, as substitute for color, an arrangement of blacks, whites, and all possible gradations of gray. The results are, of course, inferior to painting. Many of the gradations which are intended as color are lost in the process of multiple reproduction—a problem which painters do not face.

Moreover, since after all this is a motion picture, he arrives eventually at that unpleasant moment when the image, finally, must move and will disarrange its studied composition. Still photographers, for instance, have learned how to translate time into spatial terms. But in film, the problem is inverted. Space must be given meaning over time. A careful attention to some of the "art" films photographed by still photographers reveals an actual discomfort with time, and movement is most frequently merely an uneasy moment of transition, accomplished as rapidly as possible, between two static spatial compositions.

The abstract film is also derived from painting, both in principal and in the person of its pioneers. Such films are, it seems to me, not so much films as animated paintings, for the creative abstraction itself takes place on the spatial, plastic plane—the plane of painting—and is then registered, as any other reality, upon the film. To abstract in filmic terms would require an abstraction in time, as well as in space; but in abstract films time is not itself manipulated. It functions, in the usual way, as a vacuum which becomes visible only as it is filled by spatial activities; but it does not itself create any condition which could be thought of as its own manifestation. For an action to take place in time is not at all the same as for an action to be created by the exercise of time. This may become clearer later when I discuss the camera as an instrument of invention in temporal terms.

Like the rest of his work, the film of Marcel Duchamp occupies a unique position. Although it uses geometric forms, it is not an abstract film. but perhaps the only "optical pun" in existence. The time which he causes one of his spirals to revolve on the screen effects an optical metamorphosis: the cone appears first concave, then convex, and, in the more complicated spirals, both concave and convex and then inversed. It is Time, therefore, which creates these optical puns which are the visual equivalents, in "Anemic Cinema," for instance, of the inserted phrases which also revolve and, in doing so, disclose the verbal pun.

My main criticism of the concept behind the usual abstract film is that it denies the special capacity of film to manipulate real elements as realities, and substitutes, exclusively, the elements of artifice (the method of painting). It may be easier to make an abstract film by recording the movements of colored squares by ordinary photographic process; but even this is usually done one frame at a time, like a series of miniature canvasses. And it is possible to paint upon successive frames a successively larger or smaller square or circle which, when projected, will appear to approach or recede according to the plastic principles of painting. Many abstract films are painted directly on the celluloid. Any concept of film which can in theory and practice dispense with the use of both camera and editing does not seem to me to be, properly speaking, a film, although it may be a highly entertaining, exciting or even profound experience.

Realism and the artifices of other arts can be combined by photographing an imaginatively conceived action related to an obviously real location. For when the tree in the picture is obviously real, it is also understood as true, and it can lend its aura of reality to an event created by artifice beneath it. Such a delicate manipulation between the really real and the unreally real is, I believe, one of the major principles of film form.

Nothing can be achieved in the art of film until its form is understood to be the product of a completely unique complex: the exercise of an instrument which can function, simultaneously, both in terms of discovery and of invention. Peculiar also to film is the fact that this instrument is composed of two separate but interdependent parts, which flank the artist on either side. Between him and reality stands the camera . . . with its variable lenses, speeds, emulsions, etc. On the other side is the strip of film which must be subjected to the mechanisms and processes of editing (a relating of all the separate images), before a motion picture comes into existence.

The camera provides the elements of the form, and, although it does not always do so, can either discover them or create them, or discover and create them simultaneously. Upon the mechanics and processes of "editing" falls the burden of relating all these elements into a dynamic whole.

Most film-makers rely upon the automatically explorative action of the camera to add richness to their material. For the direct contact between camera and reality results in a quality of observation which is quite different from that of the human being. For example the field of vision of the human eye is comparable to that of a wide-angle lens. But the focus of the eye is relatively selective, and, directed by the interests or anxieties of the human being, will concentrate upon some small part of the entire area and will fail to observe or to remember objects or actions which lie outside its circle of concentration, even though these are still physically within the field of vision.

The lens, on the other hand, can be focused upon a plane (at right angles to the camera) within the depth of that field and, everything in that plane of focus, will be observed and recorded with impartial clarity. Under favorable light conditions, the depth of that plane can be enormously extended, so that the camera can record, in a single frame a greater richness of reality than the human eye would ever be aware of in a glance. The camera thus contributes a dimension of observation to photography by compensating for a prejudice of human vision. It does not discover, however, in the sense of revealing more than the most perfect or leisurely human vision could perceive.

It is shocking to realize how little the camera, as an instrument of discovery, has been exploited outside of scientific investigation, where the results remain in the hands of scientists as part of their data. Yet, to my mind, the sheer visual excitement of photographs taken through a microscope, for instance, transcend by far—in beauty of design, delicacy of detail, and a kind of miraculous perfection—most of the accidental or laboriously composed still lifes of vases, strings, and such objects. I refer anyone who wishes to spend an exciting afternoon to the photographs of ocean organisms, plant sections, cancerous growths, etc., which are on file at the Museum of Natural History in New York. I exclude from my criticism the handful of photographers who have, in the use of extreme enlargements, and similar techniques, shown a creative grasp of such possibilities.

The motion-picture camera, in introducing the dimension of time into photography, opened to exploration the vast province of movement. The treasures here are almost limitless, and I can suggest only a few of them. There is, for example, the photographic acceleration of a movement which, in reality, may be so slow as to be indiscernable. The climbing of a vine, or the orientation of a plant towards the sun are thus revealed to possess fascinating characteristics, qualities, and even a curiously "intelligent" integrity of movement which only the most patient and observant botanist could have previously suspected.

My own attention has been especially captured by the explorations of slow-motion photography. Slow-motion is the microscope of time. One of the most lyric sequences I have ever seen was the slow-motion footage of the flight of birds photographed by an ornithologist interested in their varied aerodynamics. But apart from such scientific uses, slow-motion can be brought to the most casual activities to reveal in them a texture of emotional and psychological complexes. For example, the course of a conversation is normally characterized by indecisions, defiances, hesitations, distractions, anxieties, and other emotional undertones. In reality these are so fugitive as to be invisible. But the explorations by slow-motion photography, the agony of its analysis, reveals, in such an ostensibly casual situation, a profound human complex.

The complexity of the camera creates, at times, the illusion of being almost itself a living intelligence which can inspire its manipulation on the explorative and creative level simultaneously. (I have just received from France a book entitled "L'Intelligence d'une Machine" by Jean Epstein. I have not yet read it, but the approach implied in the title and the poetic, inspired tone of the style in which Mr. Epstein writes of a subject usually treated in pedestrian, historical terms leads me to believe that it is at least interesting reading for those who share, with me, a profound respect for the magical complexities of the film instrument.) A running leap has, with slight variations, a given tempo; slow-motion photography creates of it a reality which is totally unnatural. But a use of slow-motion in reference to a movement which can, in parts, be performed at a variable tempo, can be even more creative. That is, one can shake one's head from side to side at almost any rate of speed. When a fast turning is reduced, by slow-motion, it still looks natural, and merely as if it were being performed more slowly; the hair, however, moving slowly in the lifted, horizontal shape possible only to rapid tempos, is unnatural in quality. Thus one creates a movement in one tempo which has the qualities of a movement of another tempo, and it is the dynamics of the relationship between these qualities which creates a certain special effectiveness, a reality which can only be achieved through the temporal manipulation of natural elements by the camera as an art instrument. In this sense, such a shot is a new element which is created by the camera for a function in the larger whole of the entire film. Another example of a uniquely filmic element is the movement created by the reversal of a motion which is not, in reality, reversible. By simply holding the camera up-side-down (I cannot stop to explain the logic by which this occurs), one can photograph the waves of the ocean and they will, in projection, travel in reverse. Such film footage not only reveals a new quality in the motion of the waves, but, creates to put it mildly, a most revolutionary reality.

Such an approach is a far cry from what is usually understood by the cliche that the province of motion pictures is movement. Film-makers seem to forget that movement, as such, is already used very thoroughly in dance, and to a lesser degree, in theater. If film is to make any contribution to the realm of movement, if it is to stake out a claim in an immeasurably rich territory, then it must be in the province of film-motion, as a new dimension altogether of movement.

I have not, myself, had the opportunity of experimenting with sound, but I am convinced that an explorative attitude, brought to the techniques of recording, mixing, amplifying, etc., could create a wealth of original film-sound elements. Even in the process of developing film emulsion itself, lives the negative image, where the inversion of all values reveals the astonishing details and constructions which fail of visual consequence in the familiar values of the positive image.

The burden of my argument is that it constitutes a gross, if not criminal esthetic negligence to ignore the immense wealth of new elements which the camera proffers in exchange for relatively minute effort. Such elements, constituted already of a filmic dynamic of space and time relationships, (related to all other accessible elements), are the elements proper of the larger dynamic of the film as a whole.

I have already pointed out that the reproduction, on film, of the other art forms does not constitute the creation of a filmic integrity and logic. Just as the verbal logics of a poem are composed of the relationships established through syntax, assonance, rhyme, and other such verbal methods, so in film there are processes of filmic relationships which derive from the instrument and the elements of its manipulations.

As a matter of fact, the very methods which result in a failure of the other art forms in film may be the basis of creative action in film itself, once the effort to carry over the values of one to the other is abandoned. Such inversion is possible largely because film is a time-space complex of a unique kind.

Film has been criticized, from the point of view of dramaturgy, as lacking the integrity and immediacy of fine theater. It is pointed out that the limitations of the stage impose upon the playwright an economy of movement, an emphasis upon the construction and development of character and situation, and a creative attention to the verbal statement upon which the immediate burden of projection rests. The very mobility of the camera, it is said, encourages a lazy reliance on an essentially decorative use of scenery and realistic detail. A plot so dull that it would not hold the attention of the theater audience for more than a moment, borrows a superficial excitement from a frequent change of location, angles and similar movements of the camera. These also permit a neglect of verbal integrity and achievement. The insistent artificiality of the processes of film-making—the complicated and intense lighting, the unresponsive machinery, the interruptions of the action—make it virtually impossible for the performer to maintain the intensity and integrity of conviction which is so central to theater, or to achieve the vitality which results from his direct contact with his human audience.

I agree. I agree absolutely that film, as theater, is less satisfying an experience than theater as theater. But, on the other hand, the sly tendency of theater to, at times, imitate the methods (however unexploited) of film by a ''realism'' of setting, frequent changes of scene, and a panoramic idea of construction is neither good theater nor acceptable film.

(In my criticism of the panoramic construction I do not intend to include vaudeville variety shows, musicals or that supremely triumphant example of such construction: ''Around the World in Eighty Days.'' These are part of a form completely separate from drama and are in the tradition of the ''word battles'' and the other contests of skills already developed to a high level (often higher than ours) in the tribal cultures of Africa, the Pacific, etc., where they also function as a socially adjusted exercise of individual exhibitionism.)

Moreover, it seems to me that many of the ''technical'' difficulties are at least compensated for by such advantages as the opportunity to repeat an action until its most perfect delivery is recorded for all time. It is true that theater does often function on a higher level than film-theater, but this is due not to technical qualifications but rather to the fact that, for theatrical presentation, plays do not gear themselves to a prescribed level guaranteed to return the amounts invested in a film. In addition and as a consequence, performers who are genuinely concerned with the profundity of their roles prefer to remain in the theater. These are the real reasons behind the loss of stature which plays so frequently suffer in being rendered into films.

This is a comparatively recent development. In the early days, the film industry was in complete disrepute: theatrical professionals considered it, for the most part, a vulgarity, and it had not yet proven its commercial

50

possibilities sufficiently to become seductive to them. It could not afford
to buy rights, hire playwrights or trained actors, or indulge in a vast personnel and a division of labor. It had, consequently, to rely upon and develop
its own resources.

The most frequent practice was to work with a very limited crew, most
of whom had no previous professional standing to lose, and would therefore
try anything. It was not uncommon, for example, to use almost everyone
except the camera-man for extras in group scenes; or for the actress to
design her own costume; or for the camera-man to suggest a preferable
action; or for the director to take over the camera; etc. In this way, the
films became a collaborative effort of the crew, rather than the current
assembly-line product of a hierarchical, myopic division of labor. Above
all, for sheer lack of writers who would deign to concern themselves with
movies, the films were often "written" on the spot by the camera, according
to a very skeletal, vague story plot. The masterpieces of Mack Sennett and
Chaplin derive precisely from this proceedure.

It was also responsible for the development of a peculiarly filmic concept,—the personality film—as in the Pickford films or the vamp films.
Although probably suggested by the vehicle plays of theater, it was actually,
for a period, extended into a qualitatively different form. The special
techniques of film—the concentrated close-up—and the special qualities of
film projection—the overwhelming, intimate experience of a face as the
sole, living reality in a total darkness—made possible an unprecedented exploitation of the very personality of an actress, from which the action of
the plot itself emanated. Although it has now fallen into an unimaginative,
pedestrian usage—as in the Grable films which must be propped up with
songs, jokes, etc.,—it also led to such achievements as "Joan of Arc"
(Karl Dreyer). In keeping with a false concept of "refinement," the
"better" films are now reverting to plays, playwrights, and play-actresses.

But I am sure that I am not alone in my deep affection for those films
which raised personalities to almost a super-natural stature and created,
briefly, a mythology of gods of the first magnitude whose mere presence
lent to the most undistinguished events a divine grandeur and intensity—
Theda Bara, Mary Pickford, Lillian Gish, Rudolph Valentino, Douglas Fairbanks, and the early Greta Garbo, Marlene Dietrich, Jean Harlow and Joan
Crawford. (For another point of view on these figures, I recommend "The
Hollywood Hallucination" by Parker Tyler.)

Moreover—to return to the dramaturgic criticisms—suppose that the
fact that a camera can stop, wait indefinitely, and then start again, was
used, not as substitute for the intermissions during which the stage scenery
is shifted, but as a technique for the metamorphosis (implying uninterrupted
continuity of time) in spatial dimension?

In the film dance which I have made, the dancer begins a large movement—the lowering of his extended leg—in a forest. This shot is interrupted at the moment when the leg has reached waist-level, and is immediately followed by a close-up shot of the leg in a continuation of its movement—with the location now the interior of a house. The integrity of the
time element—the fact that the tempo of the movement is continuous and
that the two shots are, in editing, spliced to follow one another without inter-

ruption—holds together spatial areas which are not, in reality, so related. Instead of being destructive to a dramatic integrity, the mobility of the camera and the interruption and resumption of action, here creates an integrity as compelling as that of the theater, but of a totally different quality.

There are many uniquely filmic time-space relationships which can be achieved. I can point, at random, to a sequence from another film, "At Land." A girl enters and crosses the frame at a diagonal. She disappears behind a sand dune in the foreground at the edge of the frame, and the camera, at this moment, actually stops operating. The girl walks away a considerable distance and takes her place behind a farther dune away. The camera then resumes its shooting and immediately begins to turn (in a panoramic movement) in the direction in which the girl just left the frame. Since it starts registering at the identical position at which it stopped, some five minutes before, there is no spatial indication of the time which has transpired, and consequently we expect to find the girl emerging the dune which had just concealed her. Instead, she emerges from the dune much more distant, and so the alienation of the girl, from the camera, exceeds the actual time which would have presumably been necessary. In this case, a continuity of space has integrated periods of time which were not, in reality, in such immediate relationship; just as in the previous example, time and space were inversely related, according to a similar principle.

To the form as a whole, such techniques contribute an economy of statement comparable to poetry, where the inspired juxtaposition of a few words can create a complex which far transcends them. One of the finest films I have seen, "Sang d'un Poet" (Blood of A Poet) comes from Jean Cocteau who, as a poet, has had long training in the economy of statement. It is a film which has, incidently, suffered immensely at the hands of "critics" for in its condensation it contains enough springboards for the personal, creative interpretations of a convention of "analysts." And its meaning depends upon a good many immediately visual images and realities which the literary symbolists ignore either through choice or limited capacity.

It is possible for me to go on for pages, citing one example after another, where a dynamic manipulation of the relationships between film-time and film-space (and potentially, film-sound) can create that special integrated complex: film form. But descriptions of such filmic methods are obviously awkward in verbal terms. I hope that these explicit examples suffice to clarify the principle. Above all, I sense myself upon the mere threshold of an indefinitely large, if not infinite, range of potentialities in which, eventually, there will be revealed principles beside which my concepts may seen exceedingly primitive.

Such revelations will, in their time, be as appropriate to the state of the culture—its perception of reality, the methods and achievements of its manipulations, and the complex of emotional and intellectual attitudes which attend all of these—as the problems with which I have here concerned myself, seem now to be.

The theory of relativity can no longer be indulgently dismissed as an abstract statement, true or false, of a remote cosmography whose pragmatic action remains, in any case, constant. Since the 17th century the heavens—

52

with God and His will—and the earth—with man and his desires—have rapidly approached each other. The phenomena which were once the manifestations of a transcendent deity are now the ordinary activities of man. A voice penetrates our midnight privacy over vast distance—via radio. The heavens are crowded with swift messengers. It is even possible to bring the world to an end. From the source of power must emanate also the morals and the mercies. And so, ready or not, willing or not, we must come to comprehend, with full responsibility, the world which we have now created.

The history of art is the history of man and of his universe and of the moral relationship between them. Whatever the instrument, the artist sought to re-create the abstract, invisible forces and relationships of the cosmos, in the intimate, immediate forms of his art, where the problems might be experienced and perhaps be resolved in miniature. It is not presumptuous to suggest that cinema, as an art instrument especially capable of recreating relativistic relationships on a plane of intimate experience, is of profound importance. It stands, today, in the great need of the creative contributions of whomsoever respects the fabulous potentialities of its destiny.

Contributors

Lucy Fischer is Professor of Film Studies and English at the University of Pittsburgh and Director of the Film Studies Program. Her books include *Jacques Tati, Shot/Countershot: Film Tradition and Women's Cinema, Imitation of Life*, and *Cinematernity: Film, Motherhood, Genre*, and *Sunrise*. Widely published, she has served as a curator at the Museum of Modern Art and the Carnegie Museum of Art. Professor Fischer has served as Vice-President and President of the Society of Cinema Studies.

Mark Franko is Professor of Dance and Performance Studies at the University of California, Santa Cruz. He is the author of *Dancing Modernism/Performing Politics, Dance as Text: Ideologies of the Baroque Body, The Dancing Body in Renaissance Choreography*, and coeditor of *Acting on the Past: Historical Performance Across the Disciplines*. His research has received support from the Getty Research Center, the American Philosophical Society, and the American Council of Learned Societies. He is also the director of the NovAntiqua dance company, which is based in San Francisco.

Barbara Hammer is a film and video maker of eighty works, including seven feature documentaries: *Nitrate Kisses, Out in South Africa, Tender Fictions, The Female Closet, Devotion, My Babushka*, and *History Lessons*. Her films have played at major festivals including Sundance, Berlin, Toronto, Yamagata, and Festival de Films des Femmes, Creteil, France. Among the awards she has received are an Artist Fellowship from the Japan Foundation, a New York State Council on the Arts Film Production Grant, a National Endowment for the Arts Film Production Grant, and a Radcliffe Fellowship at the Bunting Institute.

Ute Holl, film historian, is currently teaching at Bauhaus University, Weimar. She wrote her dissertation, "Cybernetics and Cinema," at Humboldt University, Berlin, and has edited a German edition of Maya Deren's writings for Hochschule für Bildende Künste, Hamburg. She is preparing a documentary film on the cultural impact of medical imaging.

Renata Jackson wrote her dissertation, "Voices of Maya Deren: Theme and Variation," at New York University. She has taught at Pennsylvania State University, Emerson College, the European Institute for International Communication in Maastricht, the Netherlands, and at New York University. She has taught critical studies in the School of Filmmaking at the North Carolina School of the Arts since 1998.

Annette Michelson is Professor of Cinema Studies at New York University. Her research addresses issues of practice and theory within the various forms and periods of the cinematic avant-garde. She is a founder of the journal *October* as well as of *October Books* and editor of *October: The First Decade*. Professor Michelson has introduced and edited *Kino-eye: The Writings of Dziga Vertov* and *Cinema, Censorship, and the State: The Writings of Nagisa Oshima*. Among her other publications are studies of Marcel Duchamp, Joseph Cornell, Andy Warhol, S. M. Eisenstein, Jean-Luc Godard, and Jean Renoir. She has organized, among other exhibitions, *The Art of Moving Shadows* for the National Gallery of Art.

Bill Nichols holds the Fanny Knapp Allen Chair of Fine Arts at the University of Rochester where he is Professor of Art History/ Visual and Cultural Studies in the Department of Art and Art History. In addition to the two-volume anthology *Movies and Methods* he has authored *Ideology and the Image*, *Representing Reality*, and *Blurred Boundaries*, along with over fifty articles on a wide variety of subjects. He is a former president of the Society for Cinema Studies and has served as an expert witness in court cases involving intellectual property rights and film. *Introduction to Documentary* is his latest book.

Maria Pramaggiore is Associate Professor of Film Studies and of Women's and Gender Studies at North Carolina State University, Raleigh. She is coeditor of *Representing Bisexualities: Subjects and Culture of Fluid Desire* and edited a special issue of *Jouvert: A Journal of Postcolonial Studies* on "Ireland 2000." She has published essays on feminism, film, and performance in *Theatre Journal*, *Cinema Journal*, and *Screen*.

Catherine M. Soussloff is Professor of Art History at the University of California, Santa Cruz, where she has held the Patricia and Rowland Rebele Chair in Art History since 1998. She currently teaches in the Department of Art and Art History at the University of Rochester where she also serves as Director of the doctoral program in Visual and Cultural Studies. She is the author of *The Absolute Artist* (1997), editor of *Jewish Identity in Art History* (1999), and currently completing *The Subject in Art*, a book about the social and historical contexts of portraiture in Vienna at the beginning of the twentieth century. Her work includes numerous essays on European art theory, historiography, and aesthetics from the early modern period to the present.

Moira Sullivan, a film critic and lecturer based in Stockholm and San Francisco, is the author of *An Anagram of the Ideas of Filmmaker Maya Deren.* She has given invited lectures at the special Maya Deren event "Dissolvenze: Maya Deren" in Italy, "Racine Noires: Recontre des Cinema du Monde Noir" in France, and "Cielo Maya Deren" in Spain. She is the author of two web sites *The Maya Deren Forum* and *Living Femme Communication.* She is also a filmmaker whose work has appeared on French television and at festivals.

Maureen Turim is Professor of English and Film Studies at the University of Florida. She is author of *Abstraction in Avant-Garde Films, Flashbacks in Film: Memory and History,* and *The Films of Oshima Nagisa: Images of a Japanese Iconoclast.* She has published more than fifty articles on cinema, video, art, cultural studies, psychoanalysis, and comparative literature. Her most recent project, *Desire and Its Ends: The Driving Forces of Recent Cinema,* examines the relation of desire to narrative in different cultural traditions.

Jane Brakhage Wodening has seven books of short stories to her credit, including *from The Book of Legends,* which contains this profile of Maya Deren. From 1957 to 1987 she was married to Stan Brakhage and featured in and assisted with most of his work during those years. Ms. Wodening has lived in a tiny cabin at ten thousand feet in the Rocky Mountains for the past ten years and snowshoes more than three miles to her car half the year.

Index

Note: Although Maya Deren's *An Anagram of Ideas on Art, Form and Film* is included in this volume, its contents are not indexed here.

Designer: Nola Burger
Compositor: Integrated Compositions Systems
Text: 10/15 Janson
Display: Janson, Stymie Condensed, Univers Condensed
Printer and binder: Data Reproductions Corporation

5902